Praise for

GOING BROKE BY DEGREE
Why College Costs Too Much

"*Going Broke by Degree* is another example of Dr. Vedder's effectiveness at breaking down public policy myths and shining the light of factual research and market truths on the process. This book shows how parents across America are picking up the tab for higher tuition costs as a result of increased spending at colleges and universities that often has nothing to do with the education of our young people."

—Governor Mark Sanford

"Professor Vedder expertly and fearlessly dissects the failings of American higher education in 2004 and persuasively shows that radical reforms are needed if this vital enterprise is to retain its strength and world standing. State legislators should pay close attention. So should Congress and the White House as they labor over the federal Higher Education Act."

—Chester E. Finn Jr., senior fellow, Hoover Institution, Stanford University, and president, Thomas B. Fordham Foundation

Going Broke by Degree

Why College Costs Too Much

Richard Vedder

The AEI Press

Publisher for the American Enterprise Institute
WASHINGTON, D.C.

Distributed to the Trade by National Book Network, 15200 NBN Way, Blue Ridge Summit, PA 17214. To order call toll free 1-800-462-6420 or 1-717-794-3800. For all other inquiries please contact the AEI Press, 1150 Seventeenth Street, N.W., Washington, D.C. 20036 or call 1-800-862-5801.

NRI NATIONAL RESEARCH INITIATIVE

This publication is a project of the National Research Initiative, a program of the American Enterprise Institute that is designed to support, publish, and disseminate research by university-based scholars and other independent researchers who are engaged in the exploration of important public policy issues.

Library of Congress Cataloging-in-Publication Data

Vedder, Richard K.
  Going broke by degree: why college costs too much / Richard Kent
Vedder. p. cm.
  Includes bibliographical references and index.

  ISBN 978-0-8447-4198-7 (paper)
  ISBN 0-8447-4197-3 (cloth)

  1. College costs—United States. 2. Universities and colleges—United
States—Finance. 3. Education, Higher—Economic aspects—United States.
I. Title.

LB2342.V43 2004
378'.3'8—dc22

2004001157

10 09 08   3 4 5

Printed in the United States of America

Contents

Illustrations

FIGURES

Acknowledgments

Somewhere around 1998, I grew sufficiently annoyed by the disconnect between my perception of what life was like in the higher education community and what university presidents were claiming about it that I wrote a column for the *Wall Street Journal* about the university cost explosion. James Taranto's willingness to publish the column began a series of steps leading to this book. At the urging of Virginia Governor (now U.S. Senator) George Allen, I wrote a longer version of the *Journal* piece for a meeting of the Boards of Visitors of various Virginia universities, followed by a still-longer piece for the Hechinger Institute of Teachers College at Columbia University and *The Long Run View*, a policy magazine of the Massachusetts School of Law.

Accepting the extreme generosity of my public employee retirement system, I entered "semi-retired status" at a relatively young age and was faced with several months free of teaching duties. The American Enterprise Institute suggested that I expand on the issues I had raised earlier, and offered to support my work through its National Research Initiative. I very much appreciate the encouragement AEI provided, and enjoyed the periods I spent at the Institute while researching and writing the book.

In proceeding, I have been aided by a lifetime of experience in the academy, mainly at Ohio University, but also as a visiting professor or scholar at a very good private university (Washington University in St. Louis), a private liberal arts college (Claremont McKenna College), and a public university (University of Colorado). Also helpful were associations with private think tanks like AEI, which carry out some of the same research functions claimed by institutions of higher education. Visits to numerous college campuses to give seminars, attend conferences, and the like have added to my perspective of the workings of American higher education. For example, while writing the book, I gave seminars on the tuition explosion at two

California universities—one public (San Jose State University) and one private (Santa Clara University)—and a presentation at AEI.

I would not have undertaken this task if I had thought others had already accomplished it. Indeed, the literature on universities is large and growing. But none of the previous studies seems to offer the perspective I felt was needed. Labor economist Ronald Ehrenberg of Cornell University wrote *Tuition Rising*, which deals with some of the issues raised here, and in some places offers observations similar to mine. But Ehrenberg views higher education cost issues from the perspective of elite private universities. Other books also view aspects of problems from the standpoint of universities themselves, or they look at narrow issues. (A good example is Derek Bok's *Universities in the Marketplace: The Commercialization of Higher Education*.) My outlook is much broader, both in terms of the type of institutions examined (all of them) and the social perspective from which policies are examined. I try to view universities with the eyes of an outsider, even though, like Ehrenberg, I have a wealth of "inside" experience.

I owe a great debt to AEI managing editor Sam Thernstrom and staff members who helped move this book swiftly through production, improving its readability along the way. My colleague and long-time collaborator, Lowell Gallaway, offered a number of insightful suggestions over lunch, as did David Klingaman. Chester Finn, of the Thomas Fordham Foundation, and Thomas Sowell, of the Hoover Institution at Stanford University, were both generous with their time and offered useful suggestions. Milton Friedman and William Bennett offered some interesting perspectives and are mentioned in the text. Three undergraduate students, Jack Keating, Ashley McCall, and Adam Shehata, read an early version of the manuscript, lending encouragement and some insight. Daniel DeLawder, president of Park National Corporation and a trustee of Ohio University, stimulated my thinking with thoughtful comments about the differences in behavior between universities and private businesses. My wife, Karen Vedder, had to endure my long absences at the office working on this book, and provided an invaluable service by helping me with some of the early editing of the manuscript. Although much of my research could be done in a lazy fashion from my comfortable office, the staff of the Ohio University Library, particularly Judith Daso and her government documents room colleagues, were of great assistance. To all of these and no doubt others forgotten, I offer my heartfelt appreciation.

Introduction

Universities are making the headlines a lot these days, and much of the publicity is distinctly unfavorable. While some bad press relates to student drinking, campus riots, athletic scandals, and the many remedial courses being taught by colleges, the dominant topic is the rapid rise in costs. Tuition is increasing far faster than the rate of inflation or even people's incomes, prompting calls from politicians and ordinary citizens to "do something" about it. This book is about the modern American university, and particularly the origins of and possible solutions to the problems of rising costs and declining efficiency that afflict the academy.

The sharp increases in college tuition in 2002 and 2003 were not unusual. This rapid growth has exceeded the inflation rate consistently for most of the twentieth century. Moreover, in modern times it has also exceeded the growth in family incomes, making college attendance an increasingly traumatic event from a financial perspective. While college administrators claim, with some justification, that "American universities are the best in the world," it is also true that they are the most expensive. Do they need to be?

College costs are soaring for a number of reasons, but one cause predominates: The productivity of university personnel is almost certainly falling, and it is clearly falling sharply relative to the rest of the economy. While it takes far less time for workers to make a ton of steel, type a letter, or harvest a bushel of corn than it did a generation ago, it takes *more* professors and college administrators to educate a given number of students.

Why is productivity falling? The basic problem is that universities are mostly nonprofit organizations, subject to only muted competitive forces, and lacking market-imposed discipline to economize and innovate. University presidents, deans, maintenance supervisors, department chairs, and other administrators do not benefit from reducing costs. Major policy issues are typically decided in committees, where advocates of the status quo (often faculty with tenure) usually have the upper hand. With third parties such as government and private donors footing much of the cost, there is little fear that higher prices will trigger a consumer backlash. It is no wonder that per-student costs of instruction are dramatically lower at the typical for-profit university, where market discipline is much stronger.

Third-party payments make consumers relatively insensitive to costs. Students receiving grants or subsidized loans are far less sensitive to tuition increases than they would be if they were paying their own way. Where entrepreneurs in a free, unsubsidized market seek to cut costs and lower their prices to lure new customers away from businesses that are raising theirs, there is very little of that in higher education. Few university presidents I know, for example, advertise on television that their institutions offer as good a product as their competitors but at a lower price. To do so would incur the wrath of other presidents, causing the offenders to be ostracized among their peers at meetings of the American Council of Education and other trade groups, and lowering their chances for academic advancement.

All of this reflects the absence of a clearly defined "bottom line" in traditional, not-for-profit higher education. Did Stanford University have a good or bad year in 2003? How would we know? A few vague indicators, such as the college rankings done by *U.S. News & World Report*, give us some hints. But in the for-profit world, constant, precise indicators, such as stock prices and frequent statements of profit and loss, give much more tangible measurements of success.

In many ways, the higher education "industry" resembles the health care industry. In both, third parties, such as government agencies, insurance companies, and private foundations, pay most of the bills, making consumers far more indifferent to the price of services than they would otherwise be. In both, many providers operate on a nonprofit basis, with a nebulous "bottom line." And in both, not surprisingly, the prices of services have risen dramatically over time, making it more difficult for society to maintain a given level of services.

In health care, a steady rise in demand for services, fueled by a growing and aging population and more third-party payments, has provided a seller's market that has allowed for tremendous price increases. As health care costs (as a percent of national output) grew in the 1990s, President Bill Clinton and his wife Hillary Clinton promoted a massive restructuring plan that failed politically, but was nonetheless followed by the growth in a large number of cost-cutting innovations, including the rise of health maintenance organizations (HMOs), preferred provider organizations (PPOs), increased insurance deductibles and copayments, and more stringent insurance or Medicare/Medicaid limits on use of prescription drugs and various medical procedures. Although Congress declined to enact legislation, the mere threat was sufficient to prompt the industry to develop its own cost-cutting measures.

Is the same thing about to happen to higher education? There are some signs it may be: nontraditional, online instruction is growing enormously, enrollments at for-profit universities are booming, and company-provided certification of skills is becoming increasingly popular in certain fields. These are all responses to the rising cost of traditional higher education. There is every reason to believe these trends will continue and intensify, prodding traditional universities into changing their ways.

Escalating tuition reflects two other developments of modern times. The first is a rise in price discrimination, which occurs when different customers pay different prices for the same service. Tuition is discounted by scholarship aid. Over time, that aid has grown substantially, so the actual average price to the consumer has risen somewhat less rapidly than stated tuition suggests. Price discrimination has allowed many universities to take advantage of the fact that affluent students are usually less sensitive to costs than poorer ones. By charging the wealthier students more, total revenues are enhanced. Also, at many selective-admissions universities, parents will often gladly pay high tuition if their child's only other option is to attend less prestigious schools. Universities have increased "sticker prices" aggressively to charge some students whatever the market will bear.

The second factor boosting tuition is an increasing cross-subsidization within universities, with institutions diverting resources away from undergraduate instruction. Professors who two generations ago would have taught twelve hours a week now teach six or possibly nine hours. The reduced teaching load is supposed to allow professors to do more research. Traditionally, undergraduate education has been heavily subsidized by third parties (through scholarships and loans); now, undergraduates are increasingly subsidizing other university expenses such as research, student activities, bigger administrative structures, and more costly intercollegiate athletic programs.

All of this leads to another issue that is often misrepresented in the popular press and by universities themselves: the nature and impact of public support. Three-quarters of students attend state universities, which receive substantial support from state governments. While the tuition charged by these schools is well below that of private universities, it has been rising rapidly. University presidents blame this on inadequate governmental support, but the evidence suggests that very little of the additional financial support recently given to state universities has actually been used to reduce the cost of undergraduate instruction. That is, more generous state support does not usually translate into lower tuition costs. Nor does it enable more students to attend college. Lavishing more state funds on higher education does not significantly affect the number of students going to college, or how much they pay for their degrees.

The evidence discussed in this book is consistent with the following scenario: University presidents ask legislatures for more funds to keep costs down for students and improve educational opportunities for those with modest financial means. Sympathetic legislators generally accede to those requests. The universities then use most of the money to fund large salary increases, add staff members (thereby lowering productivity), build more luxurious facilities, and expand research projects, instead of teaching as promised. The same thing, with some variation, occurs with respect to donations to privately endowed universities.

In their quest for funds, state university presidents also argue that higher education support is an investment in human capital, and in a knowledge-intensive economy, good universities are vital for economic growth. This sounds plausible, particularly since college graduates earn sharply more than nongraduates, and the differential has expanded over time. Yet the evidence suggests the opposite: When other factors are held equal, *the more state governments support higher education, the lower the rate of economic growth in the state.*

Why? Two explanations come to mind. First, increased government support for universities forces higher taxation on private sector activity that, on average, is produced more efficiently in competitive market environments than in university activity. Money is shifted from highly productive to less productive activity. Second, as noted above, much of the increased support does not go toward expanding students' access to learning, but rather to providing higher incomes and lighter workloads for university personnel. In the jargon of economics, the incremental funds support faculty and staff "rent-seeking"—that is, getting payments beyond the amount needed to provide goods and services—and the redistribution of income from the productive to the less productive.

How can more spending on higher education lower economic growth, though, when high wage premiums are paid in labor markets for highly educated persons? In part this relates to the diminishing returns that have set in for "investments" in universities. It is plausible that, on average, those investments are good, but at the margin they are not. That is, the first $100 billion spent on higher education is money well spent—as an economist would put it, it has a good rate of return. But the second $100 billion only has a so-so rate of return, and the third or fourth payment may have a zero or even negative rate of return, less than what could be earned by using the funds differently.

College-educated workers are relatively well-paid partly because higher education is a screening device for employers, a means of dramatically lowering the costs of searching for employees with leadership potential, technical skills, imagination and drive, and dependability and intelligence. In other words, college-educated workers earn more not because they've acquired valuable skills in college; rather, it is because the college admissions process is a valuable way of identifying talented individuals. A bachelor of arts degree from the University of Pennsylvania means something—the recipient almost certainly is literate and has high cognitive skills and moderately good work habits—qualities not always present in typical high school graduates. Employers will pay a premium wage for such a worker, knowing he or she is far more likely to have these desirable attributes (among others) than someone lacking a college degree. They are buying not just specific knowledge and skills accumulated by students in pursuit of their degrees, but broader qualities of intelligence, integrity, perseverance, and leadership that have little to do with learning acquired in college. Much of the "human capital" of the typical college graduate was not acquired in college itself.

The high earnings differential between high school and college gradu-ates means that the financial benefits of earning a college diploma typically outweigh the costs of getting it—not only the direct cost of paying for col-lege, but also the income forgone by studying rather than working. In other words, at the individual level, higher education is typically a good invest-ment, even though the marginal return to the community may be very low. Indeed, it is the high earnings differential (a college degree roughly doubles a worker's income) that has allowed universities to raise their tuition dramatically.

If university graduates can expect substantial financial benefits from their training, why should third parties like governments and private donors finance most of the cost of college? Why should low- and modest-income families through their tax payments give children from affluent fam-ilies opportunities to solidify and expand their already relatively opulent lifestyles? Why should governments subsidize education when the mar-ginal social return on that investment may be very low or even negative? Why should private individuals give money to universities to lower costs to students attending, when the students will reap huge financial benefits? Why not finance universities largely from student tuition?

Three arguments are used to justify external support of higher educa-tion. The most important is the so-called "positive externality" argument, as economists call it. According to this theory, universities have positive "spillover" effects, benefits that accrue to people other than the providers or recipients of university services. A well-educated population, for example, will likely make more informed decisions about public policies, individuals to elect to office, and so forth, leading to better governance. Yet it can be argued that colleges have negative spillover effects as well. Campus riots and disorders harm innocent third parties. "Politically correct" efforts by universities to stifle free expression can actually reduce discourse and dis-rupt the orderly communications that make democracy work. And there is an opportunity cost to supporting universities—those funds could other-wise be spent on valuable medical research, or national defense, or other highly productive areas.

Some empirical evidence suggests that the negative externalities may be greater, on balance, than the positive ones. For example, the ultimate expression of feeling toward a community comes when people move into or out of it. Moving into a community is a vote of confidence in that town, an indication that life there is better than in other locales. Similarly, out-migration is a sign that one believes life in that community is worse than elsewhere. Statistical evidence suggests that, holding other things equal, there is net out-migration from "university-intensive" states into ones where less effort (measured in various ways) is put into higher education. That is consistent with the notion that universities, on balance, have negative externalities.

The second argument in support of government subsidies is that our nation has long championed equal economic opportunity, and a college education is an important step to higher income, a necessary element of social mobility. Poor people cannot afford to go to college without state support, and will not have equal opportunities in life if they cannot afford a college education.

While this argument deserves respect, it also has severe weaknesses. If higher education conferred large financial benefits on students, banks and other lenders would readily make higher education loans without government loan guarantees—borrowing for college would be little different than borrowing to buy a business that is not making much money now but likely will in a few years. Even more important is the previously cited lack of correlation between governmental higher education support and the percentage of the populace going to college under current funding arrangements. At the minimum, the "equal educational opportunity" viewpoint argues for giving assistance to *students*, not to *institutions*, which often use funds for purposes not intended by the donors—an idea that I will return to later.

A final argument for governmental support is that universities perform functions beyond teaching that should not be charged to undergraduates. One particular function is to extend the frontier of knowledge through research. That research often leads to the development of vaccines or drugs that extend our life expectancy, innovations that enhance and diversify our productivity, and even works of art that help us define and interpret our lives.

This argument, however, is also somewhat flawed. To be sure, universities do research, some of it very useful. There is some doubt, however, whether the university is a better venue for most research than, say, private laboratories or nonprofit institutes. Much research has commercial potential, providing profits for the patent or copyright holders, and thus should appropriately be privately funded. Thus, it is not surprising that the proportion of basic research (that is, the quest for new ideas and discoveries) that is performed in university settings in America has declined over time, as private firms and other organizations take up more of this work. Besides, universities generally receive grants that ostensibly cover the cost of specific major research endeavors. Finally, some university research is relatively trivial and unproductive, done more for the sake of getting faculty members promoted than truly expanding the stock of human knowledge.

The arguments for public subsidies of higher education are, at the very least, highly debatable. A better than decent case can be made that perhaps government should, in general, largely get out of the higher education business, ending state subsidies and tax advantages for private donations. Moreover, the evidence is pretty persuasive that massive governmental infusions of funds, along with tax-sheltered private contributions, have contributed to the upsurge in higher education costs. Generous government support has also led to some unqualified students attending college. Many of them drop out, sometimes defaulting on their loans. Others linger on four-year college campuses for five or even six years at taxpayer expense.

As tuition mounts and concerns grow that American universities are not delivering their services efficiently, consumers can and do look for substitutes. More and more students are studying online. For-profit universities are growing exponentially, with the market valuation of the largest of them, Apollo Group (which runs the University of Phoenix), exceeding $13.6 billion and making roughly twenty cents on each dollar of revenue after tax. These schools are competing mainly for nontraditional adult students, but they can be expected to expand aggressively into the market for educating eighteen- to twenty-two-year-olds, a group that will stop growing in a few years. Similarly, relatively lower-cost community colleges may begin to take market share from the more expensive comprehensive universities. Computer whizzes now sometimes forgo expensive university computer science degrees, opting instead to pass company-administered examinations showing expertise with Oracle, Microsoft, or other computer-based systems.

Meanwhile, legislators and private donors have become somewhat more skeptical of university administrators' claims that they need more money. The 2001 recession and the stock market decline led to reductions in the growth of both public and private support for higher education, squeezing budgets and being offset only partly by bigger tuition increases than usual. In response, some universities are being forced to take steps to rein in their costs.

The continued growth of nontraditional alternatives to university training may make this cost-cutting exercise more than a cyclical phenomenon. It might lead, among other things, to heavier teaching loads for faculty, the slashing of administrative and other noninstructional positions, the abolition of tenure or the passing on of its implicit costs to recipients, the ending of expensive low-enrollment programs, particularly at the graduate level, the outsourcing or selling of certain noninstructional (or even remedial-instructional) operations to the market-based private sector, and the use of computers and television technology as substitutes for, not merely supplements to, traditional classroom teaching.

Yet the culture of universities is such that these changes will be resisted. Faculty will try to use their power to thwart cost-cutting moves, in some cases forming unions. Impatient legislators may try to "do something" about the problem, putting price controls on tuition, for instance, mandating minimum teaching loads, or abolishing tenure at public institutions. While most efforts will be focused at the state and local governmental level, even Congress will get involved, if the reaction to the 2002–3 tuition hikes is any indication. Congressional action is even more likely now because the Higher Education Act reauthorization is under consideration at the time this book is being released (mid-2004).

Even bolder changes in public policy might be forthcoming. Increasingly audible whispers from some politicians suggest that perhaps state universities should be privatized. A very strong case can be made for reducing public subsidies for universities gradually while increasing scholarship support for students themselves (already happening in Colorado), with this shift in emphasis taking place within five to ten years. With students paying most of the bills at public schools, university administrators likely would be more prone to pay attention to their needs, diverting fewer resources to noninstructional purposes. Fewer students would be closed out of courses (that is, not allowed to attend because of limits on class size). Fewer classes would be taught by foreign graduate assistants hardly fluent in the English language. Student price-sensitivity to tuition changes would increase, reducing the urge to raise sticker prices dramatically. Competition for students would increase in other ways as well, particularly if the vouchers or scholarships were acceptable at private colleges and universities, as was GI Bill financial aid for veterans after World War II.

Moreover, a scholarship (or voucher) program could include performance standards. A scholarship or voucher could be structured as a loan that would be forgiven if the student graduated, but would have to be repaid if the student dropped out. This would almost certainly lower attrition dramatically, as well as discourage undergraduate students from lingering on college campuses for more than four years.

Finally, such a voucher approach could be structured in a way that would appeal both to liberals on the left and libertarians on the right. Vouchers could be made progressive in nature, with larger amounts going to students from lower-income families, in keeping with the ideal of education as a vehicle to promote economic and social equality. Giving smaller vouchers (or perhaps no vouchers at all) to students from wealthy families would make them less dependent on government for financial assistance. Indeed, the voucherization of higher education largely would end the distinction between public and private universities. State universities, as we know them today, would become privatized, freed of many onerous governmental regulations.

This book expands upon and documents the assertions made above. The first four chapters lay the groundwork, outlining the magnitude of the tuition explosion and its underlying causes, and discussing the reasons for university inefficiency, productivity decline, and "rent-seeking." The section concludes with a discussion of some of the peculiarities of higher education, such as price discrimination, tenure, and the cross-subsidization of activities, and the reasons behind them.

The next three chapters place the tuition cost explosion in a broader perspective, asking such basic questions as, how have American universities changed over time? Why do we need universities? Why must universities require external support? Empirical evidence is introduced that suggests that universities have no positive impact on such quality of life indicators as growth in per-capita income or on in-migration to a region, but may well have negative effects.

In the last third of the book the emphasis turns to identifying solutions for these problems. Chapter 8 details the rise of nontraditional options, such as for-profit institutions and online instructional programs. Chapters 9 and 10 outline two different paths to change. One is evolutionary, with universities moving, reluctantly but largely of their own volition, to reform their ways. The second is more revolutionary, with change induced from outside and movement in the direction of making public support more student-centered and competitive, ultimately leading toward privatization. Chapter 11 is a final summing up and synthesis.

PART I

The Problem

1

The Cost Explosion

The cost of going to college has been going up sharply. Double-digit tuition increases at some universities have led to a rising chorus of complaints. Is the vaunted equality of opportunity that is a hallmark of American higher education threatened? Is the cost explosion a recent or long-term phenomenon? Why are costs rising so fast? Are there any signs that the problem will moderate in coming years?

Since 1978, the Bureau of Labor Statistics of the U.S. Department of Labor has maintained a college tuition and fees index as part of its compilation of the heavily used Consumer Price Index (CPI). Figure 1-1 shows how tuition has increased more than sixfold in just one-quarter of a century. To be sure, the overall CPI roughly tripled during the same period, but even on an inflation-adjusted basis, tuition somewhat more than doubled.

Table 1-1 gives the year-by-year details. Since 1981, tuition has risen faster than the overall inflation rate in every single year. In twenty of those twenty-three years, the differential exceeded 2 percent; in fifteen years, or about two-thirds of the time, the differential exceeded 3 percent. In nine years since 1981—39 percent of the total number of years—the increase exceeded the overall inflation rate by over 5 percentage points!

It is interesting to note that tuition increases are particularly large (relative to overall inflation) in or immediately after recessions. During recessions, businesses usually moderate price increases, and that tendency often persists into the early years of recovery. By contrast, universities tend to accelerate price increases in recessionary periods and the early recovery years. Note that real tuition (roughly, the difference between the rise in tuition and the overall inflation rate) rose by 5 percent or more in 1982, 1983, 1992, and 2002—all recession or early recovery years. By contrast,

3

FIGURE 1-1

THE RISE OF TUITION, 1978–2003

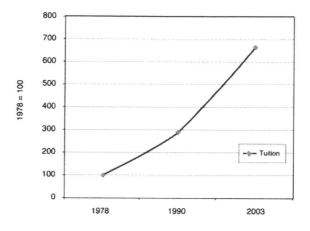

SOURCE: U.S. Department of Labor, Bureau of Labor Statistics. Underlying data are available at http://data.bls.gov/servlet/SurveyOutputServlet.

it rose by less than 3 percent in many late years of a boom, such as 1989, 1999, and 2000.

Why is that? My conjecture, based upon four decades' observation of university fiscal behavior, is that universities make up their budgets many months before each academic year, typically calling for generous spending increases; and when there are unexpected or abnormal revenue shortfalls from nontuition sources, they make up the difference by raising fees and drawing down cash reserves. In recessions and the first year or two thereafter, state appropriation increases diminish for state universities, and private universities are hit with lower contributions from private donors and, sometimes, lower investment income. As recovery begins, state appropriations typically remain depressed for a year or two, while schools can no longer draw down cash reserves. This increases the temptation to raise tuition substantially. In the private sector, by contrast, businesses try to build up sales that have declined or shown slow growth, and that makes them reluctant to raise prices. Moreover, their greater sensitivity to market forces, competition, and the carrot of the profit motive makes private businesses less willing to raise prices than universities.

TABLE 1-1

ANNUAL INCREASE IN TUITION AND OVERALL PRICES, 1979–2003

(PERCENT CHANGE)

Year	Tuition	CPI	Tuition − CPI
1979	7.90	10.70	−2.80
1980	8.26	14.43	−6.17
1981	12.23	9.79	2.44
1982	14.23	6.91	7.32
1983	10.66	3.44	7.22
1984	10.24	4.33	5.91
1985	9.11	3.57	5.53
1986	8.35	1.68	6.67
1987	7.86	3.67	4.19
1988	7.22	3.98	3.23
1989	8.01	5.28	2.73
1990	7.66	4.37	3.30
1991	9.38	5.03	4.34
1992	11.64	3.02	8.62
1993	9.67	3.22	6.45
1994	7.13	2.29	4.84
1995	6.01	3.12	2.89
1996	5.78	2.83	2.96
1997	5.25	2.24	3.01
1998	4.41	1.69	2.72
1999	4.03	2.09	1.94
2000	3.93	3.13	0.80
2001	4.60	3.62	0.98
2002	6.63	1.18	5.44
2003	7.41	2.06	5.35

SOURCE: Bureau of Labor Statistics; author's calculations. Underlying data are available at http://data.bls.gov/servlet/SurveyOutputServlet. Data are for month of May and are seasonally adjusted.

Another factor in the variability of the real rate of tuition increase (indicated roughly by the last column in table 1-1) is the inflation rate. Universities are slower than the private sector to react to changing demand and supply conditions—for one thing, tuition rates are rarely changed more than once a year. When the economy is hit with high inflation, as in 1979 and 1980, for example, costs rise less rapidly in the very short run for colleges than for most businesses, as labor and some other costs are semi-fixed.

Over the entire period 1978–2003, the mean annual increase in tuition exceeded the mean annual increase in the CPI by 3.6 percentage points. Interestingly, the variations in the CPI in an absolute and a relative sense were more pronounced than for the college tuition and fees index. The coefficient of variation (the standard deviation divided by the mean) on the tuition index was 0.332; on the CPI, it was more than twice as large, 0.724. This suggests that consumer prices in general were more volatile, and flexible, than college tuition, probably more responsive to changing underlying supply and demand conditions as influenced by general macroeconomic conditions and policies.

The relative rise in the cost of going to college did not start with the last generation. Actually, the tendency for university tuition to rise at a rate 2 to 3 percent greater than inflation goes back a century or more. In an important study done in the 1960s, economist (and later Princeton University President) William Bowen noted real tuition increases of that magnitude at major selective-admissions private universities from 1905 to 1965.[1] And Americans who attended college in the 1940s or 1950s know that tuition rose sharply faster than inflation at the selective private universities from 1945 to 1978, the first year for which the Bureau of Labor Statistics has data. During my undergraduate years at Northwestern University (1958–62), annual tuition increased over 50 percent (from $795 to $1,200), sharply more than the rate of inflation. For a while, public universities tried with some success to hold the line on inflation-adjusted tuition increases, but then they, too, succumbed, raising their fees sharply. For example, the real tuition for in-state students at Ohio University, a typical mid-size state institution, was essentially unchanged during the twelve-year period 1964–76. During the next twelve years (1976–88), real tuition rose at an annual rate of about 3.3 percent (similar to the national trend); the ascent continued during the twelve years after that (1988–2000), albeit slightly more slowly (2.4 percent a year).[2]

Price indices are difficult to construct with any degree of accuracy. There is a general consensus in the economics profession, for example, that the Consumer Price Index has systematically overstated the rate of inflation in modern times. One major commission initially estimated the overstatement at about 1.1 percentage points annually—a sizable error.[3] The same problems exist—with some additional wrinkles—for university tuition.

While a long exposition on this is beyond the scope of this inquiry, a few points are worth noting. The *quality* of higher education has changed over time. Comparing the experience of attending Harvard University or Slippery Rock College (now Slippery Rock University) in, say, 1960, with, say, 2003, is a bit like comparing apples and oranges. How do you account for qualitative changes? Also, over time, the increase in actual tuition paid by students may be less than that shown by indices because of a shift in the type of institution they attend. For example, in 2000, a much larger proportion of college students attended less-expensive public institutions than a century earlier. In the past half-century, there has been an increase as well in the proportion attending even less costly two-year colleges. The emergence of online education may accentuate that trend. As the relative price of going to expensive private universities rises, some students will migrate to less expensive substitutes.

Supporters of higher education might argue that there has been a sharp qualitative improvement in the undergraduate experience over time. Obviously, the physical facilities are better—students who in the past would have sweltered in classrooms in September or May now are likely to sit in air-conditioned comfort. Recreation centers and student unions are bigger and nicer—often with indoor jogging tracks, Olympic-sized swimming pools, and lots of fitness equipment. A *New York Times* article entitled "Jacuzzi University?" noted that university facilities increasingly rival those at fancy country clubs or exclusive resorts.[4] Computers, all but unknown thirty years ago, are usually available. PowerPoint, e-mail, and other computer-related innovations make lectures more interesting and professors more accessible. Students no longer stand in long lines to register for classes.

Yet there are some signs of qualitative decline in higher education as well. The school year has shortened somewhat over time. Increasing numbers of students take five years or more to earn bachelor's degrees, in part because of class closeouts. (To the extent that this is the case, tuition data alone *understate* the growing cost of obtaining a bachelor's degree.) The average score on the Graduate Record Examination—a standardized test taken by bachelor's degree recipients to apply for graduate school—has fallen somewhat over time, suggesting that students may be learning less than previously. The percentage of instruction offered by graduate students or part-time adjunct professors has increased relative to that offered by full-time senior faculty. All in all, it is difficult to say if, in any meaningful sense, the quality of the undergraduate experience has improved all that much—it certainly has not done so any more than goods and services generally.

In one respect, however, the tuition explosion may be exaggerated in terms of its impact on the population. As tuition has risen, so has scholarship assistance. The proportion of students receiving such assistance has increased, meaning that a smaller percentage actually pays full tuition than once was the case. The net charge—payments made after scholarship assistance—has risen somewhat less than the gross tuition itself.

Rising Tuition Costs and the Ability to Pay

Even allowing for scholarships, however, the real cost of a college education has gone up substantially for generations. This is true even for nontuition costs. For example, food and lodging costs, on average, appear higher—even after accounting for inflation. The absolute real financial burden of sending a child to college has grown substantially over time.

Moreover, that burden has grown faster than people's incomes. In 1958, the annual tuition at Northwestern University, $795, was about 15.6 percent of one year's median family income. Put a little differently, it took a bit less than fifty-seven days for a typical family to earn enough money to pay the Northwestern tuition. In fall 2003, the tuition for new students was $28,404. An estimate of the 2003 median family income (based on available data for 2001) indicates that the Northwestern tuition would be over 53.3 percent of a year's income. Instead of fifty-seven days to earn the fee, the typical family would have to spend almost 195 days. Northwestern would argue that its quality has improved since 1958 (in 2003 it tied Columbia for tenth place in the much-read *U.S. News & World Report* [*USN&WR*] national rankings of major research universities), that its fees have risen in accordance with those of other selective private universities, and that a student coming from a family with the median income would receive significant financial assistance.

All of this is true. Yet a majority of students attending even the elite private universities do not receive need-based scholarships, and much financial aid received by students from families of modest means comes in the form of loans, often putting the student in substantial debt very early in life.

TABLE 1-2

GROWTH IN TUITION AND CAPACITY TO PAY FOR COLLEGE, 1980–2000

Year	Real Tuition Fee	Real Median Family Income	Real GDP per Capita	Tuition-Family Income Ratio[a]	Tuition-GDP per Capita Ratio[b]	Tuition-GDP per Student Ratio[c]
1980	100	100	100	100	100	100
1985	129.7	101.8	111.4	127.4	114.4	115.5
1990	156.9	108.5	124.6	144.6	125.9	114.6
1995	202.7	109.9	131.5	184.4	154.1	131.7
2000	253.2	121.7	151.3	208.1	167.3	134.7

SOURCE: Bureau of Labor Statistics; Bureau of Economic Analysis; U.S. Census Bureau; author's calculations. Underlying data are available at http://data.bls.gov/servlet/SurveyOutputServlet; www.bea.doc.gov/dn/home/gdp.htm; www.census/www/statistical-abstract.us.html.
a. Col. 2 divided by col. 3 X 100.
b. Col. 2 divided by col.4 X 100.
c. Col. 2 divided by real GDP per student, not shown, X 100.

The generalization that the burden of college costs is growing does not only apply to private universities. Table 1-2 presents evidence on changes in real tuition and income over the twenty years from 1980 to 2000. The tuition index reported is based on the college tuition and fees component of the Consumer Price Index. The Bureau of Labor Statistics bases this index on fees from a multiplicity of institutions of different types and varying costs. Changes in the index are measured with relation to the figure for 1980, which is set at 100. Thus, the real tuition number for 1995, 202.7, implies that in inflation-adjusted terms, tuition slightly more than doubled from 1980 to 1995.

Two measures of the change in the capacity to pay for college are included in the table: real median family income and real gross domestic product (GDP) per capita. Each has advantages and disadvantages as a measure of financial capacity. "Median family income" represents the income received by a typical family. It may inappropriately measure the capacity to pay for college since the inflation adjustment used may understate income growth, and because the median (middle) income has risen less than the average (mean) income due to increasing income inequality. Since most college students come from families with incomes above the median, this is a matter of some importance. Per-capita GDP includes income that does not trickle down to individuals or families, such as business depreciation. Note that real median family income rose 21.7 percent, but real per-capita income grew 51.3 percent, over the two decades examined.

By any criterion, the burden of college costs grew faster than the capacity to meet that burden. Real tuition more than doubled relative to real median family income, and it increased by more than two-thirds with respect to real GDP per capita. For the last column of table 1-2, I calculated what might be the ultimate measure of ability to pay—the ratio of the real tuition to real total output (GDP) per college student. This statistic is an indicator of the amount of resources society produces for each student; a rise in tuition relative to it is clearly a sign of growing encroachment of higher education costs (as measured by tuition) on the economy. That ratio rose fairly steadily, with a pause in the late 1980s, by more than one-third over the two decades.

The rise in the ratio of tuition to output per capita or output per student cannot go on indefinitely. At some theoretical point, all the nation's resources would be devoted to higher education costs. Mathematically, therefore, at some point the ratio between tuition and GDP per capita must stop rising. Three phenomena can make that happen: GDP growth can accelerate, raising the denominator in the tuition/GDP ratio; the growth in tuition can slow down; or some combination of the first two possibilities can occur.

Perhaps this point can be more clearly made by returning to my example of the Northwestern University tuition. If the ratio of Northwestern's tuition to median family income rises by the same rate in the period 2003–48 (45 years) as it did over the previous 45 years, the tuition in 2048 will represent 1.82 years of median family income. In the context of today's economy, that would be the equivalent of a tuition rate of roughly $100,000 a year. Is such a fee sustainable? Maybe if virtually no one pays it himself, without aid, but if, as is the case now, a large number of students receive no need-based aid, private elite universities in the future will become largely preserves of the children of the very wealthy.

The rise in tuition varies somewhat with the type of college. Tuition has gone up a bit more in private than public universities, but that is largely because the rate of increase has been lower in two-year institutions, which are predominantly public (see figure 1-2).[5] The inflation rate for four-year

FIGURE 1-2
RISE IN REAL TUITION CHARGES, 1976–2001

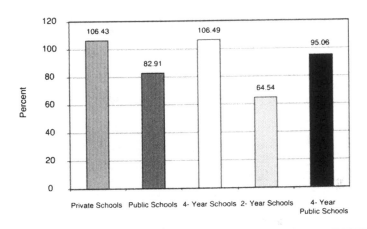

SOURCE: National Center for Education Statistics (NCES), *Digest of Education Statistics: 2002* (Washington, D.C.: Government Printing Office, 2003), table 312.

public and private schools is rather similar, although slightly higher for the private schools. All of this suggests that the "cost explosion" is greater in more research-intensive institutions, or, alternatively, that cross-subsidization of some activities in them has been increasing at the expense of others—that is, undergraduate students are being "taxed" (or at least subsidized less) to provide more resources for research, graduate education, and other purposes not directly related to their instruction. Institutions whose primary mission is teaching, such as two-year schools, have had somewhat less tuition inflation.

Higher Education Costs vs. Other Consumer Goods and Services

The rise in college tuition is greater than for any other major component in the Consumer Price Index, with the exception of tobacco products, which have risen more in price as a result of governmental and judicial actions such as litigation and tax increases. Increases in tuition far outdistance the rise in cost of the main necessities of life, such as food,

FIGURE 1-3
CHANGE IN CONSUMER PRICES, 1982–2003

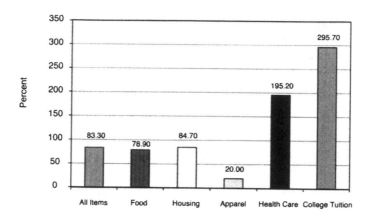

SOURCE: U.S. Bureau of Labor Statistics, http://www.bls.gov/news.release/cpi.toc.htm.

clothing, and shelter (see figure 1-3). Only in the area of medical services are the increases rivaled—those costs nearly tripled in the twenty years from the early 1980s to 2003, while tuition nearly quadrupled.

The importance of health care in the budgets of Americans has led to all sorts of changes designed to contain its soaring costs. The question is, will higher education, subject to even greater rising prices than health care and with similarly high levels of governmental involvement, face similar pressures to restructure or transform itself? Given the growing financial pressures, that seems likely.

Net vs. Gross Tuition Costs

As mentioned earlier, student financial assistance has risen sharply, so that the actual tuition paid by students (hereafter called the net tuition) is often less than the stated "sticker price," or gross tuition. While more discussion of this issue comes in later chapters, it is worth examining here the extent to which rising scholarship aid reduces the true increase in tuition. What is the rate of increase in net tuition?

FIGURE 1-4

REAL GROSS VS. REAL NET TUITION INCREASES FOR
PRIVATE SCHOOLS, 1980–95

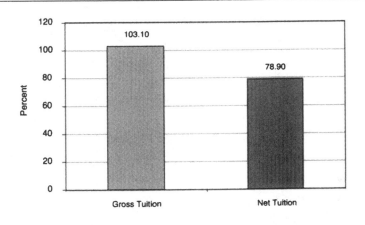

SOURCE: NCES, *Digest of Education Statistics: 2001* (Washington, D.C.: Government Printing Office, 2002), tables 316, 332, 347; underlying price data from Bureau of Labor Statistics, ftp://ftp.bls/gov/pub/specialrequests.cpi/cpiai.txt.

Since the tuition cost issue is particularly pressing for private schools, with charges often reaching $30,000 a year, I examined the ratio of scholarship assistance to tuition at private universities. Unfortunately, reliable detailed data are available only after a lengthy time lag, so the analysis could extend only as far as the 1995–96 school year. Nonetheless, it was illuminating to observe that during the 1980–81 school year, scholarship money equaled 17.55 percent of tuition revenues for private universities, increasing to 27.38 percent by 1995–96. The rising proportion of tuition met by scholarships meant that the effective net tuition on average rose less than the gross amount used in calculating price indices.

Using this information, I calculated the increase in real net charges over the fifteen-year period (figure 1-4). The increase was reduced by nearly one-fourth. On a compounded annual basis, real gross tuition charges for all universities rose 4.83 percent a year; using net tuition allowing for increased scholarship (tuition-discounting) assistance, the rate fell to "only" 3.95 percent per year. Thus, it is true that increased scholarship assistance moderates the tuition rate increases—but only modestly. Even using average real net tuition as a measure of college costs, the increase in real terms is shown to be substantial.

Why Has Real Tuition Risen? Simple Supply and Demand Analytics

Prices rise for a reason or, more often, for several reasons. We must distinguish between a general increase in prices—inflation—that occurs in large part because of certain phenomena in the whole, or macro, economy, from price increases that occur because of factors specific to a certain good or service. Here we will talk in terms of the real tuition, adjusting for inflation-induced increases that are a natural consequence of such macro-policies as, for instance, increasing the money supply or having deficit-financed government spending increases.

Putting general inflation aside, the price of a good or service goes up because the demand for it increases, the supply falls, or both happen at once. One of the most fundamental propositions in economics—the law of demand—is that consumer desire to purchase a good or service varies inversely with its price: As prices rise, the quantity demanded falls. This idea is shown pictorially as the demand curve, two examples of which are included in figure 1-5.

Looking at the line marked D_1, we see that when tuition (the price of college) is lower, the number of students wanting to attend is greater than at higher tuition levels. That is also true of line D_2, although in the latter case the impact of changing price on the quantity demanded is greater—people are more sensitive to it. While it is probably true that people may be relatively insensitive about price in deciding whether to go to college at all (demand curve D_1), they are far more sensitive about tuition when it comes to deciding on *specific* schools (demand curve D_2).

If all colleges were to increase their tuition by 10 percent, the number of students applying for college might fall by, say, 2 percent. We would say that the "elasticity of demand" is −0.20—that is, a decline in applications of 2 percent, divided by a 10 percent price increase. That is roughly consistent with D_1. However, if only a specific university, say Duke, were to raise its tuition by 10 percent while all the others kept theirs the same, the number of applications might fall by 12 percent, implying an

FIGURE 1-5

RESPONSIVENESS OF STUDENTS TO TUITION INCREASES

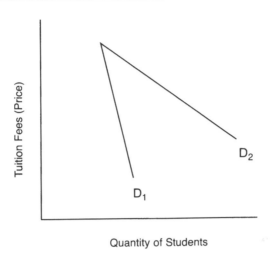

Quantity of Students

SOURCE: Author's illustration.

elasticity of demand of −1.2 (12 percent applications decline divided by a 10 percent price increase). Individuals in this example would simply substitute another school, say Northwestern or Cornell, for Duke. We would say that the elasticity of demand for individual schools is fairly high (for example, −1.2—ignoring the negative sign and speaking of a high elasticity), even while that for universities in general may be fairly low (for example, −0.2).

Tuition depends upon supply as well as demand considerations. The willingness of colleges to provide places for students is likewise dependent in part on price, with the difference being that the willingness to educate varies directly with price—the law of supply. The more money available from each student, the greater the incentive for the university to educate more students, even using expensive methods of instructing them if necessary to obtain more revenue. Figure 1-6 shows a supply curve analogous to the demand curve, drawn along with a demand curve discussed earlier.

The place where the demand and supply curves intersect (point A in figure 1-6) determines the price of goods and services in the private sector. It

FIGURE 1-6

IMPACT OF CHANGING DEMAND AND SUPPLY

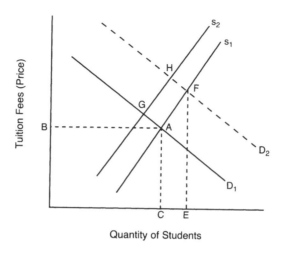

Quantity of Students

SOURCE: Author's illustration.

represents the unique price (B in figure 1-6) at which consumers (students) are able to get the services they want and suppliers (universities) are willing to provide those services. It is often called an equilibrium price, since it will tend to exist and persist until one or the other of the curves changes location.

With universities, however, sometimes prices (tuition levels) are established at below the equilibrium price level at a price where the quantity demanded, as indicated by the demand curve, exceeds the quantity that a given university is willing to supply. Consequently, some students who apply are rejected. This is the case with selective-admissions universities. For the moment, however, let us confine our analysis to open-admissions institutions—ones that accept all students who meet the minimum standards for admission. A large proportion of public institutions fits into this category.

For tuition rates to rise over time, one of three things must occur: The demand curve must shift upward and to the right (to D_2 in figure 1-6); the supply curve must shift upward and to the left (to S_2 in figure 1-6); or both shifts must occur simultaneously.

A shift to the right in the demand curve, which economists call "an increase in demand," moves the equilibrium price to a higher level (the

intersection point is at F instead of A), as does a shift to the left in the supply curve (the intersection is at G instead of A). When both shifts occur
simultaneously, the price moves up sharply (from A to H). Note that an
increase in demand will raise not only prices (tuition) but also the number of students, the exact amount depending on the sensitivity of supply
(university admissions) to tuition increases. A decrease in supply, by contrast, will lead to tuition increases but enrollment declines.

The actual history of the last several decades has been one of tuition
and enrollment increases simultaneously—consistent with rising
demand. In reality, we may have had a large increase in demand over time
and a smaller reduction in supply. Both effects lead to higher tuition, and
the demand increases predominate over the supply decreases in terms of
enrollment impacts.

Reasons for the Rise in Demand. Shifts in demand occur because something changes other than the price—or tuition, in this case. What might
account for the sharp rise in demand over time that has led to constantly
rising inflation-adjusted tuition? First, there are several factors that are
not related to public policy. One is demographic change.

Over time, the population of eighteen- to twenty-four-year-olds has
generally risen, although not in a neat linear fashion. Indeed, there have
been periods (the late 1970s and 1980s, in particular), when the pool of
eighteen- to twenty-four-year-olds declined, because of the waning of the
postwar baby boom or related factors.

University officials tend somewhat to exaggerate the importance of the
population variable. Thus, in the early 1970s, when some universities
anticipated a decline in the eighteen- to twenty-four-year-old base population, they altered their capital budgets and academic planning to meet a
corresponding decline in enrollments. They developed new programs for
adult learners and increased marketing expenditures. But the enrollment
decline never happened.

Universities' fears about adverse affects of population decline on
tuition also turned out to be unfounded. From 1982 to 1987, for example, the eighteen- to twenty-four-year-old population pool declined by
almost precisely 10 percent—a rather sharp fall for a five-year period.[6] Yet
enrollments actually went up very slightly, and real tuition rose in every

single year by more than 4 percent—above the long-term average growth. Still, the perceived demographic threat led universities to alter strategies, for example developing new programs for adult learners and increasing marketing expenditures. Rising higher education participation more than offset the demographic phenomenon of a declining cohort of traditional college age.

Also factoring into the rising demand for higher education has been a general improvement in Americans' standard of living. With substantial economic growth having persisted for at least 160 years, incomes have risen, along with desires for more education. The perceived educational requirements associated with a job at any relative earnings level also have gone up. These conditions have led increasing numbers of people to use some of their incremental income to indulge their dreams of providing more for their children than their parents did for them. In more technical terms, economists say that the income-elasticity of demand for higher education is fairly high—probably well over 1.0. This means that, with other factors being equal, a 1 percent increase in income leads to a desire to increase spending on higher education by more than 1 percent.

As further discussed in a coming chapter, it is almost certainly true that there has been a bit of a "revolution of rising expectations" in college aspirations in the past twenty years relative to the era from, say, 1945 to 1975 or 1980. In that earlier period, the income-elasticity of demand was probably high for all forms of higher education, ranging from newly formed junior colleges and technical schools to prestigious private universities. Families that had never sent anyone to college were delighted to see their progeny attend junior colleges, for example. In the past generation, however, a more affluent America has become more picky. Increasingly, two-year schools are looked upon as less desirable, and dads and moms who went to junior colleges want their kids to go to flagship state universities. Parents who went to state universities of reasonably good quality now aspire to send their children to elite private institutions.

On this basis, one would expect tuition to have risen less at the two-year institutions, the demand for which is growing less rapidly now than for their four-year counterparts. The statistical evidence presented in figure 1-2 confirms this: Real tuition has risen over 50 percent faster in four-year institutions.

At the same time, however, real tuition levels, while rising sharply, have not risen significantly more (in percentage terms) at the elite private schools than at four-year state universities in the past couple of decades. Graphic presentations such as figure 1-6, based upon traditional market-clearing assumptions, would suggest that tuition should have risen faster in the private schools if, in fact, demand for their services were rising more than for other institutions.

But it did not. Why? Selective-admissions universities, by definition, price their services *below* the equilibrium, market-clearing price. In terms of figure 1-6, assuming the demand curve is D_1 and the supply curve is S_1, the intersection point A would determine price (at level B) and quantity in a world of open admissions; this describes a large variety of institutions. Where colleges turn down significant numbers of applicants, however, tuition is set *below* price B, where the quantity demanded exceeds the quality supplied. The larger the proportion of rejected applicants, the lower tuition is relative to the equilibrium price B.

Over time, the number of applications has risen faster than the number admitted (which tends to be rather stable at the best universities), meaning that the equilibrium price has risen faster than the posted tuition charge. Why don't the selective universities take greater advantage of rising demand and raise their fees even more than they have, as a typical top-flight university rejects literally thousands of applicants?

The reason they have not is that to do so would lower their image as elite, extremely selective private universities—and lower the number of applicants. The number of applicants falls not simply because the price has risen (a manifestation of the law of demand), but because there is a perceived qualitative decline associated with accepting a larger proportion of applications. In terms of figure 1-6, there is a shift to the left and downward in the demand curve—at any given tuition level, fewer apply.

The desire of selective-admissions universities to price their services below the maximum feasible price is accentuated by the fact that college ratings, especially the influential *U.S. News & World Report* rankings, are in part determined by the degree of selectivity. A college that turns more students away is, by definition, better in the eyes of *USN&WR*. However, *USN&WR* also gives higher rankings for universities that spend more on faculty and have high alumni giving. On balance, to improve in the

USN&WR rankings, a school needs to spend more money but keep tuition as low as possible. This means that the rankings bias universities toward increasing the amount of third-party financing of their activities. Hence, universities have beefed up their fundraising efforts and appeals for both state appropriations and federal grants and engaged increasingly in commercial activities, such as licensing logos for sweatshirts or offering short-term executive education programs, designed to make a profit that can be used to finance academic activities.

Certainly, real nontuition financing of higher education has grown over time, rising roughly as fast as real tuition, as the proportion of total university funding financed by fees has remained relatively stable. *The impact of third-party financing of education is to move demand curves to the right, raising tuition.*

This is particularly true of scholarships and loans to students. Suppose a student is offered a Pell Grant or a Stafford Loan. That increases the student's ability to pay any given amount of tuition, increasing in turn the chances she or he will apply to and attend the college in question. The shift to the right in the demand curve for students—and the resulting higher tuition—has been aided and abetted by a large and proliferating number of government assistance programs—some grants, some guaranteed student loans, some work-study programs. In the 1999–2000 school year, nearly 58 percent of full-time undergraduate students in American universities were receiving some form of federal assistance, such as Pell Grants, Supplement Educational Opportunity Grants, college work study, Perkins Loans, Stafford Loans, and PLUS (Parent Loans for Undergraduate Students).[7]

In the seven-year period 1992–99, student borrowing for higher education—financed by federal or state governments, institutions, employers, and so forth—more than doubled, rising at an extraordinary compounded annual rate of 10.9 per cent—well over *triple* the rate of inflation. Even in the 1991–92 school year, over two-thirds of students received some sort of support. By the school year ending in 2000, the proportion exceeded 82 percent—only students from truly high-income homes did not get some form of assistance.[8] Since most loans to students are subsidized—given at below-market interest rates with generous payback provisions—and others are even forgiven, students do not see loans as a burden equal to the dollar amount of the principal. (Moreover, many students in their late teens are not fully conversant with the concept of meeting debt obligations.)

Another form of third-party financing of higher education has been, in recent years, the tax breaks instituted by the federal government on the individual income tax for college expenses. These breaks mean, in effect, that the federal government is subsidizing tuition payments through a loss in federal income tax revenues. In 1998, the Hope and Lifetime Learning tax credits were created, allowing credits against income tax payments of up to $1,500. Coverdell Educational Savings Accounts, or ESAs (named after the Senate sponsor of the legislation, the late Paul Coverdell), which allow tax-sheltered savings for college purposes, increased dramatically in 2002 to $2,000 per year. All states also offer what are termed 529 plans, in which families can prepay tuition at in-state public universities at guaranteed real tuition levels in a tax-sheltered fashion.

All of these things have increased the demand for higher education. The extraordinary rise in student loan programs and federal tax credits, along with traditional scholarship aid, has done to higher education what private insurance, Medicare, and Medicaid have done to health care—led to enormous increases in the price of services provided.

In a sense, much of the attempt to make college more affordable to students is ultimately self-defeating. Increased financial assistance in the form of government or private loans and grants or tax credits makes it easier for universities to raise their charges—and to use the increased incomes for a variety of purposes, some of which have relatively little to do with enhancing the undergraduate learning experience. When federal legislation was approved in the late 1990s offering tuition tax credits, I jokingly referred to it as the Faculty Salary Enhancement Act, reasoning that for every $1,000 in tuition tax credit granted, universities would raise their tuition by close to $1,000, and that professors would consequently receive larger salary increases than they would have otherwise. In coming chapters, we will show that in fact this joke has a strong factual basis, not only with respect to faculty salaries, but to other expansions in the higher education enterprise.

The Role of Supply. The simple graphics shown earlier in this chapter suggested that when prices and quantities both increased, that reflected a rise in demand relative to supply. However, it is possible that the price rises in education were at least somewhat affected by supply-side developments. An increase in supply, by itself, would have lowered tuition, so the likelihood of there having been meaningful increases in supply seems remote. Since a decrease in supply by itself would have contributed further to rising tuition, it is possible that this has happened; but supply reductions also tend to reduce quantities, which has not happened. Some supply reduction, however, would be possible along with a large demand increase, leaving a situation where tuition rises sharply and total enrollments increase moderately. This is what has happened in recent years.

Supply is largely governed by costs of production. A key factor, in turn, in determining costs is productivity: If workers every year turn out more widgets than the year before (become more productive), firms will be willing to expand output at existing prices. If, however, output per worker is falling and salaries are increasing, the willingness to supply goods or services at existing prices declines—leading to a reduction in supply. That is what has happened in contemporary American higher education.

Conclusions

The cost to consumers of higher education has risen sharply, even after adjusting for the overall rise in prices of goods and services reflecting inflationary policies. The rise in tuition far outstrips the growth in people's incomes—it takes a larger proportion of the annual (or lifetime) income of individuals to pay for college than it did, say, a generation ago. This is a trend that cannot persist indefinitely—at some point people would be working a lifetime simply to pay for college. Forces will go to work to compel a moderation in the rise in tuition relative to overall prices and to people's incomes. The last part of this book discusses the details of how that might happen.

The rise in the cost of college no doubt has elements of both supply and demand, but the increase in demand appears to play the dominant role. More students want to go to a given college at a given price today than in the past, in part for reasons related to the dynamic growth of the American economy—the growth in population and income per capita, for example.

But much of the increased demand reflects the policies of the universities themselves and of governments. Scholarship assistance has increased, so that the net cost to the student of attending college on average has fallen relative to the total amount of tuition.

Even after allowing for scholarships, however, costs have risen sharply on average for students. A hugely important factor in rising demand is soaring student loan and related assistance, largely provided by the federal government. In short, students increasingly rely on third parties— governments and private donors—to help finance their educations. This has enhanced the increase in demand, raised tuition levels, and provided new resources to universities. How have the universities utilized their enhanced revenues? This is the topic to which we now turn.

2

Why Are Universities
Inefficient and Costly?

To this point, we have described the cost explosion in American higher education—its magnitude and proximate causes. In this chapter, we will elaborate on the reasons for the inefficiencies in higher education that have contributed to that explosion. We will point out that universities operate in a radically different environment than most business enterprises, and that there are four major reasons for rising costs: third-party providers, the lack of market discipline, ineffective price competition, and government regulation.

Resource Allocation: Universities vs. Private Business Enterprise

Most large organizations create budgets upon which they base their determinations of how many resources will be used over a given time period (typically, one year), and how they will be allocated. Universities, like large business enterprises, have budgets, which they typically begin to formulate six months to a year before a fiscal year begins (although sometimes the work is not completed until a few weeks before the beginning of the year). Very often, they solicit units within the institution to state their needs, and then some central budget committee or group of administrators decides which needs are critical and which are not. The sum of all the needs approved for funding is the spending target. Tuition is then set to make up the difference between that target and anticipated income from government grants or subsidies, endowment income, and new gifts. In other words, tuition pricing is set by expenditure decisions. There are variants on this approach, and sometimes intrayear adjustments are made because of unanticipated developments.

Contrast this to private business, which faces far more uncertainty as to revenues that depend upon the volume of sales and price levels. Most universities, particularly those with selective admissions, can closely estimate the volume of business (number of students) they can expect. Tuition is set administratively and is unchanging during the year. In private business, volume fluctuates with competition, overall business conditions, and other factors, and pricing changes frequently in response to changing costs and competitive pressures. The goal is not to match revenues and expenditures, but to maximize the gap between these two (with revenues higher), so as to maximize profits, and to do so in an environment of considerable revenue uncertainty.

Businesses thus need to be flexible, to be able to reduce spending to match falling revenues, or to bolster it in areas of high demand. Resources are reallocated accordingly to accommodate changes in supply and demand in the marketplace, and cost reductions are effected as the relative price of one resource, say labor, rises relative to another. To cut costs, a grocery store may decide to put in scanners, substituting capital equipment for labor. To bolster revenues, a firm might decide to spend more on advertising. Although an overall budget exists and some spending is relatively fixed in the short run, budgeting is dynamic. The notion that prices are set annually to raise enough funds to balance predetermined expenditures is generally an alien concept in the private business world. There is a bit of truth to the notion that *in higher education, costs determine revenues, while in for-profit businesses, revenues determine costs.*

Moreover, in setting revenue needs, the president, administrators, and, ultimately, the trustees of a university are under pressure from many constituencies, including the faculty. Unlike staff in private business, the faculty has considerable power. The notion of a superior-subordinate relationship is far less firmly established, as tenured professors cannot be fired. Sometimes alumni and trustees also influence spending decisions. There is far less concern about cutting costs to meet the prices of competitors, and concerns about customer disenchantment are far fewer than with profit-making enterprises.

In private businesses, the top officials and often many of the rank-and-file staff benefit by cutting costs—the stock price goes up (making stock options extremely valuable), profit-sharing bonuses are bigger, and so forth.

In universities, there are no bonuses for cutting costs. Indeed, life is usually better if there is more staff around to do the work—having more instructors, for example, means smaller class sizes, which reduces time spent grading and counseling students. Since faculties are influential in selecting deans and other administrators, administrators tend to acquiesce at least partly in faculty spending requests, even when they lower productivity.

Four Reasons for Rising Costs

Third-Party Providers and the Vicious Circle of Funding and Spending. Chapter 1 showed how rising government and private assistance to higher education has boosted the demand for university services, raising prices (tuition) and the number of students, and greatly increasing revenues. The various university constituencies, not faced with a profit imperative, have eagerly spent these incremental funds—often to provide higher salaries, more staff, more equipment, nicer physical surroundings, and other amenities not directly related to instruction.

The key importance of third-party providers is that they have reduced resistance to rising prices on the part of first-party participants in higher education, namely, students and their families. When guaranteed student loans are readily available, or a scholarship grant is provided to reduce the amount of tuition the student must pay, universities can raise their tuition more aggressively than would be the case in a private market environment, without much loss of students.

In a sense, America has gotten itself into a vicious circle with respect to higher education financing that goes like this: In year 1, tuition goes up fairly substantially. Political pressures build to "do something" about the increases. Congress expands guaranteed student loan programs to make education more affordable, in turn increasing the demand for education and allowing universities in year 2 (or year 3, depending on the lag) to raise prices further. The result is a further expansion of student loan programs, state scholarship efforts, and other third-party funding.

The key to reform is to break the vicious circle by *not* expanding third-party payments in response to rising costs. This would push more of the cost of education directly onto the student consumer, making him or her more price-sensitive. Price-sensitive consumers of educational services will reduce the quantity demanded for them, forcing institutions to be more cost-conscious in an attempt to maintain applications for admission at current levels.

The Lack of Market Discipline. Except in the case of for-profit institutions, the incentive to perform well, reduce costs, or expand revenue by offering improved services is pretty weak in higher education. There are exceptions: Coaches are given bonuses if they achieve certain objectives, like making the NCAA Final 16 in basketball or winning a major bowl game. Often a winning football coach can move to another institution at a vastly higher salary. Occasionally, trustees will give their university president a bonus if he or she is able to raise the school to a higher level in the *USN&WR* college rankings, although this is relatively unusual. Rarely, bonuses are given for cost-saving innovations.

More often, however, the incentives work in the direction of reducing productivity and efficiency. Deans, department chairs, and heads of administrative units are always trying to increase their budgets, not minimize them, since bigger budgets mean more power and greater resources to get the job done. In a sense, they actually fight the administration for the right to *lower* productivity—to use more resources to get a given quantity of "output" measured in terms of student credit-hours and/or published research.

In the late 1980s and 1990s, American firms restructured and downsized to become leaner and meaner, to increase their competitiveness in national and, especially, international markets. For example, IBM, a profitable company that was faltering in terms of growth in profits, reduced its labor force rather abruptly by sixty thousand, or about 20 percent. Contrast that to universities, which have done no appreciable downsizing because they feel no market pressure to do so. Indeed, staffs, especially administrative, have become more bloated. My university, Ohio University, is not atypical; over the course of less than a decade, the number of "associate provosts" increased from two to seven. The University of Georgia is a fine institution that has been rising in the *USN&WR* rankings, and, by university standards, it seems ably administered. Its senior administrative staff is rather typical: one president, three "senior" vice presidents (one the provost, one for finance and administration, and one for "external affairs"), four other vice presidents, and seven associate provosts. Not only is there a "senior vice president for academic affairs" (also the provost), but there is also a "vice president for instruction." Not only is there a "senior vice president for external affairs," but there is also a "vice president for public service and outreach." Several of the associate provost titles would have been unheard of a generation ago: "associate provost and chief information officer for information technology"; "associate provost for institutional diversity"; "associate provost for institutional effectiveness"; and "associate provost for international affairs." Some universities even have their own secretaries of state!

Only when unanticipated revenue shortfalls occur, typically during or shortly after recessions, do universities do some modest downsizing. For example, Ohio University recently eliminated two associate provost positions and one vice president position, saving probably around $500,000 a year, after a (much complained about) reduction in state appropriations. Life goes on as smoothly as ever.

A big part of the problem is what the great Austrian economist Ludwig von Mises in a slightly different context once called the "calculation" problem.[1] Where profits are not pursued as the primary institutional goal, it is difficult to measure success and failure. A business is clearly a success if profits increase and is faltering when profits fall or are negative, but it is very difficult to know if a university is getting better or worse—that is why the rankings of *USN&WR* and others take on such importance.

Yet college rankings are subjective and they vary significantly, depending on criteria. Which national university offers the best undergraduate education to a bright student? As of this writing, *USN&WR* says it is Princeton, but *Princeton Review*, a guide that relies on student evaluations, says the "best overall academic experience" can be found at Northwestern—a school ranked only ninth by *USN&WR*. Northwestern, no doubt, also touts the *Business Week* rankings of business schools, since its Kellogg School is ranked number one, but *USN&WR* likes Harvard the best; and *The Wall Street Journal* favors the Tuck School of Dartmouth College.[2] Among liberal arts colleges, Wabash College ranks a respectable but not outstanding forty-fourth in the *USN&WR* rankings, but makes the top ten in the *Princeton Review*.[3] In short, quantifying excellence and success is a messy, subjective, and highly debatable business for nonprofit universities.

For the University of Phoenix, however, the nation's largest for-profit institution of higher education, the process is easy—after-tax profits, profits per share, and profit growth over time are all related measures that show the institution is doing well and getting better. The stock market price of its parent company, Apollo Group, is an excellent measure of the extent to which the investor community values this company—and of how that valuation changes over time. Top executives can acquire wealth if the stock price rises—and lose it if it falls. Their financial status is tied to the company's financial performance (and, as we will see in chapter 8, they have done very well indeed). The key to raising both profits and the stock price—and thus their own wealth—is providing a service people want to buy, satisfying their customers, and keeping costs down. That is why the cost structure of the University of Phoenix is dramatically different than that of the typical university.

A caveat is in order. It is not true that universities are totally immune to any sort of market discipline, as are most primary and secondary public schools. Universities do raise part of their income from tuition, sporting events, room and board charges, and research contracts, and thus depend on markets. Universities cannot be totally oblivious to the tuition their academic rivals charge, for example. They have to consider whether raising football game ticket prices will increase revenues—and whether it is worth the adverse publicity. Moreover, they compete in markets for resources. Well-known full professors often earn $200,000 a year or more these days, simply because of competition in the labor market for their services. (Having "star" professors on the faculty can raise rankings and enhance institutional reputation and the receipt of grants and gifts.) Still, relative to private, for-profit companies, the discipline of the market in promoting productivity growth and product improvement is pretty limited.

The difference between nonprofit institutions and, say, the University of Phoenix is illustrated by the quest for rankings. The University of Phoenix is only tangentially interested in the USN&WR and other rankings—it would be nice for marketing purposes to make the list, but real success is measured by the "bottom line" in terms of profits. However, nonprofit universities, wanting to proclaim institutional success and having no other way to do so, take the rankings very seriously. And how does one improve in the rankings? Obviously, it varies. The *USN&WR* criteria are different than those of *Kiplinger's Personal Finance, Princeton Review*, or others in the ranking game. But *USN&WR* is the best known, and it gives positive marks to schools with high levels and percentages of donations from alumni and many faculty resources. Thus, the "output" (in the form of rankings) of universities is positively correlated with the amount of money received. Success (a higher ranking) is gained by spending more money—almost the opposite of the way success is defined in market settings. The incentives for increasing efficiency and productivity are scarce indeed in the typical university community.

Ineffective Price Competition. Tell a university president that his institution does not vigorously compete with its peers, and he or she will vehemently disagree, and with reason. There is no doubt that universities vie with one another for students, faculty members, research grants, and high rankings from *USN&WR* and other organizations, not to mention on the athletic fields. Competition is alive in American higher education.

At the same time, however, price competition is muted compared with private business. McDonald's has ninety-nine-cent specials and introduces new products to try to lure business away from Wendy's and Burger King. General Motors offers rebates to try to take sales away from Ford or Toyota. Even eye surgeons advertise LASIK surgery for $499 per eye, trying to take business away from competitors who charge more. In higher education, there is some moderately vigorous competition for students, using tuition discounts as a lure. But there is very little attempt to alter sticker prices as a way to achieve a market advantage.

The top ten *USN&WR*-ranked universities all charge tuition exceeding $25,000 per year. All give substantial tuition discounts to many, though by no means all, students. If the actual tuition is, say, $28,000 a year, the average net tuition charge may be something like $19,000 (assuming average scholarship aid of $9,000 per student), much of which can be borrowed at low interest rates. A strategy that one of these universities, say Duke, could pursue that almost certainly would have the long-run effect of raising already high *USN&WR* rankings would be as follows:

Cut noninstructional costs by $1,000 per student by eliminating fifty administrative and fifty nonadministrative support positions, possibly including some faculty positions in areas of low student demand. (It is a rare university that could not do this without serious detriment to its mission.) Announce a 25 percent tuition reduction, from $28,000 to $21,000 a year. Reduce average scholarship aid to $3,000 per student, lowering average net tuition from $19,000 to $18,000 (the difference financed by reducing bureaucracy).

The university would instantly gain positive national publicity as the school bucking the trend toward more costly education. It would receive a surge in applications from children of upper-middle-class and wealthy families that receive little in the way of scholarship support but still consider tuition a significant financial obligation (say, families with incomes of $125,000 a year). Average SAT scores would rise, propelling USN&WR rankings upward. Since few of the personnel eliminated are faculty, the faculty resource measure in the rankings would be unaffected.

Why doesn't Duke (or some other school below the very top, like Columbia, Stanford, or Northwestern) do this? First of all, the strategy of cutting administrative costs would meet with some opposition within the university community, especially from top-level administrators surrounding the president who would see their staffs reduced.

Second, the university president who did this might be ostracized by fellow presidents, who get together regularly at meetings of the American Council of Education and other organizations (a practice that might be considered a violation of the antitrust laws if done in the private sector) and are friends. The club-like atmosphere in which they operate is so close that until the U.S. Justice Department intervened in the early 1990s, representatives of top universities met to discuss individual students in devising scholarship assistance strategies. The Justice Department considered that a form of price-fixing, and the universities reluctantly agreed to desist from the practice.

Third, the reduction in tuition-discounting would be viewed by some as a retreat from the stated position that no applicant would be denied admission based on financial considerations (although that argument is already weakened by the availability of low-interest-rate loans that even low-income students can obtain). For these reasons, it is rare to see price competition such as this erupt.[4]

Government Regulation. Although most college students in the United States attend government institutions, university presidents often complain about excessive government regulation. State universities often have to pay "prevailing wages" to workers constructing their buildings, adding to capital costs. Environmental rules have greatly increased the cost of waste disposal from research laboratories. The cost of complying with affirmative action, rules about research involving human subjects, regulations on the use of animals in research, and occupational health and safety restrictions is substantial. The complaints of universities in this regard are rather similar to those from businesses in the private sector.

Until the late 1960s, universities largely were exempt from the provisions of the Fair Labor Standards Act, which set minimum wages and required time-and-a-half for overtime work, among other regulations. Often college students would be hired to perform routine tasks for slightly less than the minimum wage. Now some states, such as Washington and Oregon, have state minimum wage laws that considerably exceed the federal standard, and my guess is that their existence has led to fewer students being hired, but higher overall wage payments than would be the case in an unhampered labor market.

State labor laws have in some cases led to unionization of faculty and staff at universities, raising labor costs significantly. The federal legislative mandate ending mandatory retirement for faculty has similarly increased costs and reduced productivity. Visa restrictions, tightened by national security concerns after the September 11, 2001, terrorist attacks, have raised the cost to universities of admitting foreign students and occasionally have wreaked havoc on graduate enrollments as accepted students fail to get visa approval.

More regulation is associated with Title IX legislation concerning intercollegiate athletics. That legislation and its enforcement have led to a massive increase in spending on women's sports, which arguably is good from a social standpoint, but which nonetheless has raised costs. Universities often bitterly complain (more privately than publicly) about the arbitrary and inflexible way in which Title IX is enforced.

The tremendous upsurge in litigation of recent years has not bypassed universities. University hospitals and clinics have faced enormous increases in malpractice insurance premiums. University legal departments have been expanded to deal with a variety of lawsuits ranging from wrongful employment termination to sexual harassment, legal actions that would have not occurred a generation or two ago when the "employment at will" doctrine governed labor relations and sexual harassment laws did not exist.

The Future: Factors Restricting Spending Growth

The rise in university costs will be constrained ultimately by economic reality—universities cannot continue absorbing an ever-larger proportion of the nation's output indefinitely. Several factors might reduce the growth in university revenues over time, which, in turn, will force cost-containment efforts and attempts at productivity enhancement more serious than those observed to date.

The Slowing Growth or Reversal of the College Earnings Differential. One reason colleges and universities have been able to raise their tuition enormously over time is the perception that higher educational training is a good investment. From 1970 to 2002, the earnings differential between those with four years of college and high school graduates rose sharply (tables 2-1 and 2-2). To prospective university students who view education largely as a "human-capital investment decision," the differential from acquiring extra expected lifetime incomes between high school and college graduates has increased—the financial benefits of going to college have grown, justifying spending more money to attend.

Note that the earnings differential between four-year (bachelor's degree) college students and high school graduates fell in the 1970s for men and women, a period when, not coincidentally, the rate of increase in real tuition declined a bit. That earnings differential increased sharply in the 1980s. The earnings premium associated with a college education increased in the 1990s as well, again enhancing the demand for higher education and, with that, universities' ability to raise tuition.

However, two indicators in the tables suggest that universities cannot assume that this trend, favorable from their perspective, will continue. First, the college–high school earnings differential can and does

TABLE 2-1

EARNINGS DIFFERENTIAL, MALE COLLEGE AND HIGH SCHOOL GRADS,
1970–2002[a] (IN PERCENTS)

Year	Four Years of College[b]	Four Years or More of College[b]
1970	38.64	44.99
1980	24.46	32.77
1991	52.16	61.60
2002	75.06	99.60

SOURCE: U.S. Census Bureau, *Current Population Reports*, Series P-60, *Money Income in the United States: 1970; 1980; 1991; 2002* (Washington, D.C.: Government Printing Office). The 2002 data are available at http://ferret.bls.census.gov/macro/032003/perinc/new003_000htm.

a. Full-time, year-round workers; calculated using median earnings; use of mean earnings changes trends only modestly.

b. Comparison is with high school graduates. In early years, data are for those with four years of college; in later years, data are for those with a bachelor's degree; four years or more data include those with master's, doctorates, and professional degrees in the comparison with high school graduates.

TABLE 2-2

EARNINGS DIFFERENTIAL, FEMALE COLLEGE AND HIGH SCHOOL GRADS,
1970–2002[a] (IN PERCENTS)

Year	Four Years of College[b]	Four Years or More of College[b]
1970	46.16	56.16
1980	31.26	41.82
1991	53.28	68.46
2002	64.42	73.62

SOURCE: U.S. Census Bureau, *Current Population Reports*, Series P-60, *Money Income in the United States: 1970; 1980; 1991; 2002* (Washington, D.C.: Government Printing Office). The 2002 data are available at http://ferret.bls.census.gov/macro/032003/perinc/new003_000htm.

a. Full-time year-round workers, using median earnings.

b. Comparison with high school graduates. In early years, data are for those with four years of college; in later years, data are for those with a bachelor's degree; four years or more data include those with master's, doctorates, and professional degrees in the comparison with high school graduates.

move down as well as up, as the data for the 1970s suggest. Second, the data for the 1990s show that the differential was increasing, but at a slower rate than in the 1980s, meaning that the value of expected extra lifetime earnings associated with college was growing more slowly. This, in

TABLE 2-3
U.S. POPULATION AGES 18–24 YEARS, 1960–2020

Year	Population 18 to 24 Years, in Thousands	Year	Population 18 to 24 Years, in Thousands
1960	15,604	2005	28,498[a]
1970	23,714	2010	30,163[a]
1980	30,022	2015	30,254[a]
1990	26,961	2020	29,593[a]
2000	27,143		

SOURCE: U.S. Census Bureau, *Statistical Abstract of the United States: 2003* (Washington, D.C.: Government Printing Office, 2004), tables 11 and 12. For earlier years, see *Statistical Abstract of the United States: 1988* (Washington, D.C.: Government Printing Office, 1987), table 13.
a. Projected.

combination with sharply rising college costs, could mean a lower rate of return on college human-capital investment.

There are signs that the earnings differential between college and high school graduates may be nearing a peak. From 1999 to 2002, for example, the median earnings differential fell from 65.4 to 64.4 percent for full-time, year-round female workers with bachelors' degrees compared with high school graduates.[5] Whether this decline in the earnings differential portends a reversal of the recent trend is unknown. Certainly, however, it means that further real increases in tuition likely will lower the private rate of return to individuals on their investment in higher education, at least at the undergraduate level. (There is some evidence that the differential in earnings between those with bachelors' and advanced degrees is widening. It may well be that the rate of return will continue to be high for graduate education but fall for undergraduate studies. This might increase the use of differential tuition-pricing between undergraduate and graduate education.)

Demographic Changes. Despite all the talk about higher education being a lifetime quest, a large majority of college students is still between the ages of eighteen and twenty-four. As noted earlier, the upsurge in tuition in the 1960s and 1970s was caused partly by an increase in demand arising from expanding population in this age category. The evidence suggests strongly that this growth has slowed down sharply and, except for a modest increase during the remainder of this decade, will continue to stagnate for many years (see table 2-3).

The college-age population nearly doubled in the 1960s and 1970s, but it has actually declined since then. A very slight increase in the 1990s is expected to accelerate a bit in this decade. If the fall 2004 cohort is around 28,227,000 (a linear extrapolation of the 2000–2005 data), a growth of slightly less than 5 percent (or 0.80 percent a year) is predicted to the year 2010, followed by an actual decline over the following decade. Certainly, the pool of applicants of traditional age cannot be expected to contribute much to increased demand in coming years.[6]

Slower Rise in Higher Education Participation. Historically, stagnation in the demographic pool of eighteen- to twenty-four-year-old individuals has been offset in higher education by rising participation, in the form either of an increase in the proportion of that cohort enrolled in college, or greater numbers of nontraditional students. As detailed in a coming chapter, there are some indications that the participation rate is rising much more slowly than before, perhaps approaching some saturation point. It could be that some significant proportion of the population simply is not equipped to perform satisfactorily at higher levels of learning, and we may be nearing the extent of the educable population.

While a rise in the number of international students could take up the slack, a massive increase in higher education investment overseas may in time lead to greater numbers of students attending universities in their home countries or in venues other than the United States. Moreover, factors such as terrorism and internal security concerns might hold down the size of the international student population attending American universities.

A Slowdown in Third-Party Payment Growth. Over the past several decades, the proportion of state government funding going for higher education has declined significantly. In the face of budgetary problems in the wake of the 2001 recession, many state governments reduced spending on higher education. Moreover, meteoric growth in spending for medical care and corrections has forced states either to raise taxes, which is extremely unpopular politically and potentially damaging economically, or to cut spending elsewhere. Some of the well-publicized problems of universities, such as the repression of free speech, alcohol-induced campus riots, and excesses of college athletics, almost certainly weaken public political support for higher education funding; and, as student loan obligations reach high levels, resistance to continued expansion of those programs will likely develop.

Private donations to universities have swelled significantly over time, but their growth, too, may slow down, in part for reasons discussed above, but for another one as well: The planned elimination of federal estate taxes will lower incentives for large bequests to charities. Reductions in marginal income taxes will also somewhat diminish the tax advantages of university giving. It is possible, however, that higher rates of economic growth arising from such tax reductions will offset these effects—adverse from the perspective of the universities—at least in part.

Conclusions

The university environment is radically different from that of private business. The not-for-profit nature of universities means there is no clear, unambiguous means of measuring success. There is not the passion to reduce costs or increase revenues through product enhancement that the discipline of the market provides. Unlike in the private sector, where such measures add to the "bottom line," employees have little incentive to reduce costs. *There is no obvious bottom line in higher education.* Adding to the problem is the fact that third parties pay most of the bills, reducing the sensitivity of customers to price. Thus, universities compete less vigorously on price. The increase in costs and decline in productivity have been further aggravated by greater government regulation.

The solution to these problems is not simple. A number of factors, including a declining rate of growth in the high school–college earnings differential, slowing population growth in the eighteen- to twenty-four-year-old cohort, and the crowding-out of university appropriations by other social needs may slow the revenue expansion that permits higher spending per student. Reducing reliance on third-party payments, moving toward a more market-driven model of delivering services, providing incentives to compete more on the basis of price, and easing government regulations would also help contain the continuing growth in tuition. The discussion of these and related options is a subject of the last several chapters of this book.

3

Productivity Decline and Rent-Seeking

In the first chapter, I suggested that costs to consumers of attending universities were soaring largely because of demand-induced pressures to raise tuition, a trend aggravated by the non-market-driven nature of higher education, as discussed in chapter 2. Higher demand means more students attending colleges—and paying higher prices to do so. Greatly enhanced tuition revenues, accompanied by growing governmental support and private contributions, give universities more money to spend than ever. What have they used their additional resources to buy? As the inputs to higher education have increased, what has happened to the "output," measured not only in terms of numbers of students, but also the quality of the educational experience and the production of knowledge? As money has flowed into university campuses, has some of it been siphoned off for disproportionately large increases in compensation for members of the university community? In the parlance of economics, has the higher education community been successful at rent-seeking, that is, getting payments beyond the amount needed to provide goods and services?

The Rise in Higher Education Spending

Dramatic growth in the real amount of resources devoted to higher education has occurred relative to the growth in universities' obligation to educate (as measured by the number of students) and the economy's capacity to fund it. Table 3-1 looks at the growth historically. In the 1929–30 school year—the year of the Great Crash and the beginning of the Great Depression—the nation spent one-half billion dollars on current spending for higher education, or about one-half of 1 percent of the nation's output as measured by

TABLE 3-1

SPENDING ON U.S. HIGHER EDUCATION, 1929–2000

School Year	Current Spending[a]	Real Spending in 2003 $ [ab]	Real Spending per Student ($)[b]	Spending as % of GDP
1929–30	0.507	5.513	5,008	0.52
1939–40	0.675	8.886	5,947	0.70
1949–50	2.246	17.230	6,480	0.80
1959–60	5.601	35.040	9,627	1.08
1969–70	21.043	102.346	12,786	2.09
1979–80	56.914	125.442	10,842	2.12
1989–90	134.656	192.395	14,109	2.38
1999–2000	245.278[c]	272.103	18,396	2.57

SOURCE: NCES, *Digest of Education Statistics: 2002* (Washington, D.C.: Government Printing Office, 2003), tables 171 and 342; price data from Bureau of Labor Statistics, www.bls.gov/cpi/home.htm; GDP data from U.S. Department of Commerce, Bureau of Economic Analysis, *Survey of Current Business*, August 2002, p. 123..
a. In billions of dollars.
b. Based on June 2003 seasonally adjusted Consumer Price Index.
c. Partly estimated; data for private schools are not available; assumes spending growth at those institutions relative to public schools was at levels prevailing between 1990 and 1995.

GDP. By 2000, the nation was spending in nominal dollars almost five hundred times as much—almost one-quarter of a *trillion* dollars. Since the statistics for both years ignore capital outlays, the true burden of universities on the economy is actually greater than indicated. In inflation-adjusted terms, spending rose almost fiftyfold, or by over 5.7 percent per year—dramatically faster than the growth in the nation's output. As a consequence, by 2000, higher education absorbed nearly five times the proportion of the nation's output as it had seventy years earlier.

That last statistic points to another reality: As higher education absorbs more of the nation's resources, the ability to increase that share falls. The resistance to further expansion grows as higher education crowds out more and more other forms of expenditure, and, at some point, this leads to pressures to "change the system." This is precisely what happened with respect to medical expenses, which rose from their mid-twentieth century level of perhaps 5 percent of the GDP to around 14 percent or so today. As they passed the 10 percent range, the calls for change multiplied. President Bill

Clinton and his wife, Hillary Clinton, proposed a radical new system, and while that failed legislatively, other efforts to contain costs intensified. HMOs, PPOs, Medical Savings Accounts, and other institutional innovations gained in prominence, traditional insurance benefits were restricted by employers, and copayments and deductibles rose.

It might be argued that higher education costs only one-fifth or so of what medical care does, so the pressures to contain expenses are unlikely to mount significantly anytime soon. Yet health care is a lifetime need, and people are probably willing to pay more for something that might literally save their lives than for education, which for most people is consumed only for a few years, even if it does, arguably, provide lifetime financial benefits.

Note that spending per student much more than tripled over the long time period shown in table 3-1, correcting for inflation. Since 1960, it has grown at a real rate approaching 1.8 percent a year. For a variety of reasons, the table probably *understates* spending growth per student. The Consumer Price Index probably overstates inflation. Enrollment figures are not on a full-time-equivalent (FTE) basis, meaning they include part-time as well as full-time students (and are not available on an FTE basis, as far as I know, over the entire time span indicated). Since the number of part-time, nontraditional students has become relatively more important over time, the growth in the numbers of courses taken or hours spent in class has been less than the enrollment figures seem to indicate, meaning real costs per student credit-hour have risen more than what is shown in the table. Data for the periods for which both FTE and total enrollment data are available confirm this. For example, from the 1970–71 school year to the 1995–96 school year, total enrollment rose 66.2 percent, while FTE enrollment went up 53.4 percent. Thus, real spending per student during this period rose about 13 percent, while it rose about 23 percent on the more appropriate FTE basis.

Most official statistics on real higher education spending are deflated by the Higher Education Price Index.[1] While that index has a limited legitimate purpose, it is inappropriate for evaluating the changing real burden of higher education on society. The Higher Education Price Index measures the costs to universities of the inputs used to produce their services. Those costs are determined by resource prices which, in turn, are influenced by university policy decisions. For example, if this index rose sharply over time simply because universities paid employees and contractors far more generously than before, the reported *real* rise in spending for any given nominal expenditure would be *reduced*. Yet the real burden of higher education on society—its opportunity cost—is determined by the amount of other goods society must give up to finance universities. That is most appropriately determined by a broad-based index, such as the CPI. Since the Higher Education Index has risen somewhat faster in modern times than the CPI, the National Center for Education Statistics data on the real growth in spending often show spending increases 20 percent or more smaller than indicated by the broader-based index.

A very good case can be made that the changing real cost of higher education should be measured using a very broad price index that measures all goods and services sold in the economy, not just consumer goods. The use of the GDP price deflator, the broadest-based index used in calculating the overall growth of the economy in inflation-adjusted terms, would make the reported real increases in spending per student significantly greater than those indicated in table 3-1. Indeed, using both the FTE adjustment and the GDP price deflator yields real increases in spending per student for some time periods double those indicated in the table. Spending per student has risen very substantially in modern times, growing especially rapidly since 1980.

During the 1970s, inflation-adjusted spending per student as measured in the table actually fell noticeably, an aberration in the otherwise continuous upward trend. Why? In part, the apparent decline is undoubtedly a statistical artifact, reflecting the particularly pronounced overstatement of inflation by the CPI at that time. In the 1970s significant inflation and enrollment growth occurred simultaneously. Since, as we have seen, universities are relatively slow and inflexible in reacting to inflation by raising tuition, inflation-adjusted revenues (and hence spending) lagged behind normal trends.

Note that the real spending growth rate per student, as measured in the table (which almost certainly understates it) was at about 30 percent in both the 1980s and 1990s, which translates into an annual compounded rate of increase of roughly 2.65 percent. Using FTE enrollment data, and using the GDP price deflator to adjust for inflation, the real per-student increase over the twenty years is 78.4 percent—an increase of 2.94 percent a year. Both decades were prosperous, giving rise to greater state and local government tax revenues and increasing the ability of governments to be generous in financing higher education without raising taxes. Also, rising incomes and a booming stock market increased private contributions to higher education and enhanced endowment incomes. The effect on real spending of declining rates of inflation was probably opposite that of the accelerating rates of the 1970s. This led to a somewhat higher increase in real spending than otherwise would have been the case.

Where Did the Money Go?

It is very difficult to state with precision how the resources of universities have been allocated—and reallocated—over time. To cite just one important example, faculty members divide their time between instruction (preparing for and teaching classes, grading examinations, meeting with students), research (some sponsored, some not), and other activities, often including some administration (chairing departments, running graduate programs, organizing lecture series, serving on the faculty governance body and university committees). Universities are not terribly fastidious, as a general rule, about trying to sort out the allocation of time among these various functions, so statistical compilations of categories of expenditures are necessarily subject to a good deal of error. Moreover, changes over time in the way activities are classified can lead to further distortions.

With this caveat, let us look at the evidence regarding the changing distribution of university spending over time. Although private universities lag considerably in providing data on their expenditures in the same form as those from public universities, for the period from 1929–30 to 1995–96, the following general trends are clear for all U.S. higher education:

First, the proportion of revenues devoted to instruction declined sharply, from 43.7 percent of all spending in 1929–30 to 30.3 percent by the mid-1990s. Most of the decline had occurred by the 1960s.

Second, over the very long run, research expenditures have become relatively more important, although that is not true of *outside funded* research (such as government or foundation-supported grants) if the analysis is confined to the past thirty years. However, the teaching-research mix has tilted more in favor of research over the long run.

Third, by any account, the common faculty complaint about excessive bureaucracy and administration has considerable factual basis: In 1929–30, 8.4 percent of university spending went for "administration and general expenses," compared with nearly 14.6 percent two-thirds of a century later. For every dollar spent on instruction in 1929, nineteen cents was spent on administration; that figure rose, more or less continuously, to thirty-three cents in 1959–60, forty-one cents in 1979–80, and forty-eight cents by 1995–96. Relative decline occurred in one other area besides instruction: Plant operation and maintenance went from over 12 percent of total spending in 1929–30 to well under 7 percent by the mid-1990s.

Table 3-2 looks at these trends for the period from 1976–77 to 1999–2000. It includes information only for public universities and reports spending as a percentage of "educational and general expenditures," a term that excludes the fairly considerable (often well over 20 percent) university spending carried out by hospitals, commercial operations, food and lodging services, and the like. Note that the same trends mentioned above hold true for this period: a rather considerable reduction in the relative importance of instruction and plant operations and maintenance, and a growing emphasis on research and administration. As noted earlier, more universities' funds are allocated for scholarship aid, which universities typically view as an expenditure item, but which in a real sense involves discounting student fees (reducing revenues). This is further evidence that universities are more aggressive in practicing price discrimination (charging individuals differing amounts for the same services) than previously.

Universities usually stress the need to maintain and improve instruction when they raise tuition or appeal to state legislatures or private donors. The evidence suggests, however, that that is not primarily where they use any additional funds obtained. According to National Center for Education Statistics calculations, real spending per student for instruction at public universities from 1976–77 to 1999–2000 rose 21 percent; spending for all other items per student rose 51 percent. Put differently, *only twenty-one cents out of each increased dollar spent per student went for instruction.*[2] Perhaps that explains why parents, legislators, and others are becoming more and more skeptical of requests for greater largess to finance university operations; the universities have a credibility problem—increased funds are not being used to fund instruction.

TABLE 3-2

CHANGING ALLOCATION OF PUBLIC UNIVERSITY SPENDING, 1976–2000[a]

Spending Category	1976–77 (%)	1999–2000 (%)
Instruction	38.99	33.97
Administration	12.99	14.09
Research	18.35	22.36
Student Services	3.69	3.76
Plant Operations	9.11	6.55
Scholarships, Fellowships	4.01	6.35
Other[b]	12.86	12.92

SOURCE: NCES, Digest of Education Statistics: 2002 (Washington, D.C.: Government Printing Office, 2003), table 350.
a. "Educational and General Expenditures"; excludes auxiliary, commercial operations, etc.
b. Libraries, public service, mandatory transfers.

Some insights into these trends might be offered by the theory of public choice and bureaucracy. Public-choice theorists suggest that, like others, governmental officials or nonprofit organization employees try to maximize their satisfaction in life, and they use their power accordingly.[3] As incremental resources have become available to universities, administrators have reallocated more funds to themselves, providing more administrators to ease their burdens and perhaps raising their own salaries. Faculty members, who play a significant role in governing some institutions and have considerable control over their time, do what they like best and/or what is most likely to advance their careers: research. Since research accomplishments are measurable and visible nationally and internationally, while teaching efforts are less visible and typically more localized in nature, faculty have demanded and received lighter teaching loads to allow them to do more research.

Thus, the redirection of resources away from instruction has resulted in significant part from decisions made not by the providers of those resources, but by those consuming them, in opposition to the "consumer sovereignty" concept said to dominate the market process governing most private resource allocation.

What about the rather sharp decline in spending on buildings and maintenance as a percent of university funds, which has led to a serious deterioration of old buildings on some campuses and a generally seedy appearance at others? University administrators allocating funds are beset by all sorts of pressures—from the faculty, from students, and from alumni (who may want more money spent on intercollegiate athletics). Buildings, however, cannot talk, cannot pressure administrators into meeting their needs. It is tempting to defer for another year the replacement of a roof or air-conditioning unit, or the painting of a building's facade. This is a good demonstration of what public-choice scholars call the "shortsightedness effect." University administrators, often vying for better jobs at other schools in an age when institutional loyalty is on the decline, do what they think their immediate constituencies (more the staff than the consumers) want in the short run, thinking they will not have to face the long-run consequences of poor maintenance of the physical plant.

The Increase in Personnel

Competitive profit-making businesses strive to reduce costs and improve the quality of their products. Profit enhancement requires cost reduction or revenue increases. The key to cost reduction is productivity advance—getting more output per unit (dollar) of resources used. While measuring productivity change in higher education is extremely difficult, one very important element—the amount of resources used—is relatively easy to measure. By any account, the physical quantity of resources used to support the higher education enterprise is growing faster than the number of students educated by it.

Table 3-3 shows that it took about 12.5 percent more personnel to educate one hundred students in the 1999–2000 year than it did twenty-three years earlier. For the moment, let us assume that the quality of the finished product (the college-educated student) has remained unchanged, and that there has been no substantial change in research output adjusted for enrollments. Under those conditions, we would say that labor productivity in higher education has fallen by about 12.5 percent in twenty-four years, or over 0.5 percent per year compounded. By contrast, labor productivity rose by over 1.6 percent per year in the business sector of the entire economy.

For a practical demonstration of what these numbers might mean, consider identical twins who go to work in 1976, one for a typical university

TABLE 3-3
FTE UNIVERSITY STAFF PER ONE HUNDRED FTE STUDENTS, 1976–2000

Category	1976–77	1991–92	1999–2000
All Staff	18.52	20.41	20.83
Faculty[a]	7.01	6.96	7.61
Other Professional	3.00	5.17	5.76
Nonprofessional	8.51	8.28	7.45

SOURCE: NCES, *Digest of Education Statistics: 2002* (Washington, D.C.: Government Printing Office, 2003), table 223.
a. Includes instructors and research assistants.

and the other for a typical private business. Suppose they begin with equal output per hour. By 1999–2000, assuming the twins mirrored the productivity change of their respective sectors, the one working in the private sector would be 65 percent more productive per hour than his or her twin. This, of course, is based on the untested assumption that the "output" of higher education has risen exactly proportionally with enrollments.

Returning to table 3-3, it is interesting to note that changes in the staff/student ratio have varied widely with the type of university employee considered. Over the period shown, the faculty/student ratio rose modestly (between 8 and 9 percent), while that in the "other professional" category grew by an astonishing 92 percent.[4] "Other professional" workers include administrators, librarians, laboratory technicians, computer programmers and technical support personnel, administrative assistants to administrators, affirmative action officials, nurses, counselors, and a host of others.

Academics perennially complain about administrators and about the growing presence of an administrative corps that, in their judgment, gets in the way of doing their work. Given the expenditure data reported above, it is not surprising that the category "executive/administrative/managerial" (part of the "other professional" category in the table) worker did show fairly considerable growth, going from 1.19 per one hundred students in 1976 to 1.43 twenty-three years later, an increase of over 20 percent. The administrator/faculty ratio rose, although not dramatically. I suspect, however, that some of the "other professional" workers had administrative functions as well, so that the true growth in the university bureaucracy may have been quite large relative to the growth of the student body.

I also suspect that the bulk of the "other professional" workers had little to do directly with student learning, and, in many cases, were only tangentially involved in supporting instruction. What did they do? Many supported research efforts. The sharp rise in the ratio of this category relative to enrollments, along with the relatively small change in the instructional component, adds to earlier data hinting that universities are becoming less about the dissemination of knowledge and more about the creation of it, or other activities only minimally related to the intellectual milieu, such as intercollegiate athletics.

The decline in the ratio of nonprofessional workers (secretaries, custodians, maintenance workers, and others) to students, on the face of it, might be a sign of rising productivity of those workers. But three phenomena suggest that interpretation is probably not correct. First, in the interest of greater efficiency, universities increasingly contract out some of their auxiliary support enterprises to private businesses— food service, for example, and building maintenance are more often outsourced than a generation ago. To the extent this is happening, the data on university employees understate the labor inputs into the enterprise. Second, it is my impression that there has been some increase in the proportion of students living off-campus, a trend reinforced by the rise in for-profit universities, which generally offer very little on-campus housing or food service. If so, more college students are purchasing housing and food service from private businesses, and the true growth in labor inputs per student in the last generation on typical college campuses is greater than the data on university employees alone show— very possibly over 20 percent. Finally, as indicated above, university politics do not favor putting incremental resources into some of the areas that are largely operated by nonprofessional human resources, such as plant and maintenance.

I have disaggregated the data reported in table 3-3 into public and private universities. In the interest of not inundating readers with an overabundance of statistics, I will simply summarize the findings. First, private universities are far more labor-intensive than public ones. In the 1999–2000 school year, for example, there were twenty-five full-time-equivalent employees at private universities for every one hundred students, compared with 19.23 at public ones.

Second, while the faculty/student ratio is about 15 percent higher in the private schools, the big difference is in "other professional" workers. With about five of these workers for every one hundred students in public universities and over 7.7 in the private ones, the differential is well over 50 percent. Similarly, the private universities today use about 30 percent more *non*professional workers per one hundred students than the public ones, probably in part because the private schools are more likely to be residential institutions with students living on campus.

The vast difference between public and private schools with respect to "other professional" workers is intriguing. I would speculate that it largely relates to the fact that a large proportion of the nation's top research universities are private, and they need lots of professional scientists and other support personnel who do not teach. An earlier generalization is particularly true of these schools: Teaching students is no longer the dominant activity.

As more and more resources go for noninstructional purposes, two questions arise: Does undergraduate instruction increasingly subsidize graduate instruction and research? And is it really critical to tie intensive research efforts to institutions that were founded primarily to foster the dissemination of knowledge to undergraduates? We will return to these questions later in the book.

The growth in staffing has been similar at public and private institutions. We have seen that private schools have consistently been more labor-intensive than public institutions. An even bigger difference exists between two- and four-year schools. Among public universities, which dominate the two-year sector, the two-year schools use much less labor (table 3-4). Indeed, much of the public-private school staffing differentials are explained by the fact that a much larger *proportion* of public school students attends two-year colleges than private schools. It takes less than *half* as many workers to educate one hundred students in the two-year institutions. In small part, this reflects the somewhat larger faculties of the four-year schools, but about 89 percent of the differential relates to the nonfaculty staff component.

The reason for this, as figure 3-1 shows, is that the "support staff" for each faculty member is much larger in the four-year institutions. Although I have no solid data to support the supposition, given the lighter teaching

TABLE 3-4

STAFFING PER ONE HUNDRED STUDENTS, 1999–2000, TWO- AND FOUR-YEAR PUBLIC SCHOOLS

Category	2-Year Schools	4-Year Schools
Total Staff	11.36	24.39
Faculty	5.43	6.90
Non-Faculty	5.93	17.49
Faculty as % of Total Staff	47.90	28.30

SOURCE: NCES, *Digest of Education Statistics: 2002* (Washington, D.C.: Government Printing Office, 2003), table 223.

loads in the four-year institutions I would surmise that actual class sizes, on average, are no smaller in the four-year institutions—and, indeed, probably a bit larger, since the students must be distributed among fewer classes. The lighter teaching loads in the four-year institutions are typically justified on research grounds. Thus, virtually the *entire* personnel differential between the two types of institutions is explained by noninstructional factors, presumably largely, though not wholly, research.

Is Productivity Falling in Higher Education?

The increase in labor resources per student, along with increases in other productive inputs reflected in rising per-student expenditures, is the denominator in a fraction that determines productivity change in higher education. Since productivity is determined by output divided by inputs, any serious attempt to evaluate changing university productivity must include some assessment of the change in university "output," or outcomes, over time.

Estimating changes in university output is, to put it mildly, extremely difficult—some might say impossible. Universities do many things, but their reason for existence is to create knowledge through research and disseminate it through instruction. For the sake of argument, let us assume that one half of the per-student output of universities is related to instruction, and one half to research. Let us assume that the average knowledge acquired by students today can be quantified and is the same as it was

FIGURE 3-1

NONFACULTY STAFF PER FACULTY MEMBER, 1999–2000

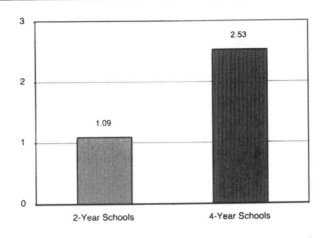

SOURCE: NCES, *Digest of Education Statistics: 2002* (Washington, D.C.: Government Printing Office, 2003), table 224.

twenty years ago. Let us assume that total research output doubled over that period (implying a very high growth rate of 3.6 percent a year), which, given enrollment growth of 27 percent on an FTE basis implies a growth in "research output per FTE student" of 57 percent. Adding together the instructional and research components yields a 28.5 percent (the average of zero and 57) growth in higher education output per student.

At the same time, the cost of resources per student, on an FTE basis adjusting for inflation with the GDP price inflator, rose 78.4 percent. Let us assume that each physical unit of resources (mostly labor, but some capital) was 30 percent better-compensated in real terms in 2000 than in 1980. That would imply an increase in productive inputs of 37.2 percent. The result? Inputs are rising faster than output (37.2 vs. 28.5 percent), indicating that total factor productivity (the relation between output and all resources used in producing that output) declined (6.4 percent).

In my judgment, the above exercise uses assumptions that bias results in favor of overstating productivity growth (or, in this case, understating productivity decline). Modest changes in these assumptions can produce fairly big changes in the results. For example, assume that the instructional component is 60 percent of the output of all institutions of higher education, and the research component is 40 percent (an allocation more consistent with the expenditure data). Then assume that research output per FTE student rose only 40 percent, and leave the other assumptions the same as before. Total factor productivity decline is a fairly sharp 15.5 percent.

The notion that productivity is falling in education is hardly novel. For at least a decade, I have gotten good laughs from legislative groups with the observation that, with the possible exception of prostitution, teaching is the only profession that has had absolutely no productivity advance in the 2,400 years since Socrates taught the youth of Athens. Caroline Hoxby of Harvard, looking at primary and secondary education, estimates a productivity decline there of an astonishing 65 percent over the past three decades.[5] According to distinguished labor economist and sometime–Cornell University administrator Ronald Ehrenberg, the failure of faculty productivity to rise over time is fundamental to rising tuition costs.[6] If faculty members on average are producing less output over time, the only way they can receive real pay increases is to increase the price that consumers of educational outputs pay. Since real compensation has indeed risen (see below), there appears to be a good bit of truth to the notion that the rising real cost of higher education is devoted considerably to increasing compensation to university employees.

Instructional Productivity

Remarkably few data offer insight into the instructional outcomes of higher education. Part of the problem is that much learning is difficult to quantify, and types of learning change over time. College graduates today, for instance, are less likely to know anything about Samuel Johnson or Peter the Great than their counterparts of a generation earlier, but they will know a lot more about computers and how to use them. There are, however, a few things we can say about what students learn. A good standardized test taken by about one-fourth to one-third of all college graduates—almost certainly above-average students—is the Graduate Record Examination (GRE), previously mentioned in chapter 1. The GRE has changed relatively little in

TABLE 3-5
AVERAGE GRADUATE RECORD EXAMINATION SCORES, 1965–2000

Year	Composite Score[a]	Biology	Engineering	Literature	Psychology
1965	1063	617	618	591	556
1970	1019	603	586	556	532
1975	1001	621[b]	592[b]	547[b]	530[b]
1980	996	619	590	521	534
1985	1019	619	615	531	541
1990	1048	612	617	523	537
1995	1030	622	596	513	544
2000	1043	629	604[c]	530	563

SOURCE: NCES, *Digest of Education Statistics: 2002* (Washington, D.C.: Government Printing Office, 2003), table 311.
a. Combined scores of verbal and quantitative components of test.
b. For 1974.
c. For 1999.

format over time, with an analytical section added in the 1980s. Besides the general test are tests specific to individual disciplines. If we assume, as others do, that the scoring has remained relatively uniform over the years, the GRE scores shown in table 3-5 can give us some sense of how the aggregate learning experience for undergraduates has changed since 1965.

Interpretation of the results in table 3-5 depends a great deal on the period examined. Looking at the entire period from 1965 to 2000, we see that the composite GRE general score declined moderately, falling significantly from 1965 to 1980, but recovering most of the decline over the next two decades.[7] Not reported, but important, is the fact that the verbal component of the test showed a significant long-term decline, while the quantitative scores rose. Arguably, this trend is predictable and even desirable, given the changing nature of the American economy and skills needed in the workplace.

It has been argued that the university is becoming more a confederation of loosely affiliated "tribes" of disciplines (represented by academic departments and even units within departments) than a coherent whole.[8] The faculty and undergraduate students are less occupied with questions of eternal common interest ("What are the arguments for constitutional representative government?" "What constitutes virtuous behavior?"), and more with specialized knowledge applicable to future vocations.[9] Given this, one might expect learning in specialized subject matter to have shown some improvement over time. The evidence here is decidedly mixed. From 1965 to 2000, scores rose in two of the disciplines (biology and psychology) included in table 3-5, but fell in two others—literature (down sharply), and engineering.

If, however, one uses as a frame of reference 1975 or 1980, the results are more favorable, showing increases in all the tests except literature, although only modest ones in many cases. The proportion of students taking the GRE rose from 1965 to 1970 but has remained relatively stable since, so the issue of the representativeness of the students taking the test is far less significant than on tests administered for undergraduate admissions, such as the SAT or ACT tests.

Of course, the level of student learning at the end of the undergraduate experience reflects not only what colleges have taught, but what the students learned in their primary and secondary schools as well. Judging by the large number of students in remedial classes in college, it would appear that the lack of strong evidence of significant gains in learning at the college level might be at least in part a function of entering students today being far less knowledgeable than those entering universities, say, thirty or more years ago.

To get some sense of the extent to which this is true, I tried to adjust for the quality of incoming college students by calculating changing SAT composite scores and comparing them with changing GRE scores from four years later (since students taking the SAT as high school seniors traditionally graduate from college four years later). This is admittedly a crude and imperfect measure, but, as was mentioned earlier, data on outcomes in education are limited.

If we compare students taking the GRE test in 2000 with those who took it in 1970, we see an improvement in the composite score of twenty-four points (from 1019 to 1043)—not a lot, but improvement nonetheless.[10] By contrast, the SAT composite scores four years earlier (1996 and 1966, respectively) fell by a moderately impressive (or perhaps one should say depressing) forty-six points. This seems to suggest that the universities were teaching a bit more by the late 1990s than they did three decades earlier, and doing so with students who were, on average, slightly less prepared academically coming into college. That implies a rise in productivity.

Several caveats are in order, however. The first, of course, is that these standardized tests have limitations in measuring learning—they do not evaluate the artistic and ethical qualities of students, for example, nor their ability to write or think about major philosophical questions. Second, each point on a test is assumed to represent the same amount of learning and knowledge over time. Third, disaggregating the data by decade shows that scores fell far more on the SAT than the GRE in the 1970s, rose significantly on the GRE in the 1980s but little on the SAT, and rose a bit on the SAT in the 1990s while falling fifteen points on the GRE. The pre-1990 data support the thesis that collegiate learning has increased, but the numbers for the 1990s do not—indeed, they argue the contrary. The data do not speak to the majority of students who do not take either test, nor to the dispersion of performance around the average value. Moreover, high school knowledge is probably not terribly relevant to some of the specific subject exams, for which virtually all knowledge is gained in college. If one were to take the average of six subject exams (the four listed in table 3-5, plus education and chemistry), the mean value actually fell slightly since the mid-1960s, with scores rising on three tests and falling on three others.[11] It is probably true that in terms of quantitative skills, students have improved, while they have lost ground with respect to verbal ones.

Adding up all the evidence from these tests, I would conclude that average student learning has not changed much since the 1960s. Learning declined early in that period, while it has risen somewhat since, but not dramatically. Little in the data suggests that students leave college with a much different stock of knowledge and skills than their parents did a generation earlier.

Moreover, it almost certainly takes the average student longer to obtain the learning that goes with a college degree. Even if "learning per student" has increased somewhat over the years it takes to get a degree, "learning per college year" may well be stable or show some decline. The "fifth-year senior" or even "sixth-year senior" is far more common than decades ago. Part of the reason may not reflect badly on either students or universities (for instance, study abroad, more frequently undertaken than in the past, sometimes extends the period needed to complete a degree), but part may reflect problems associated with the rigidity of course requirements, students being closed out of required courses, and so forth. The evidence is very good on this point at the doctoral level. In 1978–79, new recipients of the doctorate took an average of nine years from receiving their undergraduate degrees to finishing their advanced degrees. By 1999–2000, that figure had risen by 1.3 years to 10.3 years.[12]

Research Productivity

While estimating productivity change in teaching is difficult, it borders on impossible for research. Even the good statistics we have on the inputs into the research process are of somewhat questionable value owing to a large amount of informal, university-subsidized faculty research that is not well quantified. Measuring the output is even more dubious. Much research is done out of intellectual curiosity, to expand our knowledge of humankind and its environment, and to understand and offer artistic expression about various aspects of life in all its meaning. It is done to solve puzzles and challenge existing interpretations. There is no easily definable, measurable "output" from poems published in little literary magazines, research giving new insights into the life of Rutherford B. Hayes, or fresh archeological evidence on the lives of American Indians living hundreds of years ago.

This is less true of research with some direct or indirect practical (commercial) application, including, arguably, most work done in the natural and physical sciences. Most good commercial research ultimately leads to patents. To be sure, the patents result from applied research or development conducted almost exclusively by private companies, but a good deal of that builds on university basic research—that is, the quest for new ideas and discoveries.

Now let us engage in a highly speculative arithmetic exercise to estimate productivity in university research that has direct or indirect patent potential. Assume that the number of patents issued per research dollar is the same for universities as for nonuniversity researchers (for example, private companies, nonprofit research institutes, or government laboratories). Further assume that the average "output" or usefulness of patents issued remains stable over time. Under those assumptions, we can calculate the number of patents issued per billion dollars of sponsored university research. The resulting computation for 1980 is 871.44 patents; for 2000 it is 869.31 patents. There essentially is no change in the output of this research per dollar of resources put into it. Total research output roughly tripled—but so did the amount of resources used to conduct the research, adjusting for inflation. One might say that the price of university-derived patents stayed roughly constant.

With some imagination and reckless faith in the meaning of numbers, one could build an argument that total factor productivity rose in higher education from 1980 to 2000. Continuing to use the assumptions developed above, assume that research output rose by 212.8 percent from 1980 to 2000, based on university-derived patents. Next, assume that instructional output rose 27.8 percent, equivalent to the growth in FTE students (implying no change in output per student). Assume teaching absorbed two-thirds of the academic enterprise in 1980 and three-fifths in 2000, with research's share going from one-third to two-fifths. On this basis, one would calculate that the total "output" of higher education slightly more than doubled, rising 101.8 percent. Total costs in real terms (using now the broad-based GDP price deflator) rose around 128 percent.

However, inputs used to "produce" higher education (mostly labor) were more highly compensated in real terms in 2000. If average compensation per unit of input rose by 13 percent or more, the total inputs used to produce education would have risen by less than 101.8 percent, meaning total factor productivity would have risen over time. If one makes the fairly generous assumption that real compensation rose 30 percent per unit of input, the total factor productivity growth over twenty years was about 15 percent, or 0.7 percent a year. Even under these extremely tenuous assumptions, productivity was rising somewhat less rapidly than in the economy as a whole—in a relative sense, it was still declining, albeit modestly.[13]

All of the above arithmetic exercise, however, is based on a series of assumptions that are questionable. Do patents measure research output? Does the average patent change value over time? Did research not leading to patents and creative expression, such as poetry, filmmaking, or research on Rutherford B. Hayes, grow as fast as patentable research? Did university research yield as much "output" per dollar (in the form of patents or otherwise) as research conducted elsewhere? Could the rise in the number of patents be influenced by such institutional factors as changes in laws or the efficiency of the Patent Office?

These questions make me very dubious of the exercise. Even if one were to buy into the view that patents are an adequate proxy for research output in scientific endeavors, it is extremely unlikely that research in the social sciences, humanities, fine arts, education, and so forth tripled in the two decades, as that would imply dramatic increases in output per faculty member that, to my knowledge, no one has seriously suggested.

Indeed, there are grave doubts in my mind that there has been any meaningful increase in research productivity of the typical rank-and-file faculty member outside the hard sciences. As the higher education enterprise has grown in magnitude, so has the number of scholarly journals, multiplying in a typical discipline from a few dozen outlets to often several hundred. Even if faculty members are publishing at the same or a somewhat higher level than thirty years or more ago, a larger proportion of the journals are obscure, appealing to only a very small number of specialists. The increase in specialization and the use of arcane methods of communication (either in words or symbols) have made much scholarship relatively inaccessible to the bulk of the scholarly public.

With the rise of the Internet and e-mail, one wonders if the proliferation of scholarly journals serves any functional purpose that computer-based communication does not provide. Far more people subscribe (free) to EHNet, a computer-based community of economic historians that shares research results, than pay for the respected journal *Explorations in Economic History*.

Diminishing returns also apply to scholarship. The five-hundredth article on King Lear is probably going to add less insight into the human condition, Shakespeare's meaning, or the historical context of the writing than, say, the fiftieth article. The emphasis in the humanities and social sciences on race, class, and gender issues has led to a disproportionate amount of interest in these topics relative to others.

There is little doubt that total research output has risen over time. It probably has grown faster than enrollments, given the reallocation to it of resources within the university community. And there is no question American universities have contributed importantly to the growth of scientific knowledge. In the four decades of Nobel Prizes given out before the end of World War II, Americans received on average less than one such prize per year, and a small minority of the total number awarded. In the last quarter of the twentieth century, by contrast, the average number of prizes exceeded four annually, and roughly two-thirds of all prizes went to Americans.[14] American universities were at the center of this development, although some scientists were working in nonuniversity settings at the time of their research or receipt of the prize.[15]

On the occasion of the awarding of the 2003 Nobel Prizes, a spokesperson for the Royal Swedish Academy of Sciences, which awards the prizes, noted, "There's a brutal predominance for the U.S." His next observation, however, was far more debatable: "This shows that the American investments in their university system are very successful."[16] It is important to note that research, however worthwhile, is not costless. And even though the cost of financing universities rises largely because of noninstructional activities such as research, parents and other consumers are still paying about the same proportion of the total higher education bill as they did some time ago. The external subsidies for higher education are being diverted more and more from teaching to research—and to other things besides.

Overall, it is impossible to say with any precision what has happened to productivity in American higher education. Under almost any reasonable set of assumptions, university productivity has fallen relative to the private sector. It is highly plausible that it has fallen in an absolute sense as well. The exact conclusion one reaches depends in considerable part on one's assessment of the growth in research endeavors.

But it does seem safe to say that a productivity problem, probably of a substantial magnitude, exists in higher education. We are using many more resources than before to deliver our educational product, and it is highly questionable—indeed, rather doubtful—that the rise in the quality and quantity of our product exceeds the rise in the quantity of resources used to deliver it. Complicating matters is the fact that universities increasingly do other things not related to the principal purposes of higher education. They are in the food and lodging business. They are in the entertainment business, with sporting events, theaters, recreational facilities, and concerts. They run hospitals and clinics. In short, much of the business of the modern university is quite tangential to the creation and dissemination of truth and beauty.

Employee Compensation and Rent-Seeking

Earlier, I mentioned the public-choice insight that public employees try to maximize their own satisfaction, particularly in situations where institutional goals are ill-defined or where success is difficult to measure. Higher education is in this category, or at least the dominant nonprofit part of it is. Maximizing utility or satisfaction often involves salary and benefit enhancement. As funds have flowed into the universities with rising demand for their services, have faculty and others been able to capture what economists call "economic rents"—payments beyond those necessary to get them to provide their services? At the minimum, are workers sharing in the prosperity (as measured by rising real total revenues) of universities?

Before offering some evidence, I cannot resist observing that virtually everyone I have ever talked to seriously about universities during my forty-five years of involvement with American higher education would acknowledge that the employees of institutions, particularly the faculty and senior administration, play an extremely important role in ordering priorities, including financial ones. While university presidents are probably more constrained on average than the CEOs of major corporations in this regard, faculty have tenure—and that emboldens them to be assertive, often refusing to do what the senior administration truly wants. According to Ronald Ehrenberg, "Any senior administrator who recommends holding down spending, or even worse cutting spending, risks incurring the wrath of the faculty. Holding down spending increases may lead the institution's faculty salaries to fall behind the salaries of their peers at other institutions."[17]

With this in mind, how has faculty compensation changed over time? Table 3-6 brings out several trends:

- Average annual pay for all faculty shows little change after adjusting for inflation, rising just a bit more than 3 percent over the thirty-year period. Moreover, pay actually falls a bit for faculty at all major ranks during that time period, suggesting that the small rise for all faculty is a consequence of the growing proportion of the professorate in the higher-paying academic ranks, especially full professors.

TABLE 3-6

AVERAGE REAL ANNUAL PAY, FACULTY ON NINE-
MONTH CONTRACTS, 1970–2000 (IN DOLLARS)[a]

Category	1970–71	1974–75	1979–80	1984–85	1989–90	1994–95	1999–2000
All Faculty	54,163	51,063	46,553	48,734	53,508	53,514	55,888
Prof.	76,528	69,548	61,906	63,613	70,409	70,582	74,410
Associate Prof.	57,802	52,777	46,777	47,930	52,520	52,578	54,524
Assistant Prof.	47,628	43,456	38,086	39,484	43,583	43,622	44,978
Instructor	39,887	41,481	30,579	32,380	33,372	33,389	34,928
Public 4 Year	55,918	53,186	48,735	50,842	56,484	55,982	57,950
Public 2 Year	53,884	48,695	44,549	44,599	47,353	47,387	48,240
Private 4 Year	50,390	49,197	44,306	48,414	53,087	55,578	58,323

SOURCE: NCES, *Digest of Education Statistics: 2002* (Washington, D.C.: Government Printing Office, 2003), table 235.
a. Numbers are in 1999–2000 dollars, deflated by the CPI.

- After falling sharply in the 1970s, pay has generally risen in real terms since 1980.

- Pay for faculty at four-year public institutions has risen considerably relative to two-year faculty, whose pay in absolute real terms, if the data are to be believed, fell over 10 percent in the period indicated.

- Pay in private four-year institutions has risen relative to that in their public counterparts. In 1970, pay was about 10 percent higher in the public universities, but that differential has disappeared and slightly reversed.

- Some evidence supports the view that senior faculty pay is rising relative to junior faculty. The ratio of average full-professor pay to average instructor pay rose from less than 1.92 in 1970–71 to 2.13 in 1999–2000, reflecting a sharp decline in real instructor pay over time. The recent phenomenon of paying $250,000 a year or more to "superstar" faculty is only slightly hinted at in the data, but my suspicions are that updates will show continuing growth in the earnings disparity between full professors and instructors.

Is Real Faculty Pay Stagnating over Time? The suggestion that real faculty pay has stagnated over time, reached by comparing 1970 and 1999 salary levels, is almost certainly invalid for at least three major reasons. First, the stagnation is entirely the consequence of falling real salaries in the 1970s. In the twenty-year period 1979–99, real average salaries for all faculty rose slightly over 20 percent, nearly 1 percent per year. The fall in salaries in the 1970s was almost certainly due to inflation and the well-established fact that university revenues and, by extension, compensation, tend to be relatively inflexible and slower to change than is the case in the private sector.

Second, it is almost universally agreed that the Consumer Price Index has significantly overstated inflation over time, perhaps by as much as one percentage point a year over the period examined.[18] Correcting for that makes a profound difference in calculated changes in real income over time. For the 1985–99 period, simply reducing the annual measured growth in the CPI by eight-tenths of a percentage point per year, in accordance with several estimates made by professionals, nearly doubles the growth rate in real earnings.

The third reason the original data over the twenty-nine-year period understate earnings growth is that fringe benefits not included in base salary have grown relative to salary. Health insurance benefits have soared in value, and in many cases retirement contributions have grown as well. In the calculation below, I assume that fringe benefits went from being 20 percent of salary in 1979–80 to 25 percent twenty years later. That is consistent with trends in the national economy, and probably a very conservative assumption as it applies to higher education.

Figure 3-2 summarizes my revised findings. While the twenty-nine-year growth rate in real annual salary per faculty member is barely 3 percent, the twenty-year growth rate in real compensation corrected for biases in the CPI is over 45 percent. To me, that is the best true measure of the trend of real remuneration of faculty in recent times. That figure is substantial, growing at a compounded annual rate of 1.9 percent per year—

FIGURE 3-2

FOUR INTERPRETATIONS OF REAL FACULTY EARNINGS
GROWTH, 1970–99

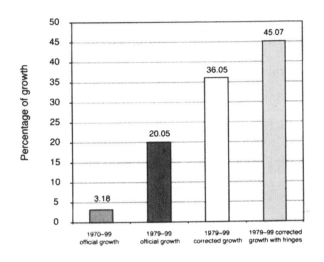

SOURCE: NCES, *Digest of Education Statistics: 2002* (Washington, D.C.: Government Printing Office, 2003), table 235; Bureau of Labor Statistics, http://www.bls.gov/cpi/home/htm; author's calculations.

almost precisely equal to the corrected growth in real hourly compensation for all workers in the private business sector.

Additional Observations on Changing Faculty Compensation. Although I cannot prove it, there is good reason to believe that the average total earnings of college professors since 1979 are rising even faster than indicated above. Since formal teaching obligations have tended downward over the long run, pay per teaching hour has risen faster than the statistics above indicate. Also, faculty members derive supplemental earnings, often very considerable, from consulting, book and patent royalties, summer teaching, government grants covering summer research, and lectures, to mention a few things. My sense is that these opportunities on balance have expanded over the years relative to nine-month university income. Private companies are more often hiring university scientists as consultants and for summer work, and an upsurge in litigation has led to a huge increase in the need for expert witnesses in legal proceedings. The economic status of college professors has been enhanced by their freedom to supplement their incomes in this manner.

When I see how college professors live today compared with forty or fifty years ago (I grew up in a university town), not only do I sense that their economic status has improved enormously in an absolute sense, but probably a bit in a relative sense as well. A larger proportion of senior professors live in what are considered the really nice homes (which are nicer than the upscale houses of a generation or two ago), and assistant professors, who fought to live on the fringes of the middle class in a sort of shabby respectability in, say, 1960, are far more likely to have perfectly nice middle-class housing and two cars of fairly recent vintage, instead of the one rather old car, as in times past. Part of this reflects general economic growth, and part reflects the rising workforce participation of faculty spouses, but some of it, I suspect, is the increasing relative remuneration of faculty compared with the rest of workers in American society. As a colleague of mine, the distinguished labor economist Lowell Gallaway, puts it, "Life in the academy is pretty good these days." To be sure, there is an "academic underclass" of adjunct instructors and others who live pretty marginally, but they are still a relatively small proportion of the academic community (although a growing one).

Conclusions

However measured, the enterprise of higher education takes immensely more resources to operate than it did a generation or two ago. Real spending has risen, even adjusting for substantial enrollment increases, and it has grown relative to the nation's productive capacity. Over time, a larger proportion of university resources has gone for research and administration, and less has gone for instruction. Costs have risen far faster in the research universities than, for example, the two-year colleges that are predominantly teaching institutions. University staffs have grown faster than enrollments.

It is difficult to say with precision what has happened to productivity in higher education, but by virtually every reasonable scenario it has fallen relative to that in the rest of the economy. Under most reasonable assumptions, it has fallen even in an absolute sense. Although the evidence is mixed and depends importantly on the period examined, in general employees have shared in the vast growth of revenues personally, seeing their incomes rise significantly in a real sense. It is very likely that the total, real work-related earnings of faculty on average have risen more than those of the American people as a whole.

The evidence here shows a trend rarely seen in the private sector—real earnings of workers (faculty in this case) rising at the same time productivity growth stagnates. Since increases in real earnings are, in the final analysis, dependent on productivity advance, this may seem surprising. Few private corporations could survive for long if their widget-makers were making no more widgets per hour over time but getting pay increases. It happens in higher education because of rapidly rising third-party payments and subsidies reflected in higher tuition, bigger grants, greater donations, and more generous state governmental appropriations. As the disconnection between the prosperity of the academy and its sluggish productivity grows, one might envision increased reluctance on the part of providers of these subsidies to continue their largess. That is a subject for the last part of this book.

4

The New Peculiar Institution

Some scholars and others refer to American slavery as the "peculiar institution," in part because of its uniqueness, and the differences between the nineteenth-century slave economy and culture and the remainder of American society.[1] One could argue that American higher education is the "peculiar institution" of contemporary times, not as morally invidious nor quite as contentious as its predecessor, but in many ways equally or more eccentric. Life within the academy is different from outside. Its inhabitants often think and act differently than individuals alien to the academic culture.

In the rest of society, an hour is a period of 60 minutes' duration. In higher education, a class that allegedly meets for an hour actually meets for around 50 minutes in most cases. A "three-credit-hour" undergraduate course often meets for 50 minutes three times a week, or a total of 150 minutes a week, which in the wider world is equal to two and a half hours. Similarly, "I went to Stanford for a year" almost certainly translates into nonacademian English as, "I attended Stanford University for a majority of the time over a ninth-month period." You typically pay for having your car fixed, your lawn mown, or your income taxes done after the services are received. In higher education, the reverse is usually true: you pay before you consume.

While many of the peculiarities of the academy are relatively trivial and quaint, others have more significant implications. In this chapter, I will discuss three of the more eccentric practices that have economic meaning, in the process extending the economic analysis of university costs introduced in previous chapters. The "peculiarities" discussed include price discrimination, tenure, and cross-subsidization of instruction, intercollegiate athletics, and food and lodging operations.

Price Discrimination

Most businesses charge all customers the same amount for goods and services. However, exceptions are fairly common and are not considered eccentric. Movie theaters often charge children less than adults, bars have "happy
hours" when they sell their liquid refreshments at lower prices, motels and
restaurants give senior citizens discounts, and so on. The most extensive
price discrimination—economist jargon for the practice of charging different prices for the same service—is no doubt practiced by the airlines. On
any given flight, there may well be over a dozen different fares paid by passengers, depending on when or with whom the flight was booked, the age
of the flier (senior citizen and youth discounts exist), or the length of stay
before return.

Colleges and universities practice price discrimination as well, but they
generally disguise it. Instead of overtly having many different tuition rates
for different classes of people, universities typically charge a single rate and
then individually offer customers discounts from it, ranging from zero to
the full amount. Scholarships (and fellowships at the graduate level) are the
major device used to implement this price discrimination.

Before we turn to scholarships, a clarification is in order. State universities typically charge out-of-state students more than in-state ones, and
sometimes universities have differing tuitions for graduate students and
undergraduate ones, or they vary fees somewhat by college or professional
program. For example, many universities run a regular, on-campus Master
of Business Administration (MBA) program at one fee, and a special week-
end Executive MBA program, very often at an off-campus site, at a higher
fee. Also, some universities in recent years, wanting to raise tuition a lot but
fearing the reaction from parents of current students, have gone to a two-
tier system, whereby new students pay a higher fee than continuing ones,
with the differential disappearing when the continuing students graduate or
otherwise leave. Finally, some universities offer online programs at a different fee level than their residential offerings.

But the major form of price discrimination is practiced through scholarship and fellowship assistance. Universities are unique in that they can
and do require intimate financial information from potential users of their
services in order to determine by how much they will discriminate. Parents

of prospective freshmen wanting financial aid are required to submit a statement on a standardized form used by hundreds of institutions that asks, among other things, about family assets, financial liabilities, income, and the like. Often, income tax returns are attached to verify information provided. *Price discrimination in the private, for-profit sector is almost entirely based on group attributes; in the university setting, it is largely based on individual attributes.*

If a private business were to try to require similar information of customers, it would likely be referred to the Attorney General or other law enforcement types for possible prosecution. The mere giving of differential rebates by the railroads in the late nineteenth century led to the earliest federal regulatory efforts. Requiring customers to surrender copies of income tax returns violates the basic concept of a right to privacy. But are universities condemned for the practice? No—to the contrary, they are praised for providing greater access to higher education via the scholarships awarded.

Before discussing in some greater detail the dimensions of price discrimination in American higher education, it is worthwhile to say something about the practice. Americans, negatively conditioned to the expression "racial discrimination" and related concepts such as "gender discrimination," in general probably view the term "price discrimination" negatively as well. Actually, economic theory and common sense suggest that price discrimination can be constructive. This is particularly true in businesses, where the marginal cost of providing one more unit of the good or service frequently is extremely low, effectively zero. In such cases, offering low prices to certain classes of customers can lead to more effective utilization of resources.

For example, the movie theater might be half-empty if all tickets were sold at the same price, but by offering discounted tickets to younger persons (or half-price tickets to Broadway shows the day of the performance), the theater owner enhances revenues and operates at a nearly full house, allowing lower prices than would otherwise be charged to those paying full price. The same principle applies with a vengeance to the airlines, which often will offer last-minute deals on tickets at bargain rates rather than let the seats go empty. Higher-capacity utilization also lowers capital costs significantly in the long run. Thus, price discrimination is socially a very desirable practice, and eliminating it via public policy would prove very costly to the nation.

Price discrimination exists because people differ in their responsiveness to changes in price. In economist jargon, they have different elasticities of demand. The general principle for a profit-maximizing entrepreneur is to charge higher prices to customers with low price elasticities, and lower prices to those with high price elasticities. That way a firm can increase revenues relative to costs, and thus enhance profits.

A simple example should drive the point home. Suppose an airline flying a 150-seat jet between two cities calculates its total costs per flight at $30,000, and that cost is the same whether it has 50 or 150 passengers. Suppose if it charges everybody $250, it can sell 100 tickets, taking in $25,000 and thus losing $5,000 on the flight. Suppose 60 of those passengers are traveling on business, and 40 are tourists. Now, in an attempt to end losses, the airline begins to price-discriminate. It prices its tickets for short-term purchase at $400, and sells 50 seats to business travelers at that price, taking in $20,000 from that group—$5,000 more than when the fare was $250. In addition, it now offers a two-week advanced ticket, bought by tourists for $150. Enticed by the lower price, the number of tourists wishing to buy tickets grows to 80, bringing in $12,000 from them ($2,000 more than before). Total revenues increase to $32,000, the flight is now profitable, and the plane flies at nearly 87 percent of capacity, rather than at 67 percent as before. The airline might even sell the last 20 seats over the Internet a few hours before the flight for $100, increasing profits still more. This is why airlines use differential pricing. The business travelers wanting to travel on short notice are rather insensitive (although not completely so) to price; their demand is price-inelastic. The tourists, however, are quite price-conscious, and their demand is elastic.

For open-admissions universities, following the same principles can increase both enrollments and revenues, giving the institutions a financial surplus over what otherwise would be the case and allowing them to hire more staff, pay their faculty more, build new facilities, and so on. They have learned this, and have increasingly used price discrimination to do precisely that.

Airlines know that sensitivity to price declines as the flight date approaches, and they use that information to price-discriminate. Universities cannot use that tactic. Since most students make their decisions on college several months before enrolling, the last-minute, high-cost admission is not a very viable option (although I am a bit surprised some colleges have not tried it). Instead, colleges use the device of scholarships as the means of getting the information necessary to price-discriminate—namely, family financial information—drawing on the fact that, other things being equal, wealthier families will be less price-sensitive than others.

To increase further the demand for services at any given tuition rate, universities can offer federally subsidized loans. Students and their families complete forms, such as the Free Application for Federal Student Aid (FAFSA), conveniently available on the Internet at http://www.fafsa.ed.gov. They have to provide information from such sources as W-2 forms, income tax returns, bank statements, and mortgage balance statements. All of this enables institutions to discriminate both with respect to the price of the university (the tuition) and the amount of loans provided to meet that cost.

Another difference exists between universities and other price-discriminators. The others explicitly price-discriminate by simply having different prices—adult fares and child fares, for example. Colleges typically set a single price and discount from that individually, offering literally hundreds of different net tuition rates depending on the income and other financial circumstances—such as having other kids in college—of students' families. Having a standard price that is widely discounted (much like booksellers with bestsellers) fits in with the myth colleges like to purvey that "everyone is treated the same."

To this point, I have discussed needs-based scholarships (tuition-discounting) at open-admissions universities. Price discrimination is also important in another context: merit-based scholarships awarded by highly selective schools. These institutions are predominantly private, but they also include some of the better state universities, such as the University of Virginia, the University of Michigan, and the University of California at Berkeley and Los Angeles. To these schools, maximizing enrollment in itself is not a goal, although increasing income while maintaining quality is. They are also deeply into what might be called prestige-maximization, which is partly achieved by raising the average SAT score and/or high school class rank of entering students, which, in turn, has a positive effect on the school's ranking in the influential *U.S. News & World Report* annual college report and elsewhere. Evidence indicates that students generally respond rather rationally to varying aid offers to maximize the return on what

Christopher Avery and Caroline M. Hoxby term their "human-capital investments."[2]

Consider two students from high-income families of similar economic circumstance. One is extremely accomplished, with an SAT composite score of 1540 (out of 1600), and ranks first in her class of two hundred. The second is also an excellent student, but not so spectacularly so, with an SAT composite score of 1300 and a rank of eighth in his class of two hundred. Suppose the first student is accepted at Yale, Columbia, and Northwestern, while the second is admitted at Northwestern, the University of North Carolina, and the University of Illinois, but is rejected by Yale.

All else being equal, the first student might well opt for Yale, since it is ranked in the top three universities by USN&WR, while Northwestern and Columbia are "only" near the bottom of the top ten. The second student likely would opt for Northwestern, easily the best-ranked of the three schools at which he is accepted, although, in the absence of financial aid, his parents might grumble a bit about the higher cost of attending that school relative to public school alternatives.

How might admissions officers at all of these fine schools react, knowing they are expected to take in a class that will improve the school's USN&WR ranking? While the first of these students is a solid admission at all three schools, she would be particularly valuable to Columbia or Northwestern, as she would have a large positive impact on the average quality of student, as measured by SAT scores and class rank. This is less true of Yale, which already admits a relatively large number of valedictorians with SAT scores over 1500. Both Columbia and Northwestern likely will offer her a generous amount of merit-based aid, hoping to win her over from Yale on the basis of price. (Columbia and Northwestern, incidentally, almost certainly do not know that Yale has accepted her, but can surmise based on her performance that she likely would be accepted at one of the top Ivy League schools.) Northwestern, the only school admitting both students, views the second student positively but not enthusiastically. Since his test scores are below the average for all Northwestern undergraduates, he might actually hurt the school a bit marginally in terms of the USN&WR (and other) rankings. So Northwestern might offer this student no grant assistance (despite the price differential with North Carolina and Illinois), but possibly some student loans (to ease the cash-flow problem of paying the higher tuition and other costs). It very well might offer a huge grant to the first student, however, essentially lowering her tuition to near zero. In terms of the earlier analysis, "the elasticity of demand" for Northwestern is high for the first student (who is inclined to go to Yale anyway), but relatively low for the second (who prefers Northwestern to the alternatives on quality grounds).

Other considerations affect universities' pricing decisions. One is race. Suppose the second student in our example above were African American. In that case, the chances are excellent that Yale would admit him, since universities view racial diversity as being crucially important (a subject of later discussion). The Yale acceptance would make the second student distinctly less enthusiastic about Northwestern, but the race consideration likely would make Northwestern distinctly more enthusiastic about him. The student's price-elasticity of demand for Northwestern would be sharply higher than if he were white, while Northwestern's "price-elasticity of supply" would be much lower. In plain English, Northwestern would now vigorously offer a huge scholarship to the student because it desperately wants him, and because that is the only way it would have a good chance of getting him. More generally, this means white students, on average, pay higher tuition to go to college, net of scholarship aid, than black students—independent of family economic circumstance. In this sense, universities are definitely "peculiar institutions"; consider the furor if businesses started offering race-based discounts to customers, on the grounds that they wanted to diversify their client base!

Universities engage in other forms of price discrimination in the admissions process. Students with athletic talent are especially favored in admissions and receive assistance ranging from deep tuition discounts to complete payment of all college expenses. While this is most prevalent at the major football and basketball schools, it is practiced to some degree at virtually every institution with intercollegiate athletic programs. Since many schools want the more talented of these athletes to improve their teams' win-loss records and national recognition, the student often has several good choices of institutions; so to the extent permissible under NCAA rules, schools sometimes compete in part by offering tuition and room and board discounts.

Other Forms of Discrimination in Admissions

Another common but moderately controversial admissions practice is the tendency for some institutions, especially highly competitive private ones, to show preference for "legacies"—the children or grandchildren of alumni. Alums often give money to their alma maters, and otherwise inadequately qualified students are admitted because the school will directly or indirectly benefit by larger contributions—in effect, the student will be paying a tuition supplement. Some argue that this undermines the concept of meritocracy that operates in most university activities and suggest that even the best of universities will compromise their standards for money.

In a great piece of investigative reporting, Daniel Golden of the *Wall Street Journal* uncovered examples of "money talking" and the seeming disregard for academic qualifications at America's premier universities.[3] Golden delved into the records of graduates of the Groton School, one of the nation's finest private secondary schools. He noted that Margaret Bass was the only one of nine Groton applicants from the Class of 1998 to be accepted to Stanford University, despite a mediocre (by elite university standards) composite SAT score of 1220—far below the scores of the other eight applicants. Her father, Robert Bass, was former chair of Stanford's Board of Trustees, and a contributor to the institution of $25 million. This is not an unusual occurrence; nearly one-half of Amherst College's applicants who are "legacies" are accepted, compared with only 17 percent of all applicants.[4] Henry Park, a Groton student and son of a Korean immigrant, was denied admission to several Ivy League schools, despite a spectacular 1560 SAT score and a high class rank (fourteenth), above that of a majority of the Groton students accepted by Ivy League schools. By contrast, Lakia Washington, an African American, ranked sixtieth in the class, had a truly poor (by Ivy League standards) SAT score of 1110, and was accepted by Columbia. Suki Park, Henry's mother, makes an interesting point: "I was naïve. . . . I thought college admissions had something to do with academics."[5]

Yet another controversial practice is "early admissions." Elite liberal arts colleges and universities often will accept students earlier than normal, provided they pledge to attend the school accepting them. This allegedly reduces hassles and worrisome waiting for the student, and helps institutions plan their admissions better. The students who apply under early admissions are typically rather well-to-do (and white) applicants, for whom the competitive offers of other schools with respect to financial aid is a secondary consideration. Some think early admissions are biased against minorities and the nonaffluent. Senator Edward Kennedy has even proposed that colleges be required to report the number of their legacy and early admission applications (somewhat ironically, since he himself was a legacy admission to Harvard).[6]

Selective-admissions schools deliberately price tuition below the market-clearing price ostensibly so they can select students who will perform well. Yet in reality that principle is breached—a lot—and money, race, athletic talent, and other nonacademic attributes seem to play a significant role in admissions. By no means is admission a strictly objective process based solely on academic potential.[7]

Tenure

Imagine the supervisor of an assembly line in a widget factory calling aside one of her employees who had worked there for six or so years and saying, "John, we like your work. We are giving you a lifetime employment contract. You cannot be fired, demoted, or have your pay reduced, and we will put it in writing. If future bosses try to fire you, you can sue them and win. If you want to work until you are eighty years old, that is up to you." This is what happens in American universities when they give tenure to members of the faculty.

The most important rationale for tenure is that it protects against infringements on academic freedom and thus helps promote diverse and lively discourse on college campuses. As an outspoken faculty member who has taken a number of stands unpopular in the university community over the years, I have felt that tenure has enabled me to say and do things I otherwise would not be able to say or do, and that academic freedom has made our universities, and, by extension, our broader American community, a better place. Of course, sometimes tenure protects scholars who use their positions to push particular political agendas and try to thwart others who hold alternative views. In such cases tenure, rather ironically, may lead to efforts to *restrict* academic freedom. It is the unfettered freedom of expression that makes universities special places, and the offering of multiple, even eccentric, views on issues helps students ponder alternative perspectives and reach educated conclusions about intellectual or policy choices

But tenure comes at a cost, and that cost may be high. I say "may be," because nowhere in university accounting systems is the financial impact of tenure on the institution evaluated, nor are other effects of the practice assessed. What are the costs?

First, tenure makes it expensive, if not impossible, to get rid of employees whose contributions to the institutional mission are declining. It is not rare for a faculty member to suffer from a progressive, debilitating long-term mental and/or physical disability and continue to work, despite diminishing effectiveness in the classroom and in his or her research. In the private sector, the worker would be dismissed, pensioned-off early, given disability retirement, or somehow otherwise let go.

These things sometimes happen in higher education, but since the worker has very strong legal protection, the cost of buying out the employee's contract can be quite high. Take a sixty-year-old professor, making salary and benefits equal to $90,000 a year, who is suffering from the early stages of Alzheimer's disease. What if he insists he plans to teach until the age of seventy? The present value of the stream of future payments to that faculty member is at least $600,000 (depending on the assumed interest rate and salary increases). Without tenure, the present value of future obligation to the faculty member might be as low as zero, and probably not more than one year's salary and benefits, or $90,000. With tenure, although chances are good that the university can ease out the sick faculty member for less than the present cash value of his future earnings, the cost will still be far greater than if tenure did not exist.[8] Most universities are not willing to make such large cash outlays. As a consequence, students are deprived of the opportunity to learn from someone who is healthier and more in the prime of his or her academic life.

Health problems aside, in a dynamic society, university resources need to change. Over time, institutions may need to shift faculty positions into teaching more courses related to information technology, for example, and fewer in medieval history. Enrollments may tumble in medieval history but soar in a management information system (MIS) course. When a large majority of faculty members are tenured, it is difficult to reallocate resources from one subject to another. Costs usually considered variable—labor—become relatively fixed. With untenured faculty, we would give the historian a year's notice, dismiss him, and add the MIS person without increasing labor costs materially on a long-term basis. With tenure, there is a tendency to keep the immovable medieval historian whose services are tepidly demanded while adding another person to teach MIS. In this instance, tenure significantly increases labor costs.

Tenure also makes university administration difficult, less efficient, and more expensive, and slows needed changes in curriculum and academic direction. Faculty who cannot be fired for their views tend to be forceful and sometimes positively uncivil about expressing them. Often they block changes desired by the administration simply because they feel their personal interests are imperiled somehow. Humanities faculty, for instance, may be able to forestall a move to allow students to meet graduation requirements by studying a computer language instead of a traditional European language.

Since the faculty must carry out the work of the university, no change in direction is possible without its cooperation. Having power relative to executive officers and managers that is unheard of in the private sector (another unique feature of higher education), they demand participation in all important decisions regarding university policy. This requires convening endless committees, where, in effect, faculty have a near-veto power on decisions (a situation dramatically less prevalent in institutions where tenure does not exist). Administrative plans to reallocate resources, change the curriculum, build new facilities, and a host of other issues are decided only after a relatively long, drawn-out committee-based process, sometimes requiring formal votes in faculty governance organizations, university committees, and other such bodies. The more distinguished the institution, the more likely this is the case. In universities with faculty unions (still very much in minority) much of this is very formally laid out in the master bargaining agreement.

Finally, tenure plays a significant role in the "balkanization" of institutions of higher education, diminishing the valuable interdisciplinary discourse that is the heart of the reason for having universities instead of research and teaching institutes narrowly focused on individual disciplines. Veteran professors and administrators at universities very often lament the decline in interest in university affairs by younger faculty and the reduction in interdisciplinary discourse across their campuses.[9] Faculty seem loyal to their disciplines, not their universities. They are appallingly ignorant of advances in other disciplines, often ones closely allied with their own, while extremely conversant on often obscure advances in their subdisciplines. Economists, for example, are clueless about what is going on in political science, and vice versa. Specialists in public finance economics increasingly cannot understand what specialists in the economics of industrial organization are talking about. Generalization and interdisciplinary synthesis are disdained; narrow technocratic specialization is de rigueur.[10]

This is not all bad. Scientific specialization has led to important advances that have raised productivity, increased living standards, and prolonged lives, not to mention adding to America's prestige and the worldwide perception that ours is the leading nation in the world. But the community of scholars spends less time discussing issues of common concern in an intelligent fashion. The economists do not spend much time talking to the historians. The philosophers and the literature professors have less interaction than in previous years. The business school faculty and the rest of the university often look upon each other with contempt.

Yet business scholarship and business itself can benefit from a historical perspective, from discussions on what separates right from wrong, from knowledge of foreign languages. And literature professors could benefit from some of the pragmatic realism and competitive spirit that the business faculty often embodies. Instead, we are engaged in a balkanized tribalism that in the university community reverses the national motto *e pluribus unum*—out of many, one—and turns it to, "Out of one comes many."

In what way does tenure help bring this about? In order to get tenure at research universities and, increasingly, good liberal arts colleges, faculty members must have published significant research in their respective professions. The proliferation of faculty over the past several decades has led to vast numbers trying to write the relatively few articles a year that are of interest to a general audience within their disciplines. The result is that most writing is done for publication in highly specialized journals appealing to narrow audiences. Thus, it is counterproductive for these persons in their formative years to interact much with those in related disciplines. It is counterproductive to serve on university committees. It may even be counterproductive to take teaching too seriously. This is bad for students, bad for scholarship that has broad social meaning, and bad for developing a university community that has common meaning. And once faculty get tenure, they are often set in their ways (often at an age approaching forty, since the median age of new PhDs in the United States is around 33), so the situation does not improve with age.

Life is full of tradeoffs, and that is quite apparent with tenure. It serves a legitimate purpose, indeed one so important that it may well trump all the negative factors associated with it. Freedom of expression is vital to the operation of great universities—when expression is suppressed, they lose much of their vitality and their reason to exist. Yet tenure can be a frightfully costly way of guaranteeing that expression, and some respected scholars have called for its abolition.[11]

There are some indications that tenure is on the decline. In 1980–81, 64.8 percent of full-time instructional faculty had tenure, but that fell marginally to 62.4 percent by 1999–2000.[12] Given that the faculty on the whole got older and moved, on average, to higher ranks, the rank-adjusted decline is moderately greater, although still well over 90 percent of full professors have tenure. Tenured assistant professors and lecturers, once fairly common, are becoming an endangered species.

Rapidly growing for-profit schools generally do not award tenure. A larger proportion of teaching is done by adjunct and part-time faculty, so the proportion of student credit-hours taught by tenured faculty is now probably well below 50 percent. Universities are finding ways to reduce the implicit costs associated with tenure. Some would argue that the rise in adjunct and part-time instructors has come at a qualitative cost. Certainly, that trend in part reflects an attempt to get around the costs associated with tenure.

Is there a "middle way" between a world where most senior faculty have tenure and one where they do not? Can there be a reasonable guarantee of academic freedom that is less costly, using some nontenure arrangement? I am not really sure, but I will discuss some options in the last part of this book.

Cross-Subsidization

Universities carry out multiple missions—undergraduate instruction, graduate instruction, contracted research, other research, the feeding and housing of students, and the fielding of athletic teams, among others. In doing so they are not distinctive or "peculiar." To use a private sector analogy, General Electric makes turbines, sells appliances, lends money, and operates a television network. Multiple-task organizations are commonplace.

Private, for-profit companies, however, expect each of their separate businesses to operate at a profit, or at least not at a sustained loss. If GE loses money for several years in a row making jet engines, it probably will exit the business. Stockholders will tire of seeing earnings dragged down, and other divisions of the company will resent, in effect, having to subsidize the jet engine business.

Universities, by contrast, will subsidize poorly performing operations for sustained periods, taking revenues that otherwise would support one activity and giving them to another that is not sustainable under existing funding arrangements. Most revenues universities receive are designated for a particular purpose. Tuition revenues are implicitly earmarked to support instruction, although seldom is there an explicit commitment that this is how they will be used. Most federal assistance for research or other purposes is also earmarked, as are most private gifts. State appropriations often are less explicitly earmarked, and universities do receive some undesignated gifts and have endowment monies available to sustain operations that are otherwise not self-supporting.

Universities engage in cross-subsidization in several areas. Let me mention three typical examples which will be discussed at length below. First, funds that most people believe are supporting undergraduate instruction often are, in fact, supporting graduate education and research activities. Second, at many universities, intercollegiate athletics are subsidized, often rather substantially, by administrators who rationalize that such subsidies have long-term payoffs in terms of alumni contributions, greater national recognition which stimulates the quality of enrollees, and other benefits. And third, I detect in some of the statistics the possibility that at some universities, food and dormitory operations are beginning to subsidize other parts of the institution.

Instructional Subsidization. It has long been accepted that in universities there are forms of instruction that need to be subsidized, since there is an institutional obligation to maintain some teaching and research in areas that are losing popularity with students, but are still important in maintaining our cultural heritage. Thus, some schools maintain classics departments with modest enrollments whose continuation might not make much sense on a strict cost-per-student, credit-hour basis. In some areas, instruction is relatively more expensive than others, either because, as in areas such as medical or business education, the salaries of professors are high relative to other disciplines, or because, as in some sciences and again, medical education, there is a need for lots of instructional support personnel or expensive equipment or supplies. In the private, for-profit sector, these dif- ferential costs are met in large part by charging different prices for services; in universities, for reasons not entirely understood by me, tuition tends to be completely or largely uniform across disciplines and colleges.

A bigger issue is the extent, if any, to which undergraduate education subsidizes graduate studies and research. It is no secret that large research universities teach freshmen and sophomores rather cheaply. Often, they attend lectures with several hundred other students, or classes taught by relatively low-paid, inexperienced graduate "teaching assistants." Meanwhile, highly paid senior professors spend generous amounts of time with advanced graduate students in small seminars, individualized discus- sion, and the like.

While this phenomenon is especially prevalent at large state universities, it is also present to some extent at expensive private schools where students pay tuition of $25,000 or more per year. I remember how struck I was a num- ber of years ago when a professional acquaintance who was a senior faculty member at Stanford University told me he was sending his son to Claremont McKenna College, where I was teaching at the time, instead of to Stanford, despite the free tuition he would receive at Stanford for his son. Speaking of his own institution, he said, "We have neglected our undergraduates for years," and, "I want him to get personalized attention and a good liberal arts education." Stanford is usually in the top five in the *USN&WR* rankings of national research universities, while Claremont McKenna—a very good school—is currently "only" thirteenth in the national rankings of liberal arts colleges. While the situation may well have improved for undergraduates at Stanford since then, the perception that undergraduates are neglected at research universities remains.

It is possible to make some rough estimates about the increase in cross-subsidization over recent decades. Confining our analysis to public universities, let us first assume that two-year institutions are only in the business of providing undergraduate instruction (a fairly realistic assumption), and that the increase of about 35 percent in their real spending per student from 1970–71 to 1999–2000 is thus entirely devoted to improving undergraduate instruction. Let us further assume that although the four-year institutions do many things besides teaching undergraduates, their qualitative effort on behalf of undergraduate learning is expanding at the same rate as the two-year colleges, or by 35 percent per student. Let us also assume that a 35 percent increase per student in the component of university activities not having to do with undergraduate education is justifiable to keep the resource allocation mix the same between undergraduate instruction and other activities. Actual 1999–2000 spending per student in public four-year universities was $1,764 higher than what those assumptions would have required—interestingly, an amount very close to the rise in real in-state tuition over that period. In total, $10.637 billion more was reallocated away from undergraduate instruction to other activities. Moreover, this was during a period in which tuition was covering a rising proportion of overall public university revenues.

Thus, over time, undergraduate student fees are covering more of the costs of higher education, but undergraduate instruction is absorbing a lesser proportion of university resources. To be sure, in 1970, the costs of undergraduate instruction were heavily subsidized, largely by state appropriations, in public universities. But the data suggest that, at the very minimum, relative to 1970, the subsidization of undergraduate instruction with monies other than fees has declined significantly as a proportion of the cost of educating students. The students are paying more of the cost of educating themselves.

This judgment may actually be an understatement of the phenomenon. According to the data available on instructional spending per student, as indicated in the last chapter, only twenty-one cents per dollar of the increased spending per student in public universities in the period 1976–77 to 1999–2000 went for instruction. Figure 4-1 shows that in-state average tuition at four-year public universities covered a significantly larger proportion of the amount spent on instruction per full-time-equivalent student at those institutions in 1999–2000 than it did a quarter of a century ago.

In the first decade of the new century, tuition rates have surged at major state universities, so data for, say, the 2003–4 school year are almost certainly going to show in-state tuition covering a majority of the direct

FIGURE 4-1

IN-STATE PUBLIC UNIVERSITY TUITION FEES AS PERCENTAGE OF
INSTRUCTIONAL COSTS, 1976–77 AND 1999–2000

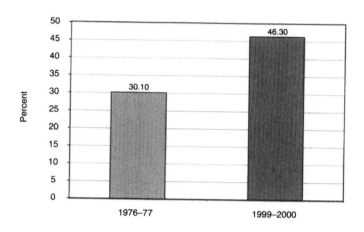

SOURCE: NCES, *Digest of Education Statistics: 2002* (Washington, D.C.: Government Printing Office, 2003), tables 312 and 350.

instructional costs at those universities. At the margin, the rise in tuition from 1976–77 to 1999–2000 more than covered the total rise in direct instructional costs—in an absolute sense, nontuition coverage of those costs declined. Moreover, out-of-state students, whose data were excluded from the calculations, saw their tuitions increase relatively more.

Furthermore, graduate students were included in the figures for instructional cost per student used in the above calculations, and graduate student instruction is vastly more expensive than that for undergraduates. While in 1999–2000, spending per full-time-equivalent student for instruction was $8,135 in public universities, my somewhat educated guess is that the additional cost of educating one more freshman is substantially less, perhaps $5,000 or a bit more per student. At some public universities, tuition exceeds that amount. For freshmen and sophomores, tuition often covers the entire instructional cost, and even a bit of the overhead administrative costs. For out-of-state students, such fees vastly exceed those marginal instructional costs for freshmen and sophomores, and probably at least cover them typically for advanced undergraduates. When other monies, for example, private support, are considered, some state universities make a considerable surplus from educating freshman and sophomore out-of-state students, which is then used to subsidize other university activities (the education of in-state students, graduate education, research, intercollegiate athletics, and so forth).

The movement of resources from undergraduate teaching to graduate education and research has probably contributed importantly to the emergence of an academic underclass of perpetual graduate students who live off modest stipends as teaching and research assistants. In the last chapter, I indicated that the median period it takes to get a PhD is now over ten years—a scandal. As the former president of Cornell, Frank H. T. Rhodes, puts it, "I believe that this pattern of ever-longer PhD enrollment is simply too much."[13] Moreover, there is some evidence that *the attrition rate for PhD candidates exceeds 50 percent.* In the core social science disciplines of economics, history, and politics, about 60 percent of entering students drop out, many of them after several years in the pipeline.[14]

At private universities, the picture is even starker. Instructional costs are somewhat higher, as those schools often do give their students more personalized attention. But my guess is that the true marginal cost of educating a freshman or sophomore at a good private university seldom exceeds $10,000 a year, and probably not $25,000 for juniors or seniors. Tuition often vastly exceeds even that higher amount, and students and their families increasingly are asked to subsidize graduate education, research, and perhaps other activities.

All of this is leading to rising discontent with universities. Much of the reallocation of resources to research and graduate education is being directed not by public policymakers or by university trustees, but by the faculty and administration of the universities themselves. Professors would rather teach graduate students than undergraduate students, and would rather write articles than teach a lot. (Of course, that is a broad generalization; there are many exceptions.)

In a recent poll commissioned by the *Chronicle of Higher Education*, 82 percent of respondents (adults) either agreed or strongly agreed with the statement, "It is very difficult for a middle-class family to afford a college education."[15] Similarly overwhelming majorities indicated support for the view that students incur too much debt to finance college, and that the colleges could reduce costs without hurting quality. Moreover, respondents even had some suggestions how to cut costs: Two-thirds were opposed to the institution of tenure, and a similar proportion thought universities devoted too much attention to athletics. Moreover, only 8 percent of respondents thought it less than important for colleges to "prepare undergraduate students for a career"; some 15 percent felt that research was less than important; and 37 percent did not feel it was important for universities to "help attract new business to the local region"—a task some state universities have appointed to themselves.

All of this suggests that the sharp increase in tuition charges cannot continue on a sustained basis. People are upset, and they may increasingly favor alternatives: online instruction, overseas or Canadian universities, nonuniversity forms of certification (to turn out "Microsoft-certified" computer gurus, for instance), attendance at cheaper community colleges instead of universities, and so on.

Intercollegiate Athletics. Intercollegiate athletics typically operates at a significant cost that must be financed, and often revenues from tickets, broadcast rights, sale of logos, and the like are not enough to cover it. My own institution, Ohio University, is an excellent example of a mid-size state university with some research emphasis whose administration wants to use sports as a means of attaining greater repute nationally. Faculty grumble about the costs, but administrators assure us that athletics lure alumni contributions, attract better applicants for admission, provide leadership skills for hundreds of students, and gain us national respect. Like most faculty colleagues, I am generally dubious that all of these "positive externalities" of intercollegiate sports exist; but even if they do, they come at a high cost.

The intercollegiate athletic budget at Ohio University exceeds $12 million a year, but less than one-fourth of that is covered by sports-generated revenues, meaning the rest of the university provides over $9 million in subsidy. Moreover, that first figure is probably an understatement, leaving out such things as depreciation of athletic facilities whose inclusion would be mandated under private sector accounting rules. The total general fund budget for the main campus, excluding auxiliary operations and some restricted grants, is around $309 million. Thus, about three cents of every dollar spent for general university purposes goes for subsidies to intercollegiate sports, an amount equal to about $500 per student. If students were asked, "Would you favor lowering tuition by $500 a year, but eliminating all intercollegiate sports?" my guess is they would overwhelmingly support the proposition. While Notre Dame, Ohio State, the University of Florida, and other popular and strong football schools may make money on football and even break even on intercollegiate athletics, many others are like Ohio University, aspiring for athletic greatness but never quite making it.

Food and Lodging Operations. During the budget crunches faced by universities after the brief 2001 recession, many schools raised not only their tuition substantially, but also their room and board charges, by far more than the rate of increase in food and lodging prices. It occurred to me that universities might be using some of the incremental increase in room and board charges to subsidize other university activities. Historically, most universities have tried to operate their dorm-related activities on a self-sustaining basis, not drawing on general university revenues to subsidize them, but also not expecting these operations to help fund the universities' other (primarily educational) enterprises.

An examination of room and board charges over time suggests that one or more of the following is probably occurring:

- The quality of food and lodging services is rising, and it is rising relative to similar services furnished by other providers.

- Because universities are relatively inefficient in providing these services, prices are rising more than for similar services provided in the for-profit sector.

- Universities are starting to generate "profits" from these operations that are now cross-subsidizing other operations.

From 1970–71 to 1999–2000, both the food and beverage and housing components of the Consumer Price Index more than quadrupled. If the price of college dormitory room and board had risen at the rate of inflation of the appropriate components of the CPI, the typical dorm room in all public institutions of higher education would have cost $1,750 in 1999–2000. The actual charge was $2,440—nearly $700, or 40 percent, more. Similarly, had the board charge for 1970–71 increased in line with the food and beverage inflation rate, the 1999–2000 charge would have been $2,173—nearly $200 less than the $2,364 actually charged. *University room and board inflation greatly exceeds that predicted by the general increase in food and housing prices.*

It is probably true that students in dorms live in somewhat better conditions and receive better food and more choices than three decades ago. More dorm rooms are air-conditioned, and more students have some kitchen facilities, either in a suite in which they live or within the dorm complex. But such qualitative improvements have occurred with housing generally, and it seems doubtful to me that a 40 percent increase in dorm charges in real terms is justified by them. Perhaps the rising costs reflect the relative inefficiency in this area of universities, which are not subject to the same market discipline as private entrepreneurs and often have a monopoly position in housing (when students are required to live in university housing). If this is so, it provides a case for privatization of those facilities. Do universities really need to be in the food and lodging business?

The data for the past few years provide very strong circumstantial support for the view that room and board charges are rising far faster than underlying inflation, and that universities are taking the surplus funds generated to do other things. This cross-subsidization, it might be argued, is the equivalent of stealth tuition increases—a backhanded way of getting more money from students without the adverse publicity associated with raising tuition.

I calculated rising average room and board charges for all institutions, private as well as public, comparing charges for academic year 2001–2 with those of two years earlier, 1999–2000. I then compared the increase in dorm charges with the increase in the "lodging away from home" component of the CPI , and the higher board charges with the increase in the "food away from home" (largely, restaurant prices) component.

The results, reported in figures 4-2 and 4-3, are pretty startling. Starting with food, the general inflation rate in the economy was slightly over 5 percent for the two years (as evaluated by the price index for outside-of-the-home food purchases), compared with over 9 percent within universities. As significant as that differential is, it pales in comparison with the rise in room charges. While the outside-of-the-home lodging prices rose less than 5 percent, university dorm charges soared over 11 percent.

FIGURE 4-2
RISE IN FOOD PRICES, U.S. ECONOMY VS. UNIVERSITIES, ACADEMIC YEAR
1999–2000 TO 2001–2

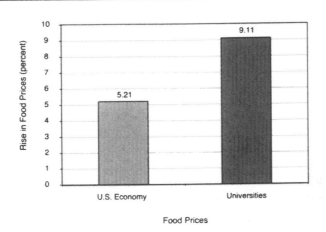

Food Prices

SOURCE: U.S. Department of Labor, Bureau of Labor Statistics, archived news releases for 2000–2003,
http://www.bls.gov/schedule/archives/cpi_nr.htm.

FIGURE 4-3
RISE IN HOUSING PRICES, U.S. ECONOMY VS. UNIVERSITIES, ACADEMIC
YEAR 1999–2000 TO 2001–2

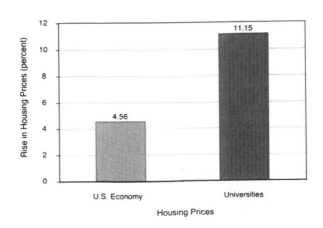

Housing Prices

SOURCE: U.S. Department of Labor, Bureau of Labor Statistics, archived news releases for 2000–2003,
http://www.bls.gov/schedule/archives/cpi_nr.htm.

Even if one accepts the argument that universities are improving their dorms and serving better food, the sharp rise in recent room and board rates in real terms suggests that some universities are leaning on their auxiliary enterprises for some relief from budget pressures that were augmented by the 2001 recession and the bear market in equities after 2000. It might be that the food and lodging operations are being forced to pay more for university overhead expenses. In any case, at the margin, it appears that some cross-subsidization of other activities is occurring.

Conclusions

Universities are peculiar in many ways. Unlike other organizations that also practice price discrimination, universities can and do legally pry into the most intimate financial information of their clients before deciding how much to charge each customer. Implicitly, universities charge whites more than blacks, nonathletes more than athletes, and, sometimes, less able students more than more able ones. They have pushed price discrimination to levels unheard of in the private sector, even in the airline industry, which is known for its aggressive use of this practice.

Universities also are nearly unique in offering large portions of their key staff—the faculty—lifetime employment contracts, a device that effectively protects academic freedom but imposes an enormous cost on higher education and, sometimes, on the quality of education received by students.

Last, universities take funds intended for one use and reallocate them to others, engaging in cross-subsidization to a degree relatively rare in other sectors, with the conspicuous exception of medicine. The external subsidies of undergraduate education have declined in relative importance as universities have reallocated funds, sometimes without the knowledge of major providers of those funds, to favored activities, such as graduate education and research, and, to a much lesser extent, intercollegiate athletics at some schools. Given growing concerns about rising costs, the continuance and expansion of these "peculiar" practices become problematic, as they contribute to the continued rise in the cost of undergraduate education.

PART II

Have Our Universities
Lost Their Way?

5

American Higher Education:
Past and Present

To this point, this book has focused on the rising costs of higher education and their causes. In the next few chapters, we put this issue into a broader context. First, in this chapter, we discuss the growing importance of the issue, looking at the growth of American universities and some of the demographic and other trends that have occurred. Then, in chapters 6 and 7, we ask some very basic questions: Why do we need universities? Can the functions of universities be performed in other ways? Even if universities are desirable institutions for disseminating and producing knowledge, why should governments and private third parties subsidize them?

In short, while the first part of this book dealt with the cost explosion in higher education, this part deals with the perceived rationale for higher education itself. It will set the stage for the final part of the book, which looks at the future of the American university.

American Higher Education Today

In many ways, this is the Golden Age of American higher education. American universities are widely perceived to be the best in the world, in marked contrast to our primary and secondary schools. Students flock to American universities from many other countries, indeed, in such numbers that the presence of foreign students was considered a potentially serious threat to national security in the aftermath of the September 11, 2001, tragedy. The winners of the most prestigious international scholarly prizes are predominantly individuals in some way affiliated with American research universities.

More than any other major nation, America has achieved the dream of providing higher education for a large proportion of its population entering adulthood. Americans devote far more resources to higher education than any other country in the world, and most persons would agree that this expenditure has resulted in a rewarding payoff: a highly educated and productive population of Americans, and of others who temporarily migrate here to take advantage of the nation's great colleges and universities.

A good deal of objective data supports what might be termed "American higher educational exceptionalism." First, the sheer numbers going to colleges, universities, technical institutes, and other postsecondary training schools are large by any standard. Table 5-1 shows the growth in enrollments for years ending in "0" since 1870.[1] Enrollments have risen continuously in absolute numbers since the first reliable estimates of total enrollments were compiled after 1870. To be sure, the American population has grown more than sevenfold since 1870. Correcting for that, however, enrollments still have increased remarkably. In 1870, barely one out of every thousand Americans was a college student; since 1980, over fifty out of every thousand are in college—more than 5 percent of the total population.

The population-adjusted numbers in table 5-1 show a steady increase in enrollments until the 1990s, although the rate varied sharply over time. It was modest in the 1880s, 1900s, and, arguably, the 1950s, for example. It was relatively large in the 1920s, and especially large in the 1960s and 1970s. The ratio of college students to population rose in decades of big wars (the 1910s and the 1940s) and economic distress (the 1930s). The huge surge in the 1960s was, in both an absolute and relative sense, easily the greatest increase of the century. During that decade, college enrollments more than doubled, implying annual average growth exceeding 7 percent per year. Old universities expanded rapidly, and many new schools were started. It was in many ways the Golden Age of university expansion.

But note the decline in the 1990s. In an absolute sense, enrollments rose modestly (about 9 percent), but they grew less rapidly than the population as a whole for the first time in modern American history. Why? It is tempting to argue that the decline was the result of rising college costs, the most important focus of this book. In fact, however, the bulk of the reason lay elsewhere—with changing demographic trends.

TABLE 5-1

ENROLLMENT IN U.S. HIGHER EDUCATION, 1870–2000

Year[a]	Enrollment	Enrollment per 1,000 Population
1870	52,286	1.32
1880	115,817	2.31
1890	156,756	2.49
1900	237,592	3.12
1910	355,213	3.85
1920	597,880	5.64
1930	1,100,737	8.93
1940	1,494,203	11.31
1950	2,659,021	17.57
1960	3,639,847	20.30
1970	8,004,660	39.39
1980	11,569,899	51.07
1990	13,538,560	54.44
2000	14,791,224	52.56

SOURCE: NCES, *Digest of Education Statistics: 2002* (Washington, D.C.: Government Printing Office, 2003), table 171; U.S. Census Bureau, *Statistical Abstract of the United States: 2003* (Washington, D.C.: Government Printing Office, 2004), table 1.
a. School year ending in indicated date.

From 1990 to 2000, the proportion of the American population in the eighteen- to twenty-four-year age group declined, reflecting falling births in the 1970s. This was the sole determinant of the fall in the percentage of Americans going to college. Table 5-2 shows enrollments for the twentieth century per one thousand persons ages eighteen to twenty-four, the prime age group attending college. In 1900, barely 2 percent (less than twenty-three per thousand population) of the prime college-age population attended college— by 1990, for the first time, a majority did. The rise in this ratio was continuous, being particularly robust in the 1920s, 1940s, 1960s, and 1980s. The sharp slowdown in the increase in college participation in the 1990s partially explains the low absolute growth in enrollments in that decade. (The other explanation is the dearth of college-age students in this time period.)

This trend has implications for future enrollment growth. Universities in the postwar era became accustomed to robust enrollment growth— but the annual percentage growth has declined in every decade after the

TABLE 5-2

HIGHER EDUCATION ENROLLMENT PER 1,000 POPULATION
AGES 18 TO 24

Year	Enrollment Per 1,000 Population Ages 18 to 24	Year	Enrollment Per 1,000 Population Ages 18 to 24
1900	22.77	1960	225.68
1910	29.99	1970	323.93
1920	46.03	1980	388.38
1930	75.54	1990	506.38
1940	96.07	2000	544.92
1950	170.05		

SOURCE: NCES, *Digest of Education Statistics: 2002* (Washington, D.C.: Government Printing Office, 2003), table 171; U.S. Census Bureau, *Statistical Abstract of the United States: 2003* (Washington, D.C.: Government Printing Office, 2004), table 1; *Statistical Abstract of the United States: 1988* (Washington, D.C.: Government Printing Office, 1987), table 13; U.S. Census Bureau, *Historical Statistics of the United States, Colonial Times to 1970* (Washington, D.C.: Government Printing Office, 1976), 15.

1960s, falling to below 1 percent in the 1990s. Changing rates of population growth play only a small role in this. Enrollment growth before 1990 resulted mainly from increasing participation of the population in higher education. As the growth in that participation slows, university enrollment change likely will be determined to a greater extent by population change, especially among eighteen- to twenty-four-year-olds. That, in turn, depends not only on birth rates but on immigration, which now contributes a significant proportion (roughly one-third) of American population growth.

In that regard, it is interesting to note that in 2001, the resident population five to nine years of age was actually slightly less than the population ages fifteen to nineteen. Thus, the traditionally important pool of eighteen- to twenty-four-year-old students one decade from now is not likely to be any larger than it is at present, unless we have an upsurge in immigration. If the participation rate of youth in higher education were to rise only a very little (as in the 1990s), enrollment gains in the next decade would be predicted to be very modest or even nonexistent in any model that emphasized the eighteen- to twenty-four-year age pool as a key determinant. Other data on, for example, college enrollments of recent high school graduates are roughly compatible consistent with table 5-2.[2]

Universities wanting to expand their numbers but aware of demographic realities and the slowing of the growth in college participation may engage in more extensive marketing efforts in years to come. Their total enrollments, however, are also affected by three other factors: the degree of participation in graduate and professional education, the growth in the importance of "nontraditional" students (outside the eighteen- to twenty-four-year age group), and international migration to American universities.

Graduate vs. Undergraduate Enrollments. Most universities (as opposed to liberal arts colleges and two-year institutions) aspire to have bigger and better graduate and professional programs. The thinking is that such programs provide prestige, greater grant opportunities, and higher subsidies from governments than undergraduate programs offer. As the traditional undergraduate student population base stagnates, graduate education offers other opportunities for universities to grow in size and reputation. The same applies to professional schools. Ambitious universities aspire to add law and medical schools and a variety of other professional postgraduate programs, as well as PhD programs, to their offerings. Professors clamor to teach graduate students, as that confers greater prestige, and arguably more intellectual satisfaction, than instructing undergraduates in basic survey courses.

With this bias toward advanced instruction, one might expect the proportion of persons seeking advanced degrees to expand significantly over time. More and more students trying to get an edge on others in job markets would try to boost their credentials with masters' or doctoral degrees, or with advanced professional training. Has this happened? Not really. While the number of graduate and professional students has risen with enrollments generally over very long-term horizons, the proportion receiving graduate or professional training has remained remarkably stable for several decades. Table 5-3 shows that 86 percent of enrollments were at the undergraduate level in both the 1969–70 and 1999–2000 school years, while the proportion of graduate students rose only very slightly, and the proportion of professional students declined a bit. What is interesting are not the differences, but rather the stability in the relationship over time.

TABLE 5-3

COMPOSITION OF UNIVERSITY ENROLLMENTS BY
TYPE OF STUDENT, 1970–2000

Year[a]	Undergraduate[b]	Graduate[b]	Professional[b]
1970	86.01	11.93	2.06
1980	85.13	12.38	2.49
1990	86.73	11.24	2.02
2000	85.73	12.22	2.05

SOURCE: NCES, *Digest of Education Statistics: 2002* (Washington, D.C.: Government Printing Office, 2003), table 177; author's calculations.
a. School year ending in indicated date.
b. All numbers are percents of all students.

One caveat is in order. In the 1990s, the graduate share of enrollment rose noticeably. Graduate enrollments rose nearly 19 percent over the decade, compared with 8 percent for undergraduates (and 11 percent for professional enrollments). Hopes of university administrators for larger relative graduate enrollments were modestly realized. Whether this was the beginning of a significant long-term trend, only time will tell. Since the financial payoff to such graduate degrees as the MBA has grown substantially over time, it is probable that the relative importance of graduate education will increase somewhat in the future.

The Increase in "Nontraditional" Students. Most persons going to college enter from high school, usually when they are about eighteen years old. They typically stay in college for four years or so, until the age of twenty-two or perhaps twenty-three. There have been brief periods in American history when the proportion of older students in universities was rather large, notably after World War II, when millions of veterans began or finished college several years older than traditional students. In the last decade or two, however, universities have talked about the increasing importance of nontraditional (generally, older) students. To what extent does this phenomenon exist?

As table 5-4 suggests, from 1975 to 1995 there was an upward trend in the proportion of college students outside the eighteen- to twenty-four-year group. The number of students over thirty-five years of age more than

TABLE 5-4

CHANGING NONTRADITIONAL STUDENT ENROLLMENTS, 1975–2000[a]

Age	1975	1980	1985	1990	1995	2000
<18	238	218	291	168	165	148
>35	1,183	1,207	1,661	2,318	2,669	2,507
25–34	2,468	2,703	3,063	3,161	3,349	3,207
All ages	10,880	11,387	12,524	13,621	14,715	15,314
Not 18–24	3,899	4,128	5,035	5,667	6,163	5,862
% Not 18–24	35.84	36.25	40.20	41.60	41.88	38.28
Δ% Total Not 18–24[b]	NA	45.17	79.77	57.61	45.33	−42.45

SOURCE: U.S. Census Bureau, *Statistical Abstract of the United States* (Washington, D.C.: Government Printing Office, various years). Tables for various years are found in section 4. Data were originally collected by the NCES..

a. Enrollments are in thousands.

b. % of increase in total enrollment over previous 5 years in age groups other than 18 to 24.

doubled, alone accounting for nearly half of the total enrollment growth in that period. In 1995, nearly 42 percent of those enrolled in college were outside the traditional student age group.

In the late 1990s, however, the upsurge in numbers of nontraditional students came to an abrupt end, and, indeed, enrollments of these students showed some decline. In the absence of a decline in enrollments of persons outside the eighteen- to twenty-four-year age group, total enrollments would have risen 50 percent more from 1995 to 2000 than actually occurred. The reason is not related to a declining population pool—to the contrary, the over-thirty-five population grew 24 percent during the 1990s. The number of college enrollees per one thousand persons over the age of thirty-five fell from 20.1 to 17.5 over the course of the decade, and even more in the last half of the decade.

I am not entirely sure why the stagnation and decline in the older student population occurred, but I can offer some educated conjectures. First, it is entirely possible that the sensitivity of older Americans to the rapidly rising tuition costs of the 1990s (the price-elasticity of demand) was greater than among traditional-age students. Why?

For younger Americans, higher education is largely an investment made to increase their lifetime incomes. This justifies borrowing large amounts to ease the financial pain of going to college. The earnings differential between college- and high school-educated individuals widened in the 1990s, justifying the payment of sharply higher tuition for those looking at college as an enhancer of income. For older Americans then returning to college at, say, fifty or sixty years of age, higher education was largely a consumption good—something attained for enjoyment and a sense of fulfillment. It was harder to justify paying the rising fees to take college courses largely for personal enrichment, especially in light of the probability that older Americans received less scholarship aid—that is, discounts from the "sticker" price. Moreover, for those seeking mainly enjoyment from learning, new or improved technologies, such as the Internet and cable TV outlets like the History and Discovery channels, and cheaper international travel, began to offer options to taking college courses that were increasingly more affordable and, arguably, as culturally fulfilling.

Second, after 1990 there was a surge in the number of workers over the age of thirty-five, increasing by 30 percent from 1990 to 2000.[3] Other things being equal, workers are less likely to participate in higher education than nonworkers. Moreover, the older student phenomenon is particularly concentrated among women. For example, in 1990, there were slightly over twice as many women of nontraditional age as men enrolled in American institutions of higher education. The rise in female labor force participation was particularly great among middle-aged women. For example, in 1990, the labor force participation rate (the percentage in the labor force) for women ages forty-five to sixty-four was 56.5 percent; by 2000, it had risen sharply to 65.4 percent—at a time when the pool of women in that age group was also rising rapidly.[4]

A phenomenon of less quantitative importance but still of some interest was the rather noticeable decline in the number of college students under the age of eighteen. If the numbers are to be believed, the absolute number fell nearly 38 percent from 1975 to 2000, despite the enactment by some states of programs allowing bright high school students to enroll in universities at relatively modest costs. One part of the explanation was the sharp increase in popularity of Advanced Placement examinations and the newer International Baccalaureate examinations, which allow students in high school to earn credits toward college graduation. As college costs continue to soar, the relative importance of substitutes for the traditional college experience can be expected to continue to grow.

The Globalization of American Universities. American universities are distinctly more international today than they were even a generation ago. American students travel abroad in programs sponsored by their own or other American universities in greater numbers than ever before. A greater international emphasis is placed on the curriculum in many schools. And, most relevant to this discussion, the number of foreign students attending American universities has risen meteorically in the last generation.

There are two dimensions to this last point. The first relates to students who are citizens of other countries who have temporarily migrated to the United States for an education; the second involves immigrants to the United States who attend American universities or have children who attend.

With respect to the first group, the number of nonimmigrant, foreign-born individuals attending American universities more than tripled in the past generation, going from less than 180,000 in 1976 to 548,000 in 2001.[5] As a percentage of total enrollments, the increase was somewhat less, going from 1.6 percent in 1976 to about 3.7 percent early in the new century, although universities with over 10 percent nonimmigrant, foreign-born enrollees are commonplace. The increase came from all parts of the globe but was concentrated heavily in Asia, which provided a majority (54 percent) of the foreign students in 1976 and an even greater proportion (nearly 62 percent) by 2001. Particularly important was rising enrollment from India, Japan, South Korea, and China (including Taiwan and Hong Kong).

Interestingly, Mexico, the large neighboring country that provides the largest number of immigrants to the United States, is a modest source of foreign students (only 11,000 in 2001—less than 20 percent of those from Latin America). Another surprise is that, in percentage terms, the biggest growth in foreign enrollments has been from Europe, which provided only 8 percent of foreign students in 1976, but nearly 15 percent by 2001—this in a period when the relative importance of Europe in immigration has declined. The end of the Cold War and the rise in incomes and educational aspirations in Europe no doubt contributed to this trend.

The internationalization of the student body has, however, been far greater than the statistics on nonimmigrant, foreign-born students indicate, as they do not reflect the large numbers of immigrants and their children enrolled at American universities. Data from the 2000 Current Population Survey suggest that, altogether, 1,766,000 foreign-born students attended American universities—between 11 and 12 percent of the total enrollment. If one were to include the children of immigrants (who grew up in homes headed by at least one foreign-born parent), the numbers rise to 3,266,000— nearly 22 percent of the individuals attending institutions of higher education in the United States.[6] In this sense, American universities have a strong multicultural dimension, with much international diversity.

The Feminization of the American University. For generations after the first institution of higher learning in the United States, Harvard College, opened in 1636, only male students were admitted to American universities. While that began to change significantly in the nineteenth century, even in 1870 fewer than 15 percent of new recipients of bachelors' degrees were female.[7] Female enrollments rose substantially in the late nineteenth and early twentieth centuries, but as late as 1955 only 38 percent of entering freshmen were women.[8]

While the very long-run trend generally has been for female enrollments to rise disproportionately, there were periods in the twentieth century when, relative to males, their enrollments fell. Startlingly, the proportion of college students that were female in 1889–90 (35.9 percent), was the same as seventy years later, in 1959–60. Nonetheless, the modern trend has been toward increasing dominance of women in college and university enrollments (see table 5-5). From 1960 to 2000, women went from being a distinct minority of less than 36 percent of students to being a solid majority of over 56 percent. As figure 5-1 shows, women have dominated enrollment growth since 1980.

Higher education is perceived by its consumers to be both a consumer good and an investment good. Some also have traditionally viewed college as a good place to meet a spouse, particularly one who has the means to provide creature comforts. This "socialization" component of university education has an obvious consumption component (having fun with one's peers), but a financial dimension as well.

TABLE 5-5

PERCENTAGE OF FEMALE STUDENTS, 1870–2000

Year[a]	Percent of Enrollees Who Were Female	Year[a]	Percent of Enrollees Who Were Female
1870	21.3	1940	40.2
1880	32.7	1950	30.3
1890	35.9	1960	35.9
1900	35.9	1970	40.7
1910	39.6	1980	50.9
1920	47.3	1990	54.3
1930	43.7	2000	56.1

SOURCE: NCES, *Digest of Education Statistics: 2002* (Washington, D.C.: Government Printing Office, 2003), table 171.
a. Fall enrollment for school year ending in indicated date.

Historically, some women "consumed" college training, indulging in the pleasures of learning and socialization in a university milieu with males of similar socioeconomic background. Others had always gone to college, some to work in occupations viewed in their times as suitable for women of culture and breeding, such as teaching. Until a generation or so ago, however, most women did not work, so university training did not have the same anticipated occupational financial advantages that it provided for men. This changed as the proportion of women seeking employment rose and women's role in the labor force increasingly converged with that of men. Women's demand for university training rose sharply.

More difficult to explain than the growing presence of women at institutions of higher education, however, is why in recent years they have significantly outnumbered men in college. In 2000, there were more than five female students for every four males, and the disparity has widened over time. Part of the gender gap relates to a female preponderance among students of nontraditional age. Among those ages eighteen to twenty-four, women constituted 54 percent of students—a majority, but a somewhat less lopsided one than suggested by the aggregate statistics. A growing tendency for boys to underachieve in high school relative to girls may also contribute to this trend.

FIGURE 5-1

U.S. HIGHER EDUCATION ENROLLMENT GROWTH BY GENDER, 1980–2000

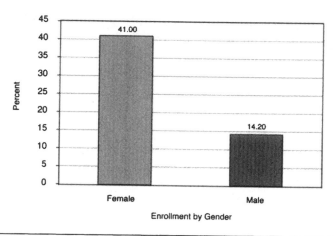

SOURCE: Author's calculations. See NCES, *Digest of Education Statistics: 2002* (Washington, D.C.: Government Printing Office, 2003), table 171.

However, the "feminization" of the university is particularly pronounced among minority groups, especially African Americans. In 2000, over 62 percent of black enrollees in higher education were women.[9] Young black men have strikingly low rates of college participation compared to their black female peers. This is probably related to another social statistic: The proportion of black men over the age of twenty who are employed is markedly smaller than for white men, while the proportion of black women over twenty who are working is actually virtually the same as for white women.[10] The statistics seem to suggest that black women seem to be more concerned about labor force prospects than black men—at least compared with whites. The high rate of incarceration among young black males also reduces the pool of potential college applicants for that group.

Racial Dimensions of Changing Enrollments. One of the most striking changes in university enrollments over time has been the extraordinary growth in nonwhite and Hispanic populations. By 2000, well over 30 percent of all college enrollees were either nonwhite or Hispanic—compared with about 18 percent in 1980.

TABLE 5-6

GROWTH IN ENROLLMENTS, BY RACE/ETHNICITY, 1980–81 TO 1999–2000

Racial or Ethnic Group	Percent Growth in Enrollment
Non-Hispanic Whites	4.4
Non-Hispanic Blacks	48.2
Hispanic Origin	179.1
Asians	217.6
American Indians	73.2
All Races	22.4

SOURCE: Author's calculations from U.S. Census Bureau, *Statistical Abstract of the United States: 1997* (Washington, D.C.: Government Printing Office, 1998), table 286; *Statistical Abstract of the United States: 2003* (Washington, D.C. Government Printing Office, 2004), table 278.

Table 5-6 shows that while white enrollments grew scarcely at all in the 1980s and 1990s, the enrollment of minority racial and ethnic groups soared. Black enrollments rose twice as fast as for the population as a whole, but the truly explosive growth occurred among other groups, especially Asians (whose enrollment more than tripled), Hispanics, and, to a lesser extent, American Indians.

The huge disparities in enrollment growth by race and ethnicity can largely be explained by differences in the population growth of the various groups, but there were also marked increases in higher education participation among nonwhites and Hispanics. However, large differences in participation still exist, as suggested by table 5-7, which looks at the number of higher education enrollees per one thousand members of the group between eighteen and twenty-four in 2000.

While in general the Hispanic and nonwhite groups have lower rates of university participation than non-Hispanic whites, it would be very difficult to argue that nonwhites are denied access to American universities, particularly given that Asian participation, so measured, is more than 26 percent higher than for whites. While it is true that black participation is still over 30 percent below that of whites, that is at least partly explainable by lower high school graduation rates and levels of academic achievement among blacks. Of particular interest is the very low rate of university participation of Hispanics—dramatically lower than even for African Americans. Since

TABLE 5-7

HIGHER EDUCATION ENROLLEES PER 1,000 POPULATION, BY GROUP, 2000

Ethnic or Racial Group	Enrollment, 1999–2000 [a]
Total Population	545.0
Non-Hispanic Whites	609.8
Blacks	416.0
Hispanics	277.5
Asians	772.2
American Indians	461.3

SOURCE: NCES, *Digest of Education Statistics: 2002* (Washington, D.C.: Government Printing Office, 2003), table 206; U.S. Census Bureau, *Statistical Abstract of the United States: 2003* (Washington, D.C.: Government Printing Office, 2004), table 13.
a. Population for group aged 18–24, 2000.

Hispanics numerically comprise the largest minority (having a more than 20 percent larger population of eighteen- to twenty-four-year-olds than blacks), their low rate of enrollment is the single most significant issue regarding minority nonparticipation in university life today.

It is tempting to argue that low rates of participation in higher education by non-Asian minorities are primarily an effect of lower income levels. While income no doubt plays some role, its importance can be exaggerated. It is true that Asians have higher incomes than whites, who in turn have higher incomes than blacks, and that Asians lead whites, who are ahead of blacks, in participation. However, the median household income of Hispanics in 2000 was almost precisely 10 percent higher than that of blacks ($33,455 vs. $30,436), yet blacks had dramatically higher rates of participation than Hispanics. Moreover, the push by universities to expand minority enrollments has led to discounted prices for attendance in the form of scholarship aid that is less readily available for whites, reducing the relative economic barrier to entry somewhat. Indeed, there is some evidence that, controlling for income differences, black participation in general is higher than for whites, particularly for those of lower socioeconomic backgrounds.[11]

Two- vs. Four-Year Colleges: Trends. About three out of every eight students enrolled in American higher education attend two-year institutions. These schools offer associate degrees, with a significant part of the training

TABLE 5-8

GROWTH IN ENROLLMENTS, BY DECADES, TWO- AND FOUR-YEAR SCHOOLS,
1970–2000 (PERCENTAGE)

Period	2-Year Institutions	4-Year Institutions	All Institutions
1970–80	95.2	20.9	41.0
1980–90	15.8	13.3	14.2
1990–99	6.7	7.2	7.0

SOURCE: NCES, *Digest of Education Statistics: 2002* (Washington, D.C.: Government Printing Office, 2003), table 173.

devoted to vocational study in specific skills. They place little or no emphasis on research, and faculty have significantly heavier teaching loads than professors at the typical four-year institution. Costs per student run one-third to one-half of what they do at the schools offering degrees at the bachelor's level or higher.

The two-year college is a product of the twentieth century. Even in 1950, fewer than 10 percent of students pursuing degrees were in two-year institutions such as junior colleges.[12] Enrollments more than doubled in the 1950s, but the heyday of the two-year college movement was the 1960s and 1970s. Enrollment much more than tripled in the 1960s, in part because of expanding market share—two-year schools increased their share from less than 13 percent to 21 percent of total college enrollments—with growth continuing robustly in the 1970s. As table 5-8 suggests, however, the growth spurt largely dissipated after 1980, and the two-year schools actually grew less than the four-year institutions in the 1990s.

I suspect these trends reflect the effect of the changing income-elasticity of demand for higher education over time. In less technical terminology, the generation after World War II included many Americans with limited education and incomes who wanted their children to have more than they had, so they sent them to relatively inexpensive two-year junior colleges, branches of four-year universities, and the like. As time passed, incomes rose generally, and the next generation wanted still more for their own children—a full four-year college education. In economic terms, a junior college education in the immediate postwar era was a normal or even a superior good—that is, as incomes rose, people wanted it more. With rising incomes in the 1970s and

TABLE 5-9

THE SHARE OF ENROLLMENTS OF PUBLIC AND PRIVATE
UNIVERSITIES, 1955–99a

Year	Percent Enrolled in Private Schools	Year	Percent Enrolled in Private Schools
1955	44.0	1980	21.8
1960	40.9	1985	22.6
1965	34.1	1990	21.5
1970	26.8	1995	22.2
1975	23.6	1999	23.5

SOURCE: NCES, *Digest of Education Statistics: 2002* (Washington, D.C.: Government Printing Office, 2003), table 172.
a. Before 1980, data refer to only students in degree programs.

beyond, a two-year education was increasingly perceived as an inferior good (one that is less desired and thus consumed less as income rises), reducing somewhat the demand for it. Adding to this was some growth in the earnings differential over time between those with two- and four-year degrees.

Type of Institution: Private, Private For-Profit, Public. While 86 to 88 percent or so of elementary and secondary students attend public schools, the importance of private institutions is far greater at the university level, with nearly one-fourth of students attending them. Considering that spending per student tends to be somewhat higher in private universities, an even larger proportion of higher education expenditures is privately controlled. Moreover, the best universities, as noted in rankings such as the *USN&WR* list, are most likely to be private schools. While many so-called "private" institutions actually receive a considerable portion of their operating funds from governments, they are not directly controlled by them. Moreover, an increasing segment of the market is in the area of for-profit institutions, owned by corporations or other forms of private enterprise.

Table 5-9 looks at the private-public university division in the past half-century. Private institutions dominated higher education in the seventeenth, eighteenth, and nineteenth centuries. As late as 1955, nearly half of all students in higher education attended private schools. It was a common

TABLE 5-10

GROWTH IN FOR-PROFIT ENROLLMENT, U.S. HIGHER
EDUCATION, 1976–99

Year	Enrollment	Year	Enrollment
1976	44,362	1990	213,693
1980	111,714	1995	240,363
1985	195,991	1999	430,199

SOURCE: NCES, *Digest of Education Statistics: 2002* (Washington, D.C.: Government Printing Office, 2003), table 172.

view in the 1950s and 1960s that public institutions would eventually dominate American higher education; indeed, many predicted the demise of the private liberal arts college. And, certainly, the market share of the private schools declined sharply during the period of rapidly expanding enrollments in the 1950s and 1960s. Yet by 1980, the market share of private schools had approached a low point. The share has stabilized between 21 and 24 percent ever since.

Indeed, there is some modest but tangible evidence of a trend reversal. Since 1990, private school enrollments have grown more than those of public schools, and the private schools have slowly but surely been adding to their market share.

These changes may be a sign that public university domination of the expansion of higher education can no longer be assumed.

The most interesting news, however, is the rapid growth of enrollments at for-profit institutions. Table 5-10 shows the enrollments at for-profit technical schools and universities in modern times. Some caution should be used in interpreting these figures, as changing definitions mean the data are not wholly consistent across years. For one thing, the numbers are for accredited schools, and some schools moved to accredited status during the period. Also, after 1995 schools are defined in terms of Title IV federal financial aid program participation. Correcting for these factors, the growth in enrollments is likely closer to a factor of five than the nearly tenfold growth recorded here.

In light of the massive subsidies received by public universities through state, federal, and even some local governmental payments, and the large endowment incomes earned by many nonprofit private institutions, how can schools compete on a for-profit basis? In later chapters, this issue is more fully explored; here, suffice it to say that the cost explosion and falling productivity of universities have given private entrepreneurs an opportunity to compete that previously did not exist.

Interstate Differences in Participation in Higher Education

The growth in higher education in the United States has not been evenly distributed throughout the country. As of March 2002, for example, the proportion of the population over age twenty-five with college degrees in Maryland was twice that in Arkansas or West Virginia.[13] Table 5-11 reports interstate variations in the proportion of the population over age twenty-five with bachelors' degrees or higher in 1980 and 2002, and indicates the growth in higher education participation by state over the two decades.

In every state, the proportion of adults who were holders of baccalaureate or higher degrees grew over time. The changes were modest in some states, such as Wyoming, Alaska, Idaho, and West Virginia, while the proportions nearly doubled in others, including Indiana, Kentucky, Maryland, Missouri, Pennsylvania, and Rhode Island. Over time, there was virtually no narrowing of interstate differences in the proportions of those with college educations (the coefficient of variation for the fifty states plus the District of Columbia falling only slightly, from .2048 to .1959). The evidence does not support any notion that ease of college access has created a uniform national involvement of young Americans in university life.

As the table shows, West Virginia and Arkansas, two states with relatively low per-capita incomes, had the lowest proportion of adult college graduates. The states with the highest proportions were Maryland, Colorado, Virginia, and Massachusetts, all relatively high-income states. Is the correlation between college participation and income very strong? I calculated the zero-order correlation coefficient between per-capita income in 2001 and the educational attainment data from the March 2002 Current Population Survey. The correlation was a very high +0.79. Income did seem to matter a great deal. Yet an interesting question is, in which direction does causality run? Does higher income lead to more people

Table 5-11

College Educational Attainment, by State, 1980, 2002[a] (percent)

State	1980	2002	Change, 1980–2002
Alabama	12.2	22.7	10.5
Alaska	21.1	25.6	4.5
Arizona	17.4	26.3	8.9
Arkansas	10.8	18.3	7.5
California	19.6	27.9	8.3
Colorado	23.0	35.7	12.7
Connecticut	20.7	32.6	11.9
Delaware	17.5	29.5	12.0
District of Columbia	27.5	44.4	16.9
Florida	14.9	25.7	10.8
Georgia	14.6	25.0	10.4
Hawaii	20.3	26.8	6.5
Idaho	15.8	20.9	5.1
Illinois	16.2	27.3	11.1
Indiana	12.5	23.7	11.2
Iowa	13.9	23.1	9.2
Kansas	17.0	29.1	12.1
Kentucky	11.1	21.6	10.5
Louisiana	13.9	22.1	8.2
Maine	14.4	23.8	9.4
Maryland	20.4	37.6	17.2
Massachusetts	20.0	34.3	14.3
Michigan	14.3	22.5	8.3
Minnesota	17.4	30.5	13.1
Mississippi	12.3	20.9	8.6
Missouri	13.0	23.1	10.1
Montana	17.5	23.6	6.1
Nebraska	15.5	27.1	11.6
Nevada	14.4	22.1	7.7
New Hampshire	18.2	30.1	11.9
New Jersey	18.3	31.4	13.1
New Mexico	17.6	25.4	7.8
New York	17.9	28.8	10.9
North Carolina	13.2	22.4	9.2
North Dakota	14.8	25.3	10.5
Ohio	13.7	24.5	10.8

(continued on next page)

(Table 5-11, continued)

State	1980	2002	Change, 1980–2002
Oklahoma	15.1	20.4	5.3
Oregon	17.9	27.1	9.2
Pennsylvania	13.6	26.1	12.5
Rhode Island	15.4	30.1	14.7
South Carolina	13.4	23.3	9.9
South Dakota	14.0	23.6	9.6
Tennessee	12.6	21.5	8.9
Texas	16.9	26.2	9.3
Utah	19.9	26.8	6.9
Vermont	19.0	30.8	11.8
Virginia	19.1	34.6	15.5
Washington	19.0	28.3	9.3
West Virginia	10.4	15.9	5.5
Wisconsin	14.8	24.7	9.9
Wyoming	17.2	19.6	2.4

SOURCE: U.S. Census Bureau, *Statistical Abstract of the United States: 2003* (Washington, D.C.: Government Printing Office, 2004), table 231; *Statistical Abstract of the United States: 1984* (Washington, D.C.: Government Printing Office, 1983), table 224.

a. Those with bachelor's degrees or more as % of population aged 25 or more.

going to college, or does more people going to college produce higher incomes? Related to this, does government spending for higher education explain a significant portion of the differentials observed in table 5-11? And, where college educational attainment rose a good deal over time, was that largely a consequence of greater state spending on colleges and universities? The answers to these questions are discussed in chapter 7.

Another way of looking at the level of university participation by state is to observe the migration patterns of students. The National Center for Education Statistics periodically publishes estimated net migration rates for new high school graduates who become freshmen at colleges and universities. In the last published survey, in 1998, five states had a significant net out-migration of students (significant being defined as 20 percent or more of residents going to other states to attend college, net of freshmen studying at colleges in the state). In other words, a significant proportion of their students studied in other states. These were Connecticut, Maine, New Jersey, Alaska, and Hawaii. Eight other jurisdictions had the opposite situation—20 percent

TABLE 5-12

UNIVERSITY EDUCATION, POPULATION 25–64 YEARS OLD, 1999

Country	% of Population with College Education
United States	27
Australia	18
France	13
Germany	12
Italy	9
Japan	18
Korea (South)	17
Mexico	12
Norway	25
Sweden	13
Switzerland	15
United Kingdom	17

SOURCE: U.S. Census Bureau, *Statistical Abstract of the United States: 2002* (Washington, D.C.: Government Printing Office, 2003), table 1317.

or more freshmen in-migration. They were Arizona, Delaware, the District of Columbia, Massachusetts, North Dakota, Rhode Island, Utah, and Vermont.

At one time, it was argued that northeastern states with a strong private university tradition but weak public colleges tended to have significant out-migration, with the cost of good local schools being too high. Today, the statistics for Connecticut (home to Yale University and other fine private schools) and New Jersey (home of Princeton) are consistent with that perspective. Yet no state has a richer private school tradition than Massachusetts, home to Harvard and many other great private universities, and yet it has significant in-migration, as do other New England states with strong private schools, such as Vermont and Rhode Island. The "private-schools-force-kids-out-of-the-state" hypothesis appears pretty weak.

American Universities in International Perspective

Americans often boast that we have the best system of higher education in the world, with "best" reflecting the generally high reputation of our universities, as well as the fact that the system provides greater access to college than is the case in other countries. That latter point is confirmed by international data on adults' attainment of university education (table 5-12).

The United States has roughly double the level of university participation of most of the other countries, with a few exceptions. Norway, for example, has nearly the same proportion of college-educated people as the United States. Moreover, since university enrollments have risen sharply in many other countries only in the past decade or two, it will take time before the impact is fully felt by the entire twenty-five- to sixty-four-year-old population. It is likely that American superiority by this measure will decline over time.

Characteristics of American University Students

Earlier we suggested that American college and university students are disproportionately female, and that 20 percent or more have significant personal or family ties to other countries, or are outside the traditional eighteen- to twenty-four-year-old age group. Minorities are underrepresented as a whole, but Asians are an important exception.

The typical college freshman today enters college slightly less educated than his or her parents, if SAT or ACT tests are accurate representations. Between 1970 and 2001, the mean composite SAT score fell 29 points, from 1049 to 1020, with the decline entirely on the verbal portion of the test. ACT scores are a bit harder to evaluate owing to a change in the scoring in 1990, but it appears that a similar decline has occurred over a generation. The decline has stopped, and modest increases have been observed since 1990.[14]

Although students are probably no more accomplished academically and arguably less so than their parents, they enter college with markedly higher grades. The typical student entering in 1970 had slightly less than a B average in high school—probably a grade-point average (GPA) of about 2.95 on a four-point scale where an A is four points, a B is three points, and so forth. The entering freshman in 2001 had on average a GPA of around 3.37, dramatically higher.[15] Grade inflation, combined with a probably smaller stock of basic knowledge, means that today's students know a bit less coming into college—but are evaluated more highly than their parents were. Many long-time college professors, this one included, would argue that in some real sense academic standards have fallen, making the job of imparting a given level of skills or knowledge more difficult than it was several decades ago. As the proportion of students going to college rises, by mathematical necessity a growing percentage will come from the middle or lower echelons of the high school grade distribution, meaning they are less prepared (in a relative sense) than the typical student of a generation earlier.

Today's typical student comes from a comfortably situated, middle-class family with a median income of $67,200, about 30 percent higher than the national median. The percentage differential is just a bit larger than it was in 1970. The belief that the typical college student would come from a relatively less well-off financial background as the proportion of high school graduates entering colleges rose simply has not come to pass—probably because of the rise in the real cost of going to college. Thus, the notion that, because of the existence of a massive system of public universities, "anyone can go to college in America regardless of economic circumstance" is somewhat questionable.

Students today are less idealistic and more indifferent to politics than their parents—in 1970, 57 percent considered it important to "keep up to date with political affairs," compared with 31 percent in 2001. They are also more politically conservative, according to self-evaluations. However, the trend toward conservatism occurred largely in the 1970s, and, if anything, students are now slightly more liberal than they were in 1985. (In 2001, around 27 percent called themselves "liberal," 50 percent "middle-of–the-road," and 19 percent "conservative.") There is a slight but noticeable trend toward more liberal views.

Students today are much more highly career- and money-oriented than their parents were—nearly 74 percent consider it important to be "very well-off financially," compared with 36 percent in 1970. This materialistic orientation may be partly responsible for a shift in college majors over time. In 1971, over half of bachelors' degrees—51 percent—were awarded to students in education, the humanities (English, foreign languages, and philosophy), and the social sciences (excepting psychology). By 2000, the proportion in those fields had fallen to less than one-fourth (24.5 percent).

By contrast, in 1971, barely 15 percent of all degrees were in business, communications, or computer or information science, but by 2000, more than 28 percent of the degrees were in those fields. The physical sciences and mathematics lost market share (from 5.5 to 2.5 percent of all degrees), while the biological sciences gained slightly (from 4.5 to 5.1 percent). Another trend shows a significant move toward students majoring in "liberal (general) studies" or "multidisciplinary studies"—from 1.6 percent of majors in 1971 to 5.1 percent in 2000. Ironically, at the same time that graduate education and research were becoming more specialized, there was a modest trend at the undergraduate level to downplay emphasis on individual disciplines somewhat.

Conclusions

Enrollments at American universities have grown enormously over time, and participation in higher education is high today, both historically and relative to other countries. Gender variations in participation have changed, with females now outnumbering males. Some racial variations exist, but not all minorities are relatively underrepresented. Interstate variations are significant and at least partly related to income differentials. The proportion of students going to graduate and professional schools is relatively stable, while two-year institutions witnessed a major upsurge relative to four-year schools that has been reversed in recent years.

While a large majority of college students are still between the ages of eighteen and twenty-four, the "nontraditional student" constituency is large. The once-forecast public university domination of higher education has not occurred to the extent many predicted, and traditional public universities conceivably are at the beginning of an era where they are losing market share. The almost certain stagnation in the size of the eighteen- to twenty-four-year-old population in the next decade makes it unlikely that university enrollments will rise dramatically, particularly since the long-term rise in the rate of university participation may be slowing down. Overall, the statistics suggest that American higher education is a vast enterprise that has grown rapidly in importance over the past century or more.

6

Why Do We Need Universities?
First Principles of Higher Education

Looking at higher education in the United States, we can say, as Charles Dickens once did, that these are the best of times and the worst of times.[1] As mentioned in the last chapter, American higher education is, in many respects, widely regarded as being the best in the world. In the *Chronicle of Higher Education* poll cited earlier, more than 90 percent of respondents either agreed or strongly agreed with the statement, "Colleges and universities are one of the most valuable resources to the U.S."[2]

Yet, as we have seen, the outlook for universities today is clouded. The cost of American education is soaring, and productivity is almost certainly falling. Universities have used public subsidies and philanthropic contributions to become less efficient, less sensitive to public opinion, maybe even more arrogant. Their respect in the community is in danger because of ethical lapses and compromised academic values. They have transferred incomes to themselves in what economists would call successful "rent-seeking" behavior. Given these problems, we might ask, "Why do we have universities?"

The Dissemination of Knowledge

Perhaps the most important responsibility of each generation is to pass on the civilization it inherited to future generations. The language, customs, history, scientific knowledge, artistic heritage, religious beliefs, and other attributes of a nation form the nucleus of its culture, and each generation must preserve that and pass it on to its children if the civilization is going to survive in some stable form. While families, churches, the media, and others all play a role in this dissemination of their legacy, a large part of the responsibility has been taken up for centuries by schools and universities.

Indeed, our society considers this function of higher education to be so important that it subsidizes it in a variety of ways, while simultaneously taxing other useful activities that provide enjoyment for people—airplane tickets, automobile sales—indeed, almost everything we consume. From the general public's perspective, the vital, noble mission of maintaining our civilization is the main job, sometimes almost the only important job, of universities.

The Production of Knowledge

Societies advance by learning to do new things in new ways. Technological development—one form of creating knowledge—is universally viewed as important in the process of economic growth. But knowledge-creation is much more than making scientific discoveries and generating related inventions. The stock of creative endeavors of authors, artists, musicians, playwrights, scientists, and others also expands over time, as they give expression to our changing lives. While other forms of education are almost exclusively concerned with disseminating knowledge and ideas, higher education has also provided an institutional setting for producing them. Thus, universities engage in research as well as teaching.

In a sense, universities are in the business of both maintaining and increasing our stock of "cultural capital." Associated with that mission is the human capital of the citizenry—the stock of knowledge and skills people possess. The teaching function of universities allows us to offset the depreciation of our human and cultural capital stock that occurs as each generation dies off. If teaching covers the *depreciation* of our intellectual capital, research is investment in expanding the *stock* of that capital.

Obviously, the highly diverse community of institutions constituting the broad category of "higher education" varies widely in the extent to which its members perform this function of cultural and human capital formation, and the ways in which they undertake it. Junior colleges and two-year associate degree institutions are more teaching-oriented than the highly research-oriented major universities. The Institute for Advanced Study at Princeton and the Hoover Institution at Stanford are examples of largely independent enclaves within academic institutions that have no students and are involved purely in research. Between these two extremes along the teaching-research continuum are other institutions, such as liberal arts colleges and the universities, whose primary teaching function also allows for the conduct of some research.

Why Universities?

It is possible to achieve the transmission of our heritage to our progeny and the expansion of the frontiers of knowledge outside the university setting. In theory, students could hire individual teacher-entrepreneurs to offer them instruction in various subjects. Those instructors, in turn, could rent lecture and office space from local landlords and charge the students tuition. Indeed, this model was sometimes used at early universities.[3]

Also, much research has been and continues to be done outside university settings. Many early scholars were independent of institutions, relying on income from wealthy patrons or their own properties, or the royalties or patents from their research. Today, corporations have large research operations trying to develop commercially lucrative products, such as new pharmaceuticals or enhanced computer technology. Nonprofit research institutes exist as well. Why, then, do we need universities?

Economies of Scale Arguments. The first rationale is that there are economies of scale, to a point, in academic endeavors. The principle of the division of labor suggests that it makes more sense to hire professors to teach what they know about and let others handle administrative chores like attracting the students, procuring and maintaining the classrooms, and collecting the fees.

Moreover, it can be argued that the modern university is a marketplace of ideas—that the give and take among knowledgeable persons is critical both to disseminating and to producing knowledge and artistic works. As John Donne said in another context centuries ago, "No man is an island entire of himself."[4] Actors need to interact with other actors (Romeo needs his Juliet), and historians with other historians. The intellectual stimulus of talking over lunch with one's colleagues can foster innovations and stimulate scholarship, as do more formal seminars and workshops. The longtime former president of Cornell, Frank H.T. Rhodes, put it well: "Without community, knowledge becomes idiosyncratic: the lone learner, studying in isolation, is vulnerable to narrowness, dogmatism, and untested assumption, and learning misses out on being expansive and informed, contested by opposing interpretations, leavened by differing experience, and refined by alternative viewpoints."[5] Arguably, there is a healthy competitive element to having "learning communities" as well. Professor A wants to maintain his reputation relative to Professor B, who publishes profusely. Thus, Professor B's presence stimulates Professor A to spend less time drinking coffee or beer with colleagues and more time working on new research endeavors.

Moreover, there is an infrastructure to research that is difficult to produce except on a large scale—libraries, expensive laboratories, massive computers, and the like. To be sure, modern technology may be changing this—the need to "go to the library" is far less in the age of the Internet, since much of the corpus of human knowledge is now obtainable with a Google search, by retrieving stored electronic journals, and the like. Yet scientific equipment ranges up to massive nuclear accelerators that cost tens or hundreds of millions of dollars, and even routine laboratories require at least hundreds of thousands of dollars in equipment.

If there are economies associated with agglomeration, how far do they go? If a community of fifty teachers and a thousand students is more efficient and productive than having fifty independent scholars contracting individually with twenty students each, is it also true that a community of a thousand teachers and twenty thousand students is more efficient and productive than the one thousand–student community? Why are universities of ten thousand professors and two hundred thousand students in a single location unknown? Where do the economies of scale end?

The answer, of course, may be that the "optimal" size of institution, one that minimizes the costs per output of any given quality, varies with the goals of the institution. For example, institutions emphasizing teaching may reach optimal size at small numbers—say five hundred or a thousand students—while research-oriented universities have to reach five, ten, or even twenty-five thousand students before "optimality" is achieved. It is also possible that there are, roughly speaking, constant returns to scale over a wide range of sizes—the cost of educating a pupil at a given qualitative level might be roughly the same in institutions of five thousand and twenty thousand students, for example. Tastes differ as well, and smallness is a virtue to some who crave individual attention, while bigness is a virtue to those wanting very specialized training, diverse campus cultural activities, such as concerts and lectures, and so on. Hence, there is a wide variation in institutional size within higher education.

Higher Education as a Screening Device. Colleges and universities perform another function that cannot easily be handled by private teacher-entrepreneurs selling their services independently. They certify when students have reached certain levels of competence. They do so, in the first instance, by the awarding of degrees. A bachelor's degree, for example, denotes that a student has successfully completed about four academic years of full-time coursework at a reasonably demanding and rigorous level. Other information is sometimes added—the student reached the degree with honors, for instance, denoting a superior or at least solid level of performance relative to other students. The student ranked 125th in a class of 600. The student achieved a cumulative grade-point average of 3.3, where four represents an A performance, and one represents a D (the lowest acceptable grade). The student had a "major" in political science, or art history, or mechanical engineering, which denotes the student studied the indicated subject a great deal.

In short, colleges and universities convey a good deal of information about the academic achievement of their students. If, as is the case, academic achievement correlates well with other attributes—cognitive ability, maturity, discipline, communication skills, motivation—college records greatly reduce the uncertainty about the character traits of students for interested persons (especially prospective employers). Thus, colleges and universities enormously lower the costs to prospective employers of gaining information about potential employees.

Moreover, employers learn which universities graduate the "best" students. They learn early that graduates of Harvard, Northwestern, or Stanford are likely to be at least a little brighter, a little more knowledgeable, and a little more motivated than graduates of, say, the State University of New York at Buffalo, Baylor University, or San Jose State University. In turn, graduates of the latter institutions are likely to have on average qualitative advantages over graduates of local junior colleges or obscure state universities or liberal arts colleges. Knowledge about institutional qualitative differences is easily obtained from ratings provided by the media (the *U.S. News & World Report* rankings being particularly well read) and various college guides.

Alternatives to Universities

While there are some persuasive efficiency arguments in support of universities fulfilling the teaching and research functions that are important to the maintenance and expansion of our heritage, it is possible to fulfill those functions in an efficient fashion through other means—and we often do. Arguments relating to economies of scale and the importance of higher education as a cost-saving screening device for businesses apply to forms of service delivery other than universities.

The Teaching Function. Businesses provide a good deal of education and training for employees, much of it specific training related to particular jobs, but some of it fairly rigorous and advanced teaching of higher-level skills. I myself, for example, have taught material traditionally covered in beginning university economics courses to newly employed university graduates in corporate training facilities, and I am by no means alone. Indeed, some corporate training programs have become so elaborate (one example is the General Motors Institute, now Kettering University) that they have received accreditation and offer degrees.

Moreover, companies are beginning to engage in credentialing, one of the strengths of universities. Through examination, one can become "Oracle-certified" or "Microsoft-certified," which may be the rough equivalent of having, say, a bachelor of science degree in computer science. Anecdotal evidence suggests that some individuals are forgoing traditional university degree programs in computer science in favor of such company-conferred certifications. More generally, just as Underwriters

Laboratories certifies the safety of privately manufactured appliances and related devices, so it would be feasible to have an independent organization certify through examination that individuals meet certain threshold levels of competence in some skills. As university costs rise, this type of alternative probably will gain more favor. The certified public accountant, certified financial analyst, and board certifications in many professional fields provide examples of other nonuniversity-directed credentialing, although in many cases a college degree is required as part of the certification process.

The Research Function. In the research area, universities carry out a small minority of all activity. Of the approximately $265 billion in research and development (R & D) spending done in the United States in 2000, only slightly over $30 billion (a little over 11 percent) went toward university research, compared with more than $197 billion spent by private business. Interestingly, federal funding of research by for-profit private sector organizations exceeded that of universities, albeit only modestly.[6]

The published data on research spending are broken down into three categories: basic research, applied research, and development. About 60 percent of total research spending is for development, putting research to work in specific applications, in which universities play a trivial role (about 1 percent of all activity). Confining ourselves to other research (basic and applied combined), we can say that slightly over 25 percent of total spending was done by universities, still sizably less than by private industry. With regard to basic research (the quest for new ideas and discoveries), in 2000 about 43 percent of spending was carried out by universities, more than by private industry (about 32 percent), but still a minority of total spending. That excludes semiautonomous labs, such as Lawrence Livermore, Argonne, and Lincoln, traditionally run by individual universities for the federal government. Even including them, however, the proportion of university-controlled basic research was less than 50 percent. Much (nearly 20 percent) of basic research was done by nonprofit research institutes other than universities, such as the Battelle Memorial Institute, the Rand Corporation, and the National Bureau of Economic Research, or by the federal government.

Prominent university officials and academics often claim that much-needed basic research will not be undertaken by private, for-profit companies. As Derek Bok, former president of Harvard University, recently wrote, "The most important inquiries in science often involve questions no company will support because the answers take the form of general laws of nature that hold no special rewards for the enterprise that funds the research."[7]

However, the proportion of basic research performed by universities is falling, if official data are to be believed. From 1980 to 1995, that proportion hovered around 60 percent, falling sharply (to 49 percent) from 1995 to 2000.[8] The reason for the decline was a very sharp increase in basic research performed and very largely financed by private industry. From 1995 to 2000, private industry spending for basic research rose from $5.4 billion to $14.2 billion. Apparently, corporations increasingly view it as a commercially viable form of investment in intellectual property. This undercuts somewhat the argument that much basic research done by universities would not occur otherwise because private business has little incentive to do it.

In sum, universities are *not* the dominant institutional means of carrying out research, even basic research, in the United States. Whatever dominance they may have had has eroded in recent years. Therefore, when colleges and universities claim that their basic research contributions are vital for economic progress and human well-being, their argument has obviously lost some of the cogency it once had.

The conclusions above require a caveat. Spending statistics are based on grant-funded research, and some research and creative activity goes on that is indirectly financed by the universities themselves from student fees, state subsidies, and endowment monies. Indeed, over time, teaching loads have declined sharply, and the rationale for this is that faculty members today do more research than in the past. In the humanities, fine arts, and possibly social sciences, probably a majority of the activities carried out to further expansions of human intellectual and artistic horizons are not funded by grants. Yet even in these fields a lot of the painting and sculpture, literature, music, philosophic musings, and so forth are done by independent thinkers and artists outside the university milieu. While very important, universities are surely not the only and probably not even the dominant means by which we extend our cultural heritage.

Conclusions

Higher education performs the important functions of disseminating knowledge at the highest levels and extending the boundaries of that knowledge. University education is becoming costly and vulnerable to new competition from alternative learning sources. Universities are learning communities, and the synergies associated with intellectuals working together, along with some administrative efficiencies, no doubt help explain their existence. Yet higher levels of learning and research—even basic research—are carried out in alternative fashions as well, and perhaps universities sometimes lose sight of this.

Are universities vital? Perhaps, but the process of learning and discovery existed before they came into being during the late Middle Ages, and it would continue, albeit perhaps on a smaller level and in a less efficient fashion, if they ceased to exist. As universities become ever more costly, they would do well to remember that they do not have a monopoly on the creation and maintenance of our human and cultural capital.

7

Universities and Society

In the United States, as in most of the Western capitalist democracies, profit-seeking entrepreneurs produce most goods and services in a market environment. Universities are different. Although there is a small but rapidly growing for-profit university sector, the mission of higher education in America overwhelmingly is carried out by nonprofit institutions. Many of them—state and municipal colleges and universities—are directly subsidized by governments, while the rest depend largely upon contributions from private donors and government grants to sustain their operations. While the consumers of higher education pay for part of the cost of the services they use, typically those payments cover less than half of that cost. As James Heckman has correctly noted, current subsidies of direct education costs at major American public universities are equal to about 80 percent of the total.[1]

Thus, universities are fundamentally different from most private businesses. We tax car producers and dealers, soap makers, and hotels, but we subsidize colleges, universities, and technical institutes. Why? Aren't those car dealers, soap makers, and hotels providing goods and services that we desire? Why are those producers treated less favorably by governmental policy than the producers of higher education services?

The Positive Externality Argument and Its Weaknesses

Two major arguments are used to justify the subsidization of higher education by third parties who are not either direct consumers or producers of higher educational services. The first is that the benefits of university education accrue only partly to the user of those services. A student profits, both financially and in other ways, from an education; otherwise, she or he would not pursue one. But others benefit, too, from there being more college graduates. An obvious example are the families of university graduates who share in the financial benefits associated with a degree.

But higher education also has "positive externalities" of a broader nature. Where the public is well-educated, communication and information costs are reduced, and productive output may consequently be increased. Higher levels of literacy mean a deeper understanding by members of society of our common heritage, something that helps bind us together and makes us better and more united citizens. Milton Friedman, no fan of large government, argued more than forty years ago that public education subsidies are justified, since collective political decisions are likely to be sounder with a well-educated electorate.[2] His view echoed John Henry Newman, writing and lecturing more than a century earlier:

> If . . . a practical end must be assigned to a University course, I say it is that of training good members of society. Its art is the art of social life, and its end is fitness for the world. . . . University training is the great ordinary means to a great but ordinary end; it aims at raising the intellectual tone of society, at cultivating the public mind, at purifying the national taste, at supplying true principles to popular enthusiasm and fixed aims to popular inspiration, at giving enlargement and sobriety to the ideas of the age, at facilitating the exercise of political power, and refining the intercourse of private life.[3]

Beyond these rather lofty purposes, it might be argued that the economic benefits of a college education accrue to the broader society in other ways. If a thousand more students go to college than before, the number of persons unemployed might eventually fall by around twenty (since unemployment rates are usually about two percentage points lower among college graduates), reducing unemployment compensation costs to employers, perhaps even those who have no contact with the new graduates.

These positive externalities are said to extend to research as well. For example, if a vaccine that cures an infectious disease is discovered at a university and many people buy the vaccine, even those who do not buy it are benefited, as the probability of contracting the disease is reduced as more and more people are protected from it. It is true that there is some incentive for for-profit businesses to engage in research to develop the vaccine. However, economic theory suggests that the resources going into its discovery probably will be below what is optimal, given that, with the potential for nonconsuming parties to benefit, profit-making entrepreneurs cannot capture all of the financial benefits of their discovery. Based on this argument, university research is funded in part with governmental funds and in part with gifts from private donors with the aim of helping society by promoting the development of vaccines and a variety of other socially beneficial undertakings that otherwise might not get the research attention they deserve.

Even some of the college and university activities not directly related to instruction or research may have positive externalities. Living in Ohio, I derive enjoyment from Ohio State University's football program, even though I am almost never a paying customer. When Ohio State won the 2002 national football championship, I was ecstatic—and I paid nothing for the pleasure. The subsidized athletic and cultural activities of universities, such as free or low-cost concerts by music school faculty or inexpensive plays put on by drama students, benefit persons otherwise unconnected with the university milieu. Perhaps that is why surveys of "best places to live" often give high marks to university and college towns.

The externality argument for higher education can, however, be attacked on at least two grounds. First, it is worth noting that scholars who are members of the higher education community itself do most of the touting of its positive externalities. While professors like to suggest that they are objective observers of reality and truth, in actuality they tend to articulate positions consistent with their own self-interest. I have known several prominent free-market academic economists who virulently oppose most forms of government intervention but fight fiercely for higher state university appropriations, more National Science Foundation funding, and so forth. Since they directly or indirectly benefit from greater funding of universities, they are not disinterested observers, and they might strain a bit to find positive externalities from universities that are either minuscule or nonexistent.

It is also possible that some of the positive externalities alleged to exist in higher education are illusory. Take the unemployment example cited above. It is true that unemployment rates are lower for college graduates than for high school graduates. In April 2004, the overall unemployment rate was 5.6 percent. For those with high school diplomas but no college, the rate was 5.2 percent, compared with 4.1 percent for those with some college (or an associate's degree) and 2.9 percent for those with a bachelor's degree or more.[4] Does it follow, however, that increasing the proportion of college graduates in the working-age population will necessarily reduce unemployment? Is unemployment low among college graduates because of the learning they did in college, or because of other attributes of college graduates—for example, their superior innate intelligence, their greater motivation and self-discipline, their greater dependability? As noted earlier, higher education is in part a screening device that identifies individuals with desirable personality characteristics that operate independent of specific amounts of learning.

Moreover, while there may be some legitimate positive externalities to higher education, there may be some negative externalities as well, and, indeed, the negative ones might offset the positive. I asked Milton Friedman if his position on the positive externalities of higher education had changed since he wrote *Capitalism and Freedom* in 1960. He replied:

> I have not changed my view that higher education has some positive externality, but I have become much more aware that it also has negative externalities. I am much more dubious than I was when I wrote *Capitalism and Freedom* that there is any justification at all for government subsidy of higher education. The spread of PC [political correctness] right now would seem to be a very strong negative externality, and certainly the 1960s student demonstrations were negative externalities from higher education. A full analysis along those lines might lead you to conclude that higher education should be taxed to offset its negative externalities.[5]

Equality of Opportunity Arguments

A second argument for external support of colleges and universities is that without it, many deserving young persons will be denied access to a university education. University education is expensive, partly because of the direct cost of providing it, partly because of the income inevitably forgone when individuals devote many hours weekly to attending class, reading, writing papers, and the like, instead of to working. America has long had an egalitarian tradition reflected in the eloquent words of its Declaration of Independence: "We hold these truths to be self-evident, that all men are created equal, that they are endowed by their Creator with certain unalienable rights, that among these are Life, Liberty and the pursuit of happiness. . . ." One might argue that for all Americans to engage in the "pursuit of happiness," they need to have equal economic opportunity, which in turn requires access to higher education for all and the removal of economic barriers that otherwise would prevent some from obtaining a college education.

Thus, some expensive private schools say that "no student will be denied admission because of economic circumstance," and elaborate scholarship aid is offered, often supported by private contributions. The same occurs at public universities, to a lesser extent. The very existence of those public universities is motivated by the desire to make college affordable to all—by governmental support of much of the cost of instructing students. There is almost universal public support for this principle. In the *Chronicle of Higher Education* poll, 91 percent of respondents gave an affirmative answer to the question, "Do you think every high school student who wants a four-year college education should have the opportunity to gain one?"[6] There can be little doubt historically that, as several tables in chapter 5 document, participation in higher education has expanded as financial resources provided by external parties have increased.

Higher Education as an Investment

In the last chapter, I argued that one might consider higher education a form of investment in "cultural capital." Teaching new generations the values, knowledge, and ideas of previous ones is necessary to keep our society's stock of cultural capital from depreciating as older persons die. University research is a form of new cultural investment, an expansion of this stock.

Our culture might be considered what economists call a "public good," one that is jointly consumed by us all. Adding one more person to the population that enjoys a public good does not increase the "cost" at the margin of maintaining it, and so consumers can "free ride"—that is, enjoy the good without paying for it. For this reason, public goods tend to be produced in too-small quantities when they are privately provided in a market environment, and governments are necessary to fill the void. National defense is a good example. Armies and navies would be nonexistent or inadequately small without governments to provide for them. Public goods are typically subsidized or produced by government, and that, arguably, explains public involvement in education in general, and higher education in particular.

By instilling ideas and knowledge in people, we make them potentially more productive. A person who cannot read or write cannot function as effectively in the workplace as one who can; similarly, a person who learns accounting at a university is more valuable to a company than one who lacks those skills. Using a term made famous by economist Theodore Schultz more than forty years ago, universities are in the business of creating "human capital."[7] Many would argue that because of positive externalities, the social rate of return of higher education is greater than the private rate of return to the individuals consuming (or investing in) it.[8]

In appealing for more government support, state university presidents sometimes like to argue that high levels of participation in colleges and universities promote economic growth, and that slow growth in incomes and wealth reflects inadequate provision of higher education services. They point out, correctly, that the earnings differential between high school and college graduates has grown over time, which suggests that the productivity of college graduates has risen relative to that of others with lower levels of educational attainment. Moreover, with rising incomes, society has placed relatively greater value on goods and services produced in a "human capital-intensive" form. Brains are becoming far more important than brawn in generating output and income.

If the total rate of return on university investment is relatively high (compared with other uses of resources), areas that invest heavily in universities might be expected to derive economic advantages. At least some evidence does seem to support that position. I developed a simple econometric model to try to explain differences among the fifty states and the District of Columbia in the rate of economic growth over the twenty-five-year period from 1977 to 2002, with economic growth measured by personal income per person.

Of course, many other things besides college education affect economic growth. In my model, I used two measures of the proportion of college-educated citizens in the population as variables, along with seven other factors introduced for control purposes. For example, one such factor was the level of per-capita income at the beginning of the period (1977). Introducing that variable allowed me to look at the relationship between college education and income growth, holding the 1977 income per-capita levels constant for all fifty states and D.C.[9]

The results, reported in table 7-1, suggest a fairly strong positive association between economic growth, as measured by real personal income per capita, and the level of university participation, and, far less convincingly from a statistical standpoint, with changes in that level of participation over time. For example, the results suggest that if the proportion of college graduates in the over-twenty-five population of a given state has been 16 percent instead of just 15 percent in 1980, its real per-capita personal income growth in the 1977–2002 period would have been over 1.91 percentage points higher (that is, 46.91 percent instead of 45 percent). Since the average state in 1980 had a per-capita income in 2003 dollars of about $17,000, that implies that an increase of one percentage point in the proportion of adults with college degrees is associated with a per-capita income growth of about $324—or nearly $1,300 for a family of four—because of the greater prevalence of university graduates. Taken literally, this would seem to imply great social benefits from university education—benefits that might well exceed those accruing to the individuals receiving the education.

Applying some simple economic theory and factual evidence, it would appear that, assuming the regression estimate is correct, only one-fourth to one-third of the income generated from a rise in college participation

TABLE 7-1

HIGHER EDUCATION PARTICIPATION AND ECONOMIC GROWTH,
1977–2002

Variable or Statistic	Coefficient or Value	T-Statistic
Constant	−3.777	0.178
% College Grads, 1980	1.915	3.404
Change in % Col. Grads, 1980–2000	1.019	1.665
Income per Capita, 1977	−0.006	3.488
State and Local Tax Burden, 1977	−1.180	0.919
Change in Tax Burden, 1977–99	−2.212	1.655
% in Unions, 1983, 1994	0.210	0.758
Age of State	0.165	4.200
% Days That Sun Shines	0.199	1.278
% Pop. over 65, 1981	1.912	2.717
Adjusted R-squared	0.722	
F-Statistic	15.409	

SOURCE: Regression equation generated by author; see text and note 9.

accrues to the new college graduates themselves. For example, assume that a 1 percent increase in college participation leads to a 0.75 percent increase in the labor resources utilized in producing goods and services. That 0.75 percent estimate is based on the fact that, as of 1980, college graduates earned roughly 75 percent more than high school graduates (less than that for those with associate degrees, but more than that for those with less than a high school education).[10]

Further assume that a 1 percent increase in labor arising from greater human capital leads to a 0.70 to 0.75 percent increase in output. This is based on the fact that labor resources command about 70 to 75 percent of the national income and are compensated, according both to theory and empirical evidence, on the basis of their marginal productivity. This would imply that a 1 percent increase in the proportion of adult workers who are college graduates would lead to an output increase of around 0.55 percent (0.70 X 0.75 = 0.525; 0.75 X 0.75= 0.5625). Since total output is estimated to have risen 1.915 percent for each 1 percent increase in college participation, this implies that about 28 percent (0.55 divided by 1.915) of the output growth associated with a 1 percent rise in college participation would go to increased labor compensation to the college graduates themselves, while the other 72 percent would go to other members of society—comprising the positive economic externalities mentioned earlier. Since external parties pay roughly that proportion (72 percent) of college costs, it could be argued that the system works about right.

There are, however, numerous potential problems with that conclusion. First, observe that the variable measuring the impact of the change (growth) in college participation from 1980 to 2000 has a much smaller coefficient. It implies that a 1 percent increase in the proportion of adults in college from 1980 to 2000 was associated with only a 1.019 percent increase in economic growth. The result, in fact, is not statistically significant at the 5 percent level using a one-tailed test (although it nearly is, and is significant at the 10 percent level). The smaller coefficient relative to the variable measuring the impact of the level of 1980 participation is anticipated by economic theory. The law of diminishing returns says that when you add an amount of a resource while you hold other resources constant, output will rise, but by diminishing amounts. That is what is happening here. In a practical sense, more college participation almost certainly means that a higher proportion of students with fewer cognitive and motivational skills are attending college—students who are less likely to benefit from higher education.

Thus, even if there were very high apparent positive externalities in 1980 from participation in higher education, it does not necessarily follow that *increases* in that participation would have the same externalities. In this particular case, there was also an apparent rise in the internal (or private) benefits of college education, as the college–high school earnings differential rose after 1980.[11] Thus, the calculation of the proportion of the benefits received from education showed that about 28 percent of them in 1980 went to the student graduating from college (0.55 divided by 1.91), but that by 2000 that figure approached 70 percent. Much of the measured positive externalities had been internalized—that is, received by the student.[12]

Figure 7-1 depicts the trend. The individual benefits of going to college have risen—but the contributions of additional college students in terms of overall output growth have declined. The internal benefits have grown relative to external benefits. If the trend were to continue, the case for extensive third-party support of universities would become considerably weaker

FIGURE 7-1

CHANGING BENEFITS OF COLLEGE OVER TIME

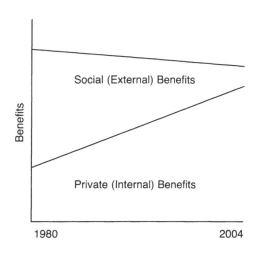

SOURCE: Author's illustration.

(although some external support for research efforts might continue to be justified).

Moreover, it is possible that the positive externalities as measured above may be overstated because of the implicit assumption that the causation in the regression runs from college participation to higher income. It is plausible that the causation is at least as much in the opposite direction: people with college educations migrate to areas with high economic growth.[13]

Although they are of only tangential relevance, it is interesting to note some other factors that seemed to influence economic growth. Growth was greater in states whose incomes were low to start with—a sign that states are converging on one another, as predicted by neoclassical economic theory (also known today as the "old" growth theory). Older states (as measured by date of statehood) grew faster than newer ones, a result contradicting at least one well-known hypothesis.[14] For some reason, when other things are equal, the larger the proportion of elderly living in a state, the higher the rate of economic growth. Also with other things being equal, higher taxes meant lower growth, although the results here were not terribly strong statistically.

The scenario of falling positive economic externalities following from the regression is both plausible and somewhat supported empirically, and indeed is even rather consistent with some recent trends in the financing of higher education, such as tuition rising as a percentage of total university revenues. But caution should be used in accepting it uncritically. Alternations in the regression model will no doubt lead to somewhat different estimated results which may not be consistent with this outcome. Sensitivity analysis (trying alternative variables, time periods, and ways of estimating the equation) is desirable.

The point here, however, is that a reasonable, simple, straightforward model does suggest there are, indeed, positive externalities to university education, but that they have diminished considerably over time. This is an area for further research. Moreover, the regression suggests that, other things being equal, increased taxes were associated with lower rates of growth. It may well be that some, conceivably all, of the positive growth effects of universities are offset by the negative incentive effects of the taxes levied to finance them.

That leads to the claim by university presidents at state schools that economic growth is enhanced by giving these institutions more appropriations, presumably, at least in part, on the grounds that more state assistance leads to smaller increases in tuition, making colleges and universities more accessible and allowing for greater positive economic externalities. This view is often cited uncritically but without empirical support by academics, including economists. Ronald Ehrenberg, for example, has said, "State governments need to be educated so that they understand the role that higher education plays in economic development and in boosting the incomes of state residents."[15] This notion is a testable proposition. Does enhanced governmental support to universities lead to greater student participation in higher education? Does it lead to higher rates of economic growth?

Using ordinary least squares (OLS) regression techniques, I report in table 7-2 the results of a simple cross-sectional analysis of variations in the rate of economic growth among the fifty states and the District of Columbia, similar to that shown in table 7-1. For a measure of state and local support of higher education, I took the average of state and local government higher education spending as a percent of personal income for two years, one near the beginning (fiscal year 1979–80) and one near

TABLE 7-2

STATE/LOCAL GOVERNMENT SPENDING FOR HIGHER EDUCATION,
AND ECONOMIC GROWTH, 1977–2002

Variable or Statistic	Coefficient or Value	T-Statistic
Constant	35.837	1.172
Higher Education Spending[a]	−11.933	3.570
1977 Income per Capita	−0.004	1.957
Taxes as % of Income, 1977	1.402	1.070
Change in Taxes % of Inc., 1977–99	0.091	0.064
% Workers in Unions	−0.476	1.582
Age of State	0.164	4.362
% of Days Sun Shines	0.152	0.831
% Pop. over 65, 1981	0.912	1.177
Adjusted R-squared	0.641	
F-Statistic	12.170	

SOURCE: Author's regression calculations using U.S. Census Bureau and other government data.
a. Average of state and local higher education spending as % of personal income, 1980, 2000.

the end (fiscal year 1999–2000) of the period in question (1977–2002). State support of higher education varied dramatically, being less than 1 percent of personal income in three northeastern states (Connecticut, Massachusetts, and New Jersey) and in the District of Columbia, but above 2.4 percent in five states (Mississippi, New Mexico, North Dakota, Utah, and Alaska). I included seven variables used in table 7-1 for control purposes (to approximate more closely the usual assumption of "holding everything else constant").

The results are startling. *A priori*, I expected either a statistically significant positive relationship between public support of higher education and economic growth (the conventional wisdom in the academic community) or no statistically significant relationship whatsoever (the positive effects of the apparent human capital investment being offset by the negative effects of the taxes needed to finance it). The results, however, are *significantly negative* (at the 1 percent level)—increases in the proportion of a state's income used to support higher education are associated with *lower* rates of economic growth. Moreover, the estimated negative growth effects, more than being statistically significant, are fairly powerful. Calculated at the means, the results suggest an elasticity of economic growth with respect to public higher education spending of −.52. That means that with other factors in the model being held constant, a 10 percent increase in state support of higher education is associated with a 5.2 percent reduction in the rate of economic growth (that is, from 40 percent to slightly less than 38 percent). It implies that state government investment in higher education has a negative rate of return, and that if economic externalities exist, they are negative.

Such strong results in the direction opposite from conventional wisdom need to be verified by more testing. I will do some of that below. First, however, it is interesting to speculate on how a negative relationship between higher education spending and economic growth might arise. Particularly puzzling is that the results in table 7-2 seemingly contradict the results in table 7-1 that show a positive relationship between the proportion of the population with college degrees and economic growth.

There are several possible reasons for the contradiction. One, of course, is that the findings in table 7-2 are a statistical fluke that do not withstand more intensive econometric scrutiny. I deal with that below, again concluding that the negative relationship seems fairly robust statistically. A second possible explanation, strange as it might seem, is that there is either no association or a negative one between the state and local effort to finance higher education and the proportion of the adult population that completes college.

This explanation is also testable. In table 7-3, I use OLS regression procedures to explain variations in the average proportion of the population over the age of twenty-five in college in the years 1980 and 2000. The key independent variable is the average percentage of personal income devoted to state and local governmental funding of higher education (Government Funding in table 7-3). While the key variable does have the positive sign that conventional wisdom would predict, the coefficient is statistically insignificant at conventional confidence levels. Moreover, even if significant, the estimated relationship is rather weak. The estimated elasticity of college graduates (as a percentage of the adult population) with respect to state and local government funding is 0.14. A 10 percent increase in state funding for universities is associated with a

TABLE 7-3

STATE/LOCAL HIGHER EDUCATION FUNDING AND THE PERCENT
OF COLLEGE GRADUATES

Variable or Statistic	Coefficient or Value	T-statistic
Constant	−14.392	−2.453
Government Funding	1.045	1.447
Av. Real per Capita Income	0.001	6.281
Age of State	0.021	3.037
% Days Sun Shines	0.076	2.529
% Pop. over 65, 1981	0.212	1.461
Adjusted R-squared	0.544	
F-Statistic	12.938	

SOURCE: Author's regression using U.S. Census Bureau and other government data.

1.4 percent increase in the proportion of adults with college degrees (that is, from 20 percent to slightly less than 20.3 percent).

This latter finding suggests that increased state subsidies for universities at best only marginally increase access, via lower tuition or more scholarship aid. Arguably, the funds are used to effect qualitative improvements to the educational experience of those attending college. Yet other evidence, presented earlier, calls this conclusion into question. In modern times a large proportion of incremental funds is used for non-instructional purposes. As we have seen, it is possible, for example, that incremental funds largely go to support research or auxiliary activities, such as intercollegiate sports. It is also possible that the funds simply are redistributed to members of the higher education community in the form of higher salaries and amenities, or what economists call economic rent (payments that have no positive incentive effects on economic behavior). In other words, the incremental funding is a means of redistributing, income from the taxpayers to the university community. All of these explanations are disturbing, given the typical state university president's assertion that enhanced state support of universities is necessary for maintaining and improving access for lower-income individuals (table 7-3 does show a very strong positive correlation between income and college graduation rates).

While the discussion above provides some explanation for the absence from table 7-2 of the expected positive relationship between economic growth and higher education spending by state and local governments, it does not explain the presence of the negative relationship. In order to do so, first assume that most spending on higher education is, in reality, for consumption. The touted "human capital formation" claims are, for the most part, illusory. The positive association between the percentage of college graduates and economic growth (table 7-1) does not reflect "human capital investment" provided via university training. Rather, it merely reflects the fact that states with relatively high proportions of college graduates have populations with relatively high levels of innate intelligence, positive work habits, desires to achieve economically, and so forth.

If, in fact, universities are merely informational devices that help employers find innately able people rather than training grounds that provide vital skills, the finding in table 7-2 is not terribly surprising, particularly since the financing of higher education means taking resources away from the private sector, with its relatively high and rising productivity subject to the discipline of markets and profit imperatives, and giving them to the university sector, with its lower and falling productivity subject to little market discipline and no profit imperatives. The redistribution of income from the productive private sector to less-productive public enterprise, according to this scenario, is the root cause of the negative relationship between state and local government spending on higher education and the rate of economic growth.

Additional Testing

The statistical relationships in tables 7-2 and 7-3 are so contrary to conventional wisdom that the burden of proof in demonstrating their veracity is greater than is perhaps customary in scholarly inquiry. I altered the regression models extensively to see if the observed relationships were replicated.

Turning first to the relationship between economic growth and university spending, I modified the model in table 7-2 in quite a number of ways. One involved, first, dividing the critical variable (higher education spending) into two: the level of spending as a percentage of personal income in 1979–80 (near the beginning of the period) and the change in that spending level over the next two decades. It was possible that the negative association observed for the single spending variable might change with this alternative formulation. To deal with a possible problem of omitted-variable bias, I added two independent (control) variables that seemed appropriate. One was the proportion of the population in 1980 (near the beginning of the period) who were between the ages of eighteen and twenty-four (the age group for most college students). The other was a variable measuring energy production near the beginning of the period, since economic growth at that time was affected by energy prices—that is to say, when oil prices were on the rise, oil-producing states had high rates of income growth. I also simplified the tax variables into a single variable (the average tax rate for the beginning and end of the period), and eliminated two control variables that were relatively weak in table 7-2, and whose exclusion actually raised the model's explanatory power as measured by the adjusted coefficient of multiple determination (r-squared).

The modified results, shown in table 7-4, are consistent with those already reported. Both higher education spending variables have negative signs, and one is negative at a high level of statistical significance. I then modified the sample to eliminate Alaska, Hawaii, and the District of Columbia, jurisdictions often excluded in interstate social science research because of their special characteristics. Those results, not reported here, are similar to those in table 7-4, except that the variable measuring the change in higher education spending over time is negative at a significance level of 5 percent (and the variable measuring the level of higher education spending in 1980 is still significant at the 1 percent level).

Higher education spending in the tables above was measured in terms of a percentage of personal income. According to this measure, Mississippi spent much more than Connecticut. Yet income levels per capita were nearly twice as high in Connecticut, so on a per-capita basis Mississippi's state and local government higher education spending were not dramatically higher than Connecticut's. A case can be made for defining the spending variables in per-capita terms (spending on higher education per capita in 1980, and the inflation-adjusted change in that

TABLE 7-4
GOVERNMENT HIGHER EDUCATION SPENDING AND
ECONOMIC GROWTH, 1977–2002

Variable or Statistic	Coefficient or Value	T-Statistic
Constant	44.570	1.760
Higher Ed. Spending, 1980	−13.002	4.431
Change in Higher Ed. Spend., 1980–2000	−6.583	1.533
% 18–24 Years Old, 1981	1.186	0.561
Income Per Capita, 1977	−0.004	2.397
Av. Tax Burden	2.320	1.875
Av. % in Unions, 1973, 1984	−0.705	2.214
Age of State	0.130	4.213
Energy Prod., 1977	−0.232	2.649
Adjusted R-Squared	0.690	
F-Statistic	14.925	

SOURCE: Author's regression using U.S. Census Bureau and related government data.

spending from 1980 to 2000). Estimating the model in table 7-4 with those changes, using forty-eight observations, I still observe negative relationships between the higher education spending variables and economic growth, with the variable measuring the level of per-capita spending in 1980 being statistically significant at the 1 percent level. However I defined the model, higher government spending for higher education is associated with lower, not higher, economic growth.

Likewise, I tried a quite different model to evaluate the earlier assertion that the association between state and local government university spending and college participation is very weak (although probably positive). The original statistical measure of college participation used in table 7-3 was the percentage of college graduates among the population over age twenty-five. A problem with that measure is that included in the base are large numbers of older persons clearly not affected by current funding levels. In other words, there is a long lag between increases in state funding and its material impact on the statistic chosen to measure college participation.

To deal with that, I looked at 1999–2000 school year college enrollments (not graduates) as a percentage of the current population ages eighteen to twenty-four (ENROLL in the results reported below). I regressed that against state and local government higher education spending in fiscal year 2000 as a percentage of personal income (SPENDING in the equation below), personal income levels per capita (INCOME), and the percentage of the population over twenty-five with college degrees (GRADS), since presumably children of college graduates, other things being equal, are more likely to attend college. With all fifty states and the District of Columbia in the sample, the results statistically are clearly not significantly positive, but excluding Alaska, Hawaii, and D.C., they are very nearly so for SPENDING:

ENROLL = 11.225 + 4.417 SPENDING + 0.001 INCOME + 0.650 GRADS,

   (1.021) (2.011)   (1.593)   (2.083)

   adjusted r-squared = .338, F-statistic = 8.993,

where the numbers in parentheses are t-statistics.

While the results do show the expected positive relationship between government higher education spending and enrollments, it is extremely weak. The estimated elasticity of enrollments with respect to spending, calculated at the means, is only .043. Suppose a state has 54 percent of its eighteen- to twenty-four-year-old population in college, and it increases higher education funding by a very large 20 percent. The results here suggest that the proportion of individuals going to college would rise to about 54.5 percent. Put differently, it takes a 20 percent spending increase to reduce the proportion of nonattendees by 1 percent. Using a per-capita spending measure (instead of measuring spending as a percentage of personal income) yields even less positive results, clearly not statistically significant at the 5 percent level, and even weaker in terms of the estimated impacts even if one assumes that the observed positive results truly exist and are not a statistical fluke.

In short, a good deal of model manipulation does not change the basic conclusion. We clearly reject the claim that state and local spending on universities promotes economic growth, finding it far more likely that the reverse is the case. The claims that more funding materially improves student access to college are, at the very minimum, hugely exaggerated if these results are valid. If there is any positive association between government spending and enrollments, it is decidedly very weak.

To be sure, I do not expect this to be the last word on the subject. More sophisticated econometric analysis, using, for example, computable general equilibrium models or at least multiple-equation regression procedures, might yield findings more favorable to universities. Other possibilities for research include evaluating different time periods or using time series as opposed to cross-sectional analysis. Nonetheless, the assertions that universities exude huge positive economic externalities manifested in greater community income are just that—assertions—and do not have an obvious empirical basis. Similarly, the notion that incremental university funding by state and local governments materially increases the proportion of persons attending universities is also highly suspect. At the very minimum, more research by truly objective scientists into these questions is needed.

Government University Support and Economic Growth: Case Studies

Many readers without a statistical bent may well be unconvinced (and bored) by the statistical evidence suggesting an actual negative relationship between state and local governmental support for higher education and the rate of growth of per-capita income. Accordingly, some examples discussed in narrative form of this actually occurring might be interesting. The approach here is to look at states that are similar in many ways in terms of their differing experiences with respect to support of higher education and economic growth.

North Dakota vs. South Dakota. It would probably be hard to find two states more similar than the Dakotas—both are low-population-density farm states with rather harsh climates. Yet over the past generation, South Dakota has far outdistanced North Dakota by most growth measures— total personal income growth, growth in income per capita, population growth (reflecting net migration), and so forth.

Interestingly, even in 1977 North Dakota invested a sharply higher proportion of its personal income in public higher education than its neighbor to the south—2.78 vs. 2.03 percent. Over the next two decades, North Dakota not only maintained but actually increased the share of its income going for state support of higher education, to 2.88 percent in fiscal year 2000—the highest of any state in the Union. By contrast, South Dakota reduced rather sharply the proportion of its income going for higher education, from 2.03 to 1.56 percent, going from above to below the national average.

Did North Dakota's high and rising "investment" in higher education pay off, while South Dakota's parsimony in subsidizing universities caused economic problems? Not if the data are to be believed. Per-capita income in inflation-adjusted terms rose more in South Dakota than North Dakota. Moreover, other measures confirm the trend. For example, total real personal income rose nearly 57 percent in South Dakota, compared with a little over 35 percent in North Dakota. From 1990 to 2002, North Dakota had a significant net out-migration of native-born Americans, while South Dakota had in-migration.

Moreover, the much larger subsidies for higher education in North Dakota did not even lead to much greater college participation. In the 1999–2000 school year, 55 percent of North Dakotans ages eighteen to twenty-four were in college—compared with 54 percent in the southern neighbor spending barely half as much of its income on support for universities. One reason may have been that because income per person rose more in South Dakota, the ability of South Dakotans to afford university training for their progeny was rising faster.

To be sure, many other factors no doubt also influenced these trends. For example, South Dakota did not have an income tax, while North Dakota did, and research has shown a negative correlation between state income tax burdens and economic growth. Nonetheless, the experience is highly consistent with the statistical results showing that state governmental spending for higher education actually discourages growth—and does little to improve college access.

Illinois vs. Michigan vs. Ohio. The Dakotas are small agricultural states with a combined population that is barely one-half that of Chicago. Let us compare the three largest Midwestern states, Illinois, Michigan, and Ohio. All are among the nation's ten most highly populated states. All have large industrial centers as well as small but vibrant agricultural sectors. Of the three, Illinois has for decades been the most affluent, having the highest per-capita income, but all three have been considered relatively prosperous.

In 1979–80, Illinois spent on state and local governmental support for higher education a proportion of its personal income more than one-third smaller than did Michigan, and about 15 percent less than Ohio. Over the remainder of the century, Michigan dramatically increased its already above-average commitment (as measured by the percentage of personal income devoted to governmental support) to universities, to the point that it ranked sixth in the nation by that indicator in fiscal year 2000. Illinois, by contrast, only very marginally increased its proportional support. In 2000, Michigan devoted 2.34 percent of its personal income to governmental university support, nearly double Illinois' 1.26 percent. (The corresponding figure for Ohio was 1.58 percent.)

Yet the growth experience was precisely in the opposite direction. Illinois had the highest rate of economic growth. This is particularly surprising, since both economic theory and the national experience of the period suggest that lower-income states tended to converge on higher-income ones. Yet by 2002, Illinois' advantage in per-capita income compared with Michigan—over 10 percent—was almost precisely double what it was a generation earlier. The state most committed to higher education—Michigan—had the least growth, while that with the least commitment, Illinois, had the most; Ohio was in the middle. Moreover, Illinois' low public investment in higher education did not deter students from attending college—in 2000, the ratio of college enrollees was higher in Illinois than in either of its two large neighbors. Again, it is obvious that other, noneducational factors are changing as well, but the pattern still suggests that the notion of state support of universities promoting growth is exceedingly questionable.

New Hampshire vs. Vermont. New Hampshire and Vermont are neighboring, small New England states, both with a reputation for a bucolic, semirural ambiance envied by weary urban commuters. Vermont's approach to higher education, however, has been dramatically different than its neighbor's. In 1979–80, Vermont spent 2.39 percent of its income on governmental support of universities, compared with 1.30 percent in New Hampshire. Although both states reduced their proportion of higher education spending in the next two decades, New Hampshire reduced it more, so the differential actually increased.

New Hampshire's relative neglect of its state universities, however, did not cost it in terms of economic growth. New Hampshire, already the more affluent state, increased its per-capita income advantage over Vermont from less than 12 percent to over 16 percent. While Vermont had a modestly larger proportion of its eighteen- to twenty-four-year-old population going to college at the end of the period than its neighbor, New Hampshire's proportion was well above the national average—despite a significantly lower level of higher educational effort (as measured by the proportion of personal income spent by state and local governments) than was typical nationally.

Space does not permit detailed further examples. High-university-support Oregon grew more slowly than neighboring Washington, which was less supportive of the public universities. The same is true of Kentucky (big support for its universities) relative to Tennessee, which had higher economic growth but much less public subsidization of colleges. Taking the ten states in the contiguous United States with the lowest economic growth from 1980 to 2000 and comparing them with the ten with the highest growth, I find that median state and local government spending for higher education in 1980 was 1.80 percent of personal income in the low-growth states—more than one-third more than in the high-growth states (1.31 percent). Moreover, while spending expanded modestly in the high-growth states (from 1.31 to 1.44 percent of personal income), it exploded in the low-growth ones (from 1.80 to 2.21 percent). It almost appears as though those states doing poorly economically accepted the arguments of state university presidents that with greater higher education investment they could revive their relative economic fortunes. It did not work.

Higher Education and the Quality of Life

While the alleged external economic benefits of higher education seem more illusory than real, that does not necessarily mean there are no positive externalities to universities. As noted earlier, many observers have commented on the high quality of life in college towns, noting the cultural and other activities readily available at moderate prices on college campuses. While concepts like "quality of life" and even "happiness" are almost impossible to measure, there is one good quality of life indicator that is quite measurable—net migration.

When more people move into an area than move out of it (positive net migration), it is a sign that individuals are "voting with their feet" to relocate to a place where they feel they will likely be happier. Similarly, net out-migration from an area suggests that, on balance, people are finding that jurisdiction less likely to produce a high quality of life than others. The U.S. Census Bureau estimates net migration by states on an annual basis. Is there any association between net migration and the intensity of support for higher education, or the presence of universities or college graduates? If universities have positive externalities, either economic or noneconomic, one would expect a positive association between the intensity of higher education (however defined) and net migration.

Again, I used ordinary least squares regression to analyze the variations in net domestic migration among the fifty states and the District of Columbia over the period 1990 to 1999. Domestic migration excludes the in-flows of immigrants. I analyzed many variants of models containing one or the other of two higher education variables: the percentage of personal income spent by state and local governments on higher education in fiscal year 1990, and the percentage of the population age twenty-five or older with college degrees as of the 1990 census. A host of other different independent variables were introduced for control purposes, and I ran a number of regressions with all fifty-one observations, as well as some with just the forty-eight contiguous states in the sample.

The results were unambiguous. In every single regression estimated, the relationship between the university variable (based either on spending or on college graduates) and net domestic migration was negative, although in no case significantly so. The best way to interpret the results is to conclude that there was no observed statistical relationship between the university variable and net domestic migration. Using a broader definition of migration including new immigrant arrivals does not change the conclusion. If the presence of college-educated persons provides positive externalities to a community, with other things being equal people should move into a state to take advantage of them. Yet there is absolutely no evidence that this in fact occurs.

Conclusions

Most funding of American higher education comes not from the consumers of university services, but from outsiders—governments, foundations, or other private donors. They provide funds to universities because they believe universities serve society beyond the benefits received by the students in attendance. There are "positive externalities." Presumably economies grow faster because of universities, and some of the incremental income accrues to others besides the consumers of university services.

Although some evidence suggests that this is the case, it also suggests that the marginal benefits of expanding enrollments are falling—as are positive externalities. More shockingly, the relationship between economic growth and governmental support for universities in recent years is actually negative. The notion that expanding university support is a good "investment" in the economy is not supported—indeed, the results would suggest we are already "overinvested" in colleges.

The notion that increased support of state universities increases access to college for the financially less fortunate is also highly suspect, with any improvements in access being very small for any given increment in spending. That might be an argument in support of an alternative notion that governmental assistance to higher education is better directed to the students than to the institutions themselves, a subject for a later chapter.

The initial observation that economic growth tends to be greater where there are more college graduates does not seem to square with the evidence that incremental state and local governmental financial support for the universities is actually harmful economically. Part of the reason for this is that higher funding does not, in any material way, increase the number of graduates. As detailed earlier, the money given to colleges tends to be used largely for things other than instruction—perhaps research, perhaps greater salaries and perks for employees. The findings are also consistent with the view that earnings are higher among college graduates not because of the skills acquired in school, but because they have other attributes desirable to employers—motivation, perseverance, high innate intelligence, and so forth. Colleges are, according to this view, rather expensive "screening devices" whose presence lowers information costs to employers, at considerable cost to society.

The empirical evidence presented in this chapter implies that much of the increase in funding to universities has bought little that is socially useful. To be sure, that proposition needs further examination, using different data sources and methodologies. Nonetheless, there is much straightforward evidence that raises questions about the continued increasing public support of our universities.

PART III

Solutions

The Future of American Higher Education

8

New Alternatives to Traditional Higher Education

When something becomes expensive, people tend to look for substitutes—alternative products or services that serve the function of the original good. When oil and petroleum derivatives became expensive in the 1970s, people sought alternative fuel and heating sources, or moved to energy-saving devices to reduce their demand for oil and gasoline. As the price of stamps has risen and technology has evolved, so people have increasingly used e-mail instead of "snail mail" to correspond with one another. Likewise, as universities become expensive, people can be expected to look for alternatives—and they are.

In this chapter, I will discuss three major developments that could radically transform higher education, or at least force traditional universities to become serious about cost-cutting. The first is the extraordinary growth of for-profit universities, institutions that offer an attractive service and are disciplined by market forces to be efficient. The second is the rise of distance learning, particularly online computerized instruction. Last, we will briefly discuss a nonuniversity option—private certification of competence in skills, bypassing traditional higher education as the primary means for certifying high-level skills and academic accomplishments.

For-Profit Higher Education

The most dynamic dimension in American higher education today is the proprietary or for-profit sector. For-profit universities are growing by

151

leaps and bounds, and many of them are extremely profitable. Wall Street has noticed, and several companies have stock that trade at very high multiples to earnings, suggesting that market participants believe these firms have a bright future. I will discuss in some detail the largest of these companies, Apollo Group, which operates the University of Phoenix (UOP) and several other institutions and has controlling interest in the University of Phoenix Online. I will offer more abridged descriptions of four other companies, and point out differences between these institutions and mainline traditional not-for-profit colleges and universities.

The University of Phoenix—Higher Education's Financial Success Story. While Harvard, Yale, Princeton, and a few other schools vie to be designated America's best universities in popular rankings, Apollo Group, owner of the University of Phoenix, is clearly America's most successful university in a financial sense. A person investing $10,000 in Apollo common stock in January 1995 (shortly after the company went public) would have an investment of over $9.5 *million* as of February 23, 2004.[1] Apollo has shrewdly exploited opportunities provided by generous student loans and rapidly rising tuition in not-for-profit institutions to offer an affordable alternative to traditional universities. As of this writing, the market value of Apollo Group common stock approximates $13.5 billion; by this criterion, it is one of the richest American universities, probably second only to Harvard in market valuation of its assets. Its stock trades at well over fifty times its earnings, an extremely high price-to-earnings ratio that suggests market participants are extremely optimistic about rapid, sustained, profitable growth in future years.

The University of Phoenix was founded by Dr. John Sperling in 1981, becoming a public company thirteen years later. Its current CEO, Todd Nelson, age forty-four, received over $4.5 million in direct compensation in 2003, many times the salary of any not-for-profit university president. Nelson also exercised stock options worth $28.8 million. Company insiders own well over $2 billion in stock.

As figure 8-1 shows, enrollments at the University of Phoenix are growing almost exponentially. Enrollment growth of over 20 percent per year has been accompanied by revenue growth approaching 30 percent and per-share earnings growth exceeding 35 percent. Enrollment in

FIGURE 8-1

ENROLLMENT GROWTH, APOLLO GROUP SCHOOLS, 1998–2003

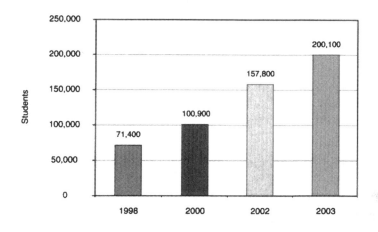

SOURCE: Yahoo Finance, http://finance.yahoo.com/q?s=APOL&d=t.

degree-granting programs, over two hundred thousand at the end of 2003, is scattered among more than two hundred campuses and learning centers, a majority having fewer than a thousand students. There is also a rapidly growing online business, discussed below.

The University of Phoenix, the major business of the Apollo Group, provides education for working adults in about half the United States, Puerto Rico, and British Columbia, Canada. Degrees offered include associate's or bachelor's degrees in business, general studies, criminal justice administration, human services, health care services, and information technology. The school also offers a few master's degree programs in such fields as education, organizational management, business administration, nursing, and counseling. The emphasis is on providing vocationally related training at prices well below those of private, not-for-profit universities, and often only modestly higher than the tuition at major state universities. Most students finance their participation through federal loan and other subsidy programs.

To date, the UOP has not sought to compete directly for traditional college-age students, although there are early indications that that might be changing. In addition to the UOP, Apollo runs Western International

FIGURE 8-2

NET AFTER-TAX INCOME, APOLLO GROUP, FISCAL YEARS 1998–2003

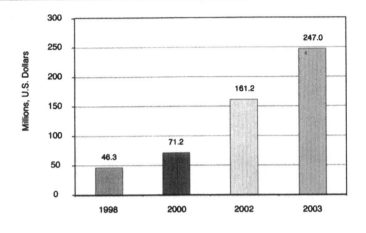

SOURCE: Yahoo Finance, http://finance.yahoo.com/q?s=APOL&d=t.

University, an Arizona-based institution; the Institute for Professional Development, which contracts with private, not-for-profit colleges wishing to offer adult education programs; and the College for Financial Planning, which trains people to attain certified financial planner (CFP) certification.

The Apollo Group is immensely profitable and becoming more so over time. Figure 8-2 shows that after-tax profits (income) much more than quintupled from 1998 to 2003. Figure 8-3 shows that pretax profits as a percentage of revenue have steadily increased, going from slightly less than 20 percent in 1998 (already an extraordinarily high profit margin in most businesses) to almost precisely 30 percent in 2003—about as high as it gets for American business. On a per-student basis, after-tax profits rose dramatically as well, going from $648 in 1998 to $1,235 in 2002.

Rising profits reflect two factors: rising revenue per student and some cost-savings from economies of large scale. It appears that the UOP raises its tuition annually somewhat less than the not-for-profit universities, but since it has better cost containment and no productivity reduction over time, it is able to increase its profit margins—while gradually narrowing the differential between its tuition and that of state universities. This suspicion is supported by the fact that revenues per student rose about

FIGURE 8-3

PRETAX PROFITS AS A PERCENT OF REVENUES, APOLLO GROUP,
FISCAL YEARS 1998, 2001, AND 2003

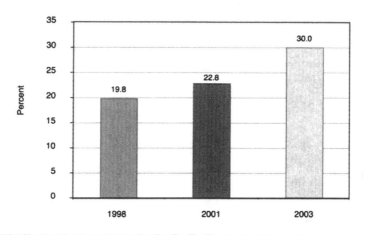

SOURCE: Yahoo Finance, http://finance.yahoo.com/q?s=APOL&d–t.

16.5 percent from 1999 to 2003—well below the average tuition increase in that period, but more than the rise in consumer prices generally.[2]

The revenue of for-profit universities gets disbursed in a radically different fashion than that of typical not-for-profit institutions. To begin with, the traditional institution almost always spends somewhere between ninety-nine cents and a dollar of each one dollar in revenue, and in bad times may dip into cash reserves and spend a bit more on various expenses incurred in pursuing its mission. By contrast, Apollo Group spends only seventy cents out of every dollar—with thirty cents being profit, out of which part goes for income taxes of about eleven cents per dollar of revenue. Whereas the typical state university is a recipient of income tax receipts, the for-profit schools are disbursers (although they benefit mightily from guaranteed student loan and related tax-financed programs).

Based just on funds disbursed as "costs and expenses," we can see that the two types of universities behave very differently. In 2002, Apollo Group spent sixty-six cents of each dollar on "instructional costs and services," compared with thirty-four cents spent at public universities in 1999–2000. To be sure, the definitions of categories may differ a bit, but

it is virtually certain that the for-profit universities devote a far larger proportion of their budgets to instruction than the not-for-profits. Although
marketing and selling expenses are vastly greater at the for-profits—
Apollo spent almost 20 percent of its budget on these expenses in 2002,
while I suspect that it is a rare not-for-profit institution that spends more
than 10 percent—they spend nothing on research, and far less than traditional universities on administration. Less than eight cents of each dollar goes toward administrative costs at for-profits, versus fourteen cents
for the public universities, despite paying senior administrators far higher
salaries. For-profits also spend next to nothing on things such as buildings and grounds and libraries.

The for-profits like the UOP have one mission: to educate students in
a profitable fashion. There are no research aspirations, no athletic teams,
no sense of obligation to provide community services. As detailed in earlier chapters, the traditional universities have diverted resources from
instruction to such undertakings. It is roughly true at some state universities that state subsidies cover the costs of these "other things," while
tuition covers the costs of instruction. Thus, schools like the UOP, without direct state subsidies but not needing them for "other things," can be
rather competitive in a cost sense even with the students paying all the
bills. Since the faculty teaching at the for-profits are largely untenured
and, in a majority of instances, part-time, and since they teach heavier
loads (given the lack of research expectations), the faculty costs per student can be reduced from those at traditional universities.

Career Education Corporation. Apollo Group is not the only very successful
postsecondary, for-profit provider of educational services. Some other companies rival or even surpass Apollo in terms of financial success. Career Education Corporation, headquartered in a Chicago suburb, did not exist ten
years ago, and public trading in its stock began only in 1998. A person putting $25,000 in its stock at that time would now have shares worth over
$500,000. Not even traded seven years ago, this company has a market valu-
ation in excess of $5 billion. Revenues are rising faster than for Apollo, and
profit margins are increasing as well. In its 2003 fiscal year, the company
earned about $119 million (after taxes) on sales of nearly $1.2 billion. Pretax
profit margins are around fifteen cents on the dollar—not as high as Apollo,

but still rather impressive (about a 20 percent rate of return on equity). Enrollments have been expanding at an impressive rate, rising 63 percent from January 31, 2003, to January 31, 2004, and reaching 83,200 by the later date.

Career Education Corporation offers programs at dozens of campuses for various degrees (through the master's) and diplomas, but confines itself primarily to five career-related areas: visual communication and design technologies, information technology, business studies, culinary arts, and health education. The company has a growing e-learning division, called American InterContinental University-Online. It places a very strong emphasis on obtaining jobs for its graduates and devotes a good deal of resources to placement services. Unlike Apollo, Career Education has a very significant international presence, with campuses in Canada, France, the United Kingdom, and the United Arab Emirates.

Corinthian Colleges, Inc. Like many for-profit firms, Corinthian Colleges began as a privately held company. (Several fairly large for-profits still are privately held.) In the five years since it went public in 1999, its stock price has risen more than tenfold. Its return of stockholder equity in 2003 well exceeded 30 percent—at least double that of a typical corporation. Like those who bought shares in Apollo Group and Career Education Corporation, someone who became a fairly large investor in this company early on would be wealthy today.

Corinthian is growing by leaps and bounds, and in the 2003 *Fortune Magazine* rankings of America's one hundred fastest-growing companies, it ranked sixth, above such dot.com icons as eBay. In 1998, its last year as a private company, Corinithian had revenues of $106.5 million and net income of $1.2 million (1.1 percent of sales). By 2003, sales had nearly quintupled to $517.31 million, and profits had grown by more than fifty times, to $65.9 million (more than 12 percent of sales). Pretax profit margins approximate 20 percent. Market capitalization is $2.7 billion.

In one sense, Corinthian is a smaller version of the University of Phoenix, opening small "campuses" (usually a single, medium-size building) in dozens of locations, a large proportion of them in Sun Belt states like California and Florida. By 2003, over fifty-nine thousand students were enrolled. Most were in associate degree and diploma programs, suggesting that Corinthian competes mainly against community colleges.

Like Career Education Corporation, Corinthian places a large emphasis on marketing and on placement. In mid-2002, it had about 140 professionals working in its placement service, which is many times the ratio of placement professionals to students at the traditional university. Even more unusual by traditional university standards is that it employed 464 admissions representatives, maybe twenty times the typical number for a fairly large state university. In 2003, its director of admissions (actually the senior marketing executive) made nearly $1 million for orchestrating the company's remarkable growth.

Students at Corinthian clearly view their enrollment as an investment, a means to the end of a higher income and a better job. A majority of Corinthian employees are faculty (compared with one-third or less at the traditional university). Students who register full-time for a bachelor's degree pay a tuition of around $9,000—above that charged to in-state students at most state universities, but less than that typically charged at the not-for-profit, private institutions.

DeVry University and Associated Businesses. Incorporated in 1973, DeVry, Inc. is one of the more mature companies in the for-profit higher education business. With sales of about $700 million, it is highly profitable, although less so than the institutions mentioned above, and slower growing. DeVry operates career-oriented programs emphasizing technology across the United States and Canada. In 2002, it merged the various DeVry Institutes and its Keller Graduate School (emphasizing graduate management education) into a single entity, DeVry University. DeVry also operates the Becker Conviser Professional Review, a well-known firm that prepares candidates for major postgraduate examinations, such as those for certifications as CPA (certified public accountant) and CFA (chartered financial analyst). Thus, it supplements and sharpens the learning experience of students who have already attended traditional colleges and universities.

Like Corinthian, DeVry is trying to grow through acquisition. In March 2003, it bought the company operating the Ross University School of Medicine and the Ross University School of Veterinary Medicine. Like most for-profit universities, DeVry has a very strong balance sheet, with virtually no debt. While traditional university presidents bemoaned rising cost pressures and inadequate state appropriations or private contributions, this for-profit firm, not subsidized in any direct sense, was able to pay $310 million for its new acquisition.

Strayer Education, Inc. Not all for-profit universities are large national or international entities. Strayer University (which also owns Education Loan Processing, Inc.) is a highly successful regional firm with a presence in the Washington, D.C. area and North Carolina. With revenues in 2003 of $147 million, Strayer is much smaller than the previously mentioned providers. But it is extremely profitable, making after-tax profits of over 22 percent of sales, and, unlike the other companies, it pays a regular dividend. A $25,000 investment in Strayer at the time of its going public as a company in July 1996 would have increased to over $250,000 by the summer of 2003—not quite as spectacular as the growth in value of Apollo or Corinthian, but certainly far better than the market performance as a whole. Its $1.1 billion valuation in the market is some seven times existing sales, an impressive multiple suggesting that investors view Strayer as a growth stock more akin to the dot.com stocks before the technology bubble burst than to conventional service industry stocks.

Strayer is conservatively but aggressively expanding, planning new ventures in Tennessee and Pennsylvania as it expands beyond its metropolitan Washington base. Two things impress me about Strayer. First, although it has large marketing costs like the other for-profits, its instructional costs seem low in relation to tuition revenue—between 35 and 40 percent. The company keeps them well-contained, perhaps by having heavy teaching loads, being less extravagant than not-for-profits in providing fringe benefits, not awarding tenure, and using less expensive part-time faculty. Second, Strayer historically has invested some of its profits in financing the educations of its own students—Education Loan Processing, Inc., in reality is in the business of lending to Strayer students who prefer to pay as they go rather than to wait until after graduation.

Distinguishing Characteristics of For-Profit Colleges and Universities. The five companies discussed above are not the only players in the for-profit higher education market, but together they probably represent a large majority of the market valuation of for-profit providers.[3] What are some common characteristics of these institutions, and how do they differ from traditional not-for-profit providers?

- To this point, most for-profits have focused on the adult market—individuals outside the traditional eighteen- to twenty-four-year age group that dominates enrollments. They appear to have been reluctant to compete directly and too vigorously with the traditional universities, which may explain the rather muted objections to their presence by the not-for-profits. As the adult market becomes more saturated, the for-profits will either have to expand geographically (that is, to foreign countries) or start competing more directly for students of traditional college-attending age.

- For-profits have emphasized the vocational aspects of higher education training much more than traditional schools, with the exception of some community colleges. They train persons in specific specialties—computer programming, information technology, culinary arts, human resource management—and give short shrift to the basics of a liberal education, such as instruction in philosophy, history, literature, foreign languages, anthropology, or the basic sciences.

- For-profits operate in modest but comfortable buildings in many locations, rather than in one large, centralized campus. Enrollments are often measured in the hundreds or, at most, a few thousand, on any given campus. Almost all of their facilities are directly related to instruction or administration—there are few, if any, of the recreational facilities, art galleries, concert halls, research laboratories, or libraries that are features of the typical university campus.

- For-profits are purely teaching institutions. Faculty members typically have heavy teaching loads, no tenure, and few non-teaching responsibilities. Many of the faculty are part-time, often individuals with other full-time jobs (sometimes as professors), or perhaps retired faculty members from other institutions. The senior, tenured faculty member with a lot of power is a rarity at for-profit universities.

- For-profits place far more emphasis than the typical traditional university on recruiting students and placing graduates in jobs. They want to attract customers and to have them leave satisfied so as to attract future customers. They are very much motivated by market forces, specifically the need to maximize revenues (hence their large marketing expenses) and minimize costs (hence the no-frills approach with little noninstructional emphasis).

My wife, a high school guidance counselor, recently received this e-mail from a counselor at the University of Phoenix Online:

Dear Potential Student, I wanted to give you some great news! We are offering a promotion for enrollment into our October 23 and 30 programs!! What that means to you is we will waive the application fee and *buy your books for your first course.* (A value up to $200.00). Classes filled at a record rate in our May promotion and we expect the same response in October. Please respond by clicking below to reserve your spot in class in October and take advantage of this opportunity.[4]

How many not-for-profit schools offer "May promotions" and free books if you enroll now?

Finally, and relevant to the previous point, for-profits use technology for cost containment, making heavy use of computerized instruction and online services. Often they have a relatively standard curriculum for all classes in a subject, with readings and work assignments developed at the headquarters rather than individually by each instructor.

The discussion above is not exhaustive, and it neglects one component of for-profit private higher education: Many large companies have training programs that, in effect, provide the equivalent of college instruction for some of their students. For example, I have taught basic economic principles at one of the nation's largest banks to students with backgrounds primarily in the humanities and social sciences. Some corporations, such as General Motors, even have their own institutions offering college-level instruction. The General Motors Institute, begun around 1920, provided training for GM employees. It has evolved into an independent institution, Kettering University, which still has close ties to GM. (It is named after Charles Kettering, a long-time top GM official who ran GM's research efforts.)

Also, the above discussion omits the many for-profit companies that provide vital inputs into learning on each campus, such as textbook publishers and computer software companies. Even traditional college campuses increasingly rely on for-profit outside contractors for some of their services, such as food and maintenance. Lastly, do not forget that the raters of colleges who play an increasingly prominent role in defining some sort of "bottom line" for many institutions are private, for-profit institutions, some of which, like *The Princeton Review*, are publicly traded.

Distance Learning

For generations, universities have tried to reach beyond their main campuses to serve populations in other areas. State universities in particular have viewed this as part of their mission, and the Morrill Act of 1862 establishing land-grant universities had as its philosophical foundation the view that state universities should serve a broad public, not just a small number of traditional-age college students. In the twentieth century, many universities developed correspondence programs, through which students could read materials and complete assignments and even take examinations by mail. Often, extension divisions of universities became fairly large operations, sometimes largely self-sustaining from the tuition paid by participants.

In the 1950s, 1960s, and 1970s, distance learning began taking on new dimensions, with greater use made of television (or occasionally radio). Interactive television instruction began to take hold in the 1980s, by which students could communicate in real time with their instructors located miles (sometimes thousands of miles) away. It was the advent of personal computers after 1980 and the increasingly widespread popular use of the Internet in the 1990s, however, that enormously expanded the potential of distance learning, as communications costs fell and new technology provided powerful and effective instructional aides that could be utilized over long distances.

Computer usage among college students has soared. In 1993, only 55 percent of students reported they regularly used computers; eight years later, the proportion of nonusers had fallen by more than half, and nearly 79 percent were computer users.[5] The use of computers and participation in distance learning, however, are two different things. In the school year ending in 2000—the most recent for which data are available—about 8 percent of undergraduates took distance-learning courses, with a large majority (about 60 percent) Internet-based.[6] Those numbers exclude traditional correspondence courses. Enrollment was proportionally larger among nontraditional adult learners than students of traditional college age.

Enrollments in online and other distance-learning courses increased rapidly after 2000, and the number of students enrolled in some form of online education now probably exceeds 3 million.[7] That is about 20 percent of the enrollment of traditional residential schools. Among the institutions enrolling over twenty-five thousand students are the University of Maryland University College (which claims to be the nation's leader), SUNY (State University of New York) Learning Network, Old Dominion University (including three thousand U.S. Navy personnel in a Ships at Sea program), and the University of Phoenix Online.

The statistics suggest that computer-based instruction among college students at the present is not the consequence of a drive to reduce costs, but serves rather to supplement and enhance traditional learning techniques. The potential economic benefits of distance learning come from lowering the number of faculty and reducing the amount of other instructional inputs needed to educate a given number of students, and from saving students traveling, food, and lodging expenses. The evidence to date shows that while distance learning of this sort exists, is growing, and is even moderately important, the substitution of capital and technology for labor in the instructional process at traditional universities is proceeding very slowly. Indeed, instead of saving money, many universities are arguing that they need more fee revenue to pay for technology. (Imagine your car dealer trying to add a "technology fee" to the price of the Chevy you want to buy, in order to pay for new machines used at General Motors.) They argue that new technology is a burden on costs, not a relief.

While it is difficult to get a precise handle on the growth of the online higher education industry, it is stratospheric in magnitude—and very big business. For example, the online operations of the University of Phoenix (UOP) are performed through a separate company, University of Phoenix Online, which is controlled by Apollo Group. As of this writing, the market capitalization of the company exceeds $5 billion. In the twenty-seven months from the end of August 2001 to the end of November 2003, enrollments more than tripled, going from about twenty-nine thousand to around ninety-one thousand students. This implies an annual enrollment rate growth of roughly 65 percent! Annual revenues are expected to reach $800 million, and after-tax earnings are now running well in excess of 20 percent of sales, a truly extraordinary record. The stock price has increased tenfold since 2000. While other online universities are no doubt less successful financially, the UOP story reveals that online instruction is popular, profitable, and gaining market share.

Perhaps the greatest pioneer in distance education is Britain's Open University, which now has over two hundred thousand students taking some 150 different courses in many countries besides the United Kingdom. Using several distance-learning technologies, such as interactive television and computer instruction, the Open University is growing less frenetically than UOP Online, but still solidly; enrollments have risen one-third or so in the past eight years. On several occasions, publications have rated the quality of the learning experience at the Open University in the top ten of British universities.

UOP Online and other distance-learning options do not offer the quality of experience that one would get at, say, Harvard or Princeton. There is something about personal contact that motivates students and stimulates the spirit of inquiry and the acquisition of insight into the world. Like many other professors who have taught for decades, I am taken aback occasionally by the students who say I importantly changed their lives by some almost offhand remark I made to them. This experience is difficult to replicate online. However, e-mail has led to far more effective and extensive written communication between students and faculty than previously. Moreover, there is a lot of knowledge that can be conveyed efficiently and cheaply online. The better professors can reach larger audiences at lower cost. As cost becomes an ever-bigger issue, distance learning will pose a greater threat to the old ways of instruction.

Moreover, this threat may be approaching faster and more powerfully than university presidents think. Anyone who works with interest compounding knows that numbers can grow quickly from modest to very large if the growth rate is high, as it is with respect to distance learning. Suppose the online higher education business is growing from 35 to 40 percent a year, and that this is expected to continue for six more years. What that means is that in 2010 the online instruction component of higher education will be eight times as large as it is today. Increases of this magnitude could force the administrators of traditional universities to make radical alterations to their operations to meet a truly powerful threat.

Alternative Forms of Certification

There is no question that the certification function of universities is extremely important in explaining their popularity. As discussed earlier, by issuing degrees, universities greatly lower the cost to prospective employers of finding out about the intellectual and academic skills of job candidates. The earnings differential that college graduates receive may reflect less the actual learning that occurs in college than the other attributes of college graduates that are viewed positively by employers (or, in some cases, professional or graduate schools).

To be sure, some professions do not believe that a bachelor's (or master's) degree in a given subject is sufficient certification for employment, and they have accordingly devised additional tests. The CPA examination is a good example. Graduates of law, medical, and some other professional schools similarly must pass examinations to receive licenses to practice in their professions. But as a general rule, college graduation is a prerequisite for taking the examinations for licensure, so colleges still play a major role in the certification process.

But certification can occur through other approaches, and the information technology field is paving the way for noncollege-related certifications. Major companies like Microsoft, Cisco, Oracle, and Novell have their own certification programs. Students passing examinations can demonstrate mastery of the technology associated with the relevant computer application. Thus, students seek designation as Microsoft-certified systems engineers, Microsoft-certified solutions developers, Microsoft-certified database administrators, Cisco-certified network associates, Cisco-certified network professionals, Oracle-certified application developers, Oracle-certified database administrators, certified Novell administrators, certified Novell engineers, or literally dozens of others. Armed with these certifications, prospective employees can go to employers and say, "Look, I can handle your Oracle and Microsoft applications well"—indeed, clearly with more competence than a person with a generic bachelor's degree in computer science, who may or may not have the very specific skills needed.

As anyone knows who is acquainted with bright high school students who are clever with computers, the level of formal education needed to master computer skills is not high, although the skills themselves are of a fairly high order. The new certification programs in the information technology industry potentially threaten the near-monopoly of universities in certifying persons for highly skilled positions.

To be sure, the universities themselves are trying to share in this market. Many extension divisions now offer training, often online, designed to help students pass the requisite examinations. However, they are competing with a bevy of for-profit private training operations for this business.

If the costs of universities continue to rise, more nonuniversity forms of certification can be expected to develop, particularly demonstrating the mastery of reasonably specific occupational skills. Organizations like Underwriters Laboratories, for example, which certify the safety of equipment, may start certifying the competency of human resources providers. As Plato said more than two millennia ago, "Necessity is the mother of invention," and rising costs combined with the quest for efficiency and minimal search costs will likely expand the emerging movement toward nonuniversity-based certification.

Conclusions

As traditional universities continue to raise their prices, reflecting relatively low and probably declining productivity, they generally have ignored the possibility that alternatives to their services exist. Three such alternatives are for-profit universities, distance learning, and nonuniversity occupational certification. As the costs of traditional learning grow, people are searching for substitutes. The spectacular popularity and commercial success of for-profit university training and distance learning suggest that the mainstream market of traditional students may increasingly forgo expensive onsite training for these newer alternatives.

9

Evolutionary Change on the Campus: One Scenario

As indicated in previous chapters, the sharply rising cost of college to its consumers is not sustainable in the long run. Moreover, a series of factors suggests that the demand for traditional higher education may begin to grow at a slower rate or even stop growing altogether, leading, most likely, to smaller tuition increases and forcing universities to halt the decline in productivity that has characterized modern higher education. Indeed, since real wages in other professional occupations have been rising along with productivity, college teaching will not remain a comparably well-paid profession unless university productivity begins increasing as revenue growth slows. In short, significant changes will be needed.

Change can evolve naturally over time, with only modest governmental involvement. If government support for higher education grows slowly or not at all, financial pressures could hasten self-imposed changes within the academy. If government support grows robustly for awhile, the internally generated changes will come more slowly and perhaps not at all for a number of years. But given the rising pressures for more state government spending on competing social services, especially Medicaid, I suspect that sometime in the next decade there will be some move toward greater change in public universities.

In this chapter, we will discuss some of the things universities might do to make themselves somewhat more efficient in the face of rising competitive pressures.

Reducing Instructional Costs

The instructional component of university budgets has declined in relative importance over time, but it is still large, amounting to one-half or more of the total at some community colleges and more than one-quarter at most universities. The dominant component of "instructional costs" is faculty salaries. Can economies be made here? There are at least four ways these costs can be reduced: by increasing the student-faculty ratio; by ending or modifying tenure; by increasing the use of part-time or adjunct faculty; and by using more capital-intensive instructional techniques.

Increase the Student-Faculty Ratio. We pay faculty members at major universities upwards of $100,000 annually on average, including fringe benefits, to teach four to six courses a year—or, on average, close to $20,000 a course. The number of hours faculty spend in the classroom is relatively small—typically less than 200 hours per year at major research universities, somewhat more (perhaps 250 hours) at medium-quality schools with some research emphasis, and 300 to even 350 hours at institutions whose primary mission is teaching. At two-year colleges, teaching loads can get still a bit heavier, but it is the rare college professor who is in the classroom for more than 500 hours a year. By contrast, teachers in primary and secondary schools have two or three times that amount of classroom contact.

University professors will argue long and hard that lighter teaching loads are justified because they need to spend a good deal of time keeping up with work done in their fields and working to extend the frontiers of knowledge through more research. Yet if college professors were to spend 250 hours a year teaching, another 250 hours preparing for class and advising students, 500 hours in research (the same as in teaching-related activities), and 200 hours in service activities such as serving on committees, they would still be working a total of only 1,200 hours a year—at least one-third less than the typical full-time employee in other professions or in the labor force at large.

Of course, faculty work only a nine-month "year" typically, unless they teach summer school or have summer grant support dedicated to research. Yet one might ask why college campuses operate on a much-reduced basis for several months a year. That means that capital costs of classroom buildings, student laboratories, computer and library facilities, dormitories, and other facilities are relatively high, as buildings are utilized far less than comparable facilities in the private sector. Alternatively, if faculty members insist that a three-month summer vacation is necessary to revive and recharge themselves intellectually every year (a somewhat dubious contention, in this author's judgment), then it may not be unreasonable to expect them to work relatively long hours (45 to 50 hours per week) during the academic year. Working 48 hours a week for thirty-five weeks a year would mean a total work year of 1,680 hours, allowing at least 400—possibly 500—hours for teaching, with time available for some research, advising of students, reading, and the like. This would imply teaching loads of 12 to 15 hours a week during the standard academic year, instead of the 6- to 9-hour loads that most faculty have today (less at some top institutions, more at some lesser-known schools).

Faculty would cry mightily that such loads would stifle research and end their ability to keep up on the literature. It is interesting that at the middle of the twentieth century, teaching loads more closely approximated those suggested above, with 9-hour loads prevailing at major research universities, 12-hour loads at medium-quality state and private schools, and 15-hour teaching assignments common at somewhat lesser-known institutions. Teaching loads fell in the 1950s and 1960s (when faculty were in high demand), and they have stayed down since. The instructional savings from heavier teaching loads can be dramatic. Suppose a mid-size university teaches 1,500 courses each academic term, with 750 instructors teaching on average two courses each (6 hours per week if the school offers courses of three semester-hours; remember, an academic "hour" is usually fifty to fifty-five minutes). Suppose now that the average teaching load is increased to three courses. The same number of classes can now be taught with 500 faculty members—one-third less. Very significant savings in instructional costs are possible from increasing teaching loads.

The same type of savings can come by reducing the number of courses and increasing the average class size. For example, a liberal arts college that teaches 200 freshmen each term in ten sections of 20 students each could move to teaching those students in eight sections averaging 25 students. Rather than teaching principles of economics to 1,500 students in fifteen classes averaging 100 students each, teach them in six sections averaging 250 students.

To be sure, there are costs to either approach. Other things being equal, students and professors alike prefer small rather than large classes.

There may be greater learning with a smaller class size, although a massive literature for primary and secondary education suggests that the learning advantages to small classes are modest at best.[1] Heavier teaching loads will likely mean reductions in published research. But it can be argued that the "publish or perish" atmosphere of modern times has led to a good bit of very marginal research with minimal social value. Moreover, for many, heavier teaching loads will simply mean that professors will work harder. While I know many workaholics who spend, say, 250 hours a year teaching, 500 hours preparing for class and advising students, 1,000 hours doing research, and 400 hours in committee work and other university functions, for a total of 2,150 hours a year, I know about as many who teach 250 hours, spend 250 hours on other instructional duties, 400 hours doing minimal research, and 100 hours on campus activities, for a total of 1,000 hours—25 hours a week for forty weeks a year. Heavier teaching loads for these faculty members would merely cut into time they now use to play golf, do leisurely reading, or perhaps engage in lucrative private consulting.

An interesting case study of the impact of heavier teaching loads is taking place at Fort Hays University in Hays, Kansas. The university's longtime president, Dr. Edward H. Hammond, decided to increase teaching loads greatly in the face of declining state support following the 2001 recession.[2] The typical load was increased to six courses a semester, or 18 hours per week. Since Fort Hays' salary levels are also relatively low, its per-class instructional costs are now dramatically lower than other state schools, indeed, probably competitive with such for-profits as the University of Phoenix. To assist further in dealing with his financial problems, President Hammond vigorously pushed online instructional programs in a province of China, providing Fort Hays with over a million dollars in additional annual cash flow.

The heavier teaching loads allowed Dr. Hammond to recommend a *much* smaller tuition increase than those implemented at such sister Kansas institutions as the University of Kansas and Kansas State University, thereby greatly increasing the school's relative attractiveness to prospective students. As a consequence, the fall 2003 enrollment went up around 15 percent over the previous year. Also, the large increase in classes taught allowed a reduction in class size, enhancing the school's marketing appeal.

To be sure, the changes promoted by Edward Hammond have not been without cost. The faculty, predictably, was up in arms and, indeed, successfully formed a union. Kansas, however, is a right-to-work state, which weakened the union's potential power. An eighteen-hour teaching load, even with small classes (most have fewer than twenty students), leaves relatively little time for faculty members to do research, or even keep up on what others are doing and saying in their disciplines. Yet serious cutting-edge research has never been present to a high degree at schools like Fort Hays, and arguably all that Dr. Hammond has done is sharply reduce the school year leisure time of the instructional staff.

An unanticipated plus from the Fort Hays move came with regard to hiring faculty. The higher enrollments and associated additional tuition revenues allowed Fort Hays to add faculty at a time when other schools were retrenching. Because of the dismal state of the academic job market in this environment, Fort Hays was able to acquire some new, relatively high-quality faculty. Bucking conventional wisdom can pay dividends in academia, as it does it business.

Use Technology to Reduce Instructional Costs. Most teaching in universities is done the way Socrates did it 2,400 years ago, but probably not as well. Professors get up in front of a group of students and talk. To be sure, the talking might involve using a blackboard, an overhead projector, a PowerPoint presentation, or even an instructional video, but the professor still is presiding over a group of students in a room. The system works, and I think works fairly well, but it is increasingly expensive as real labor costs rise over time.

As indicated in the previous chapter, the introduction of computers and television has not lowered the costs of instruction to this point in time. We have merely superimposed new technology onto the classroom without altering the system in any fundamental way. Thus, if anything, the new technology has added to costs. There are two ways, however, that technology can potentially reduce instructional costs. First, instructors can reach a larger audience, not limited to a single location. Call this a technology-induced spatial expansion of teaching. Second, by recording in some fashion the wisdom that the instructor wishes to convey, the "lecture" can be repeated many times—a replication expansion of teaching also induced by technology.

The major obstacle to this happening has not been technological, nor the cost of capital needed to use the new techniques. Rather, it has been staff opposition. Professors would rather teach live to students they can see, and students would rather see their instructors in the flesh as well. The latter point is particularly meaningful—if students are willing to pay for very expensive live instruction compared with far cheaper televised or computerized instruction, then they should be allowed to do so. However, it is altogether another issue whether such expensive instruction should be subsidized by third parties.

Staff objections to new technology are overcome in the for-profit sector, where there is no tenure, and shared governance does not exist. Profit-sharing and stock options also soften the objections of instructors, and certainly of administrators, to moving to new technologies. As costs constrain traditional universities more, they, too, will probably develop incentive systems to nudge their staffs into participating more enthusiastically in the use of technologies that raise the student-faculty ratio.

Change Tenure. As indicated in earlier chapters, tenure imposes real financial costs on universities, as well as possibly some loss of quality when inadequate faculty members continue to work because of it. Tenure reduces the flexibility of universities to reallocate resources with changing needs. It promotes sometimes obstructionist behavior on the part of faculty who feel little negative consequence of opposing structural or other changes that might promote efficiency. The power it gives to faculty forces administrations into governance arrangements that are very expensive in terms of human resources—it seems that nothing important is done in universities without a multitude of committee meetings.

Yet there is absolutely no question that universities exist to promote free and unfettered inquiry into all sorts of issues. If the freedom to inquire is stifled, universities lose much of their vitality. The frontiers of knowledge may expand more slowly, and students may become less expressive, imaginative, and resourceful. Academic freedom is very important indeed, and tenure does most definitely help maintain it.

In reality, there has been some chipping away at the institution of tenure slowly over time. Schools that do not provide tenure, including, typically, the for-profit institutions, are growing faster than those that grant it.

Tenure-granting institutions have increased the proportion of the faculty who work on a part-time, adjunct basis, or who have nontenure-track term appointments, sometimes running three to five years. More recently, some schools, often under compulsion from state government or regulatory authority, have experimented with loosening tenure, notably with post-tenure review.

While post-tenure review procedures vary, they might involve a substantial peer evaluation of the performance of tenured faculty members every five years after the award of tenure. In the case of faculty adjudged weak and inadequate, the review might identify areas where improvement is needed, and perhaps even suggest some ways of remedying the problem. The faculty member in question then has a period of perhaps two years to deal with the weaknesses. A second evaluation is conducted. If the faculty member is still found deficient, he or she might be terminated from employment with one year's notice or, in a "softer" version, given one further year to improve prior to a third evaluation. Often, faced with the embarrassment of a poor post-tenure review, faculty members choose to resign or retire.

There are two sorts of criticism of post-tenure review—one along the lines that it does not go far enough, and the second that it goes too far. Those complaining about the inability of universities to expeditiously weed out unproductive or unneeded faculty might argue that post-tenure review often means taking several years to rid the institution of an unproductive employee—less than if no review occurred, but a long period nonetheless. Those concerned with academic freedom will argue that post-tenure review provides a means of ridding universities of individuals with unpopular views, or those who are disliked by senior faculty and administrators. Its existence will make faculty more cautious in what they say, what they research, and what they write. That impinges upon true, freewheeling academic debate.

As a person who has spent a lifetime offending people with my speaking and writings, I am very skeptical about eroding tenure. At the same time, I think post-tenure review is a reasonable approach to dealing with a problem. Some safeguards can be introduced, for example, making it illegal to dismiss a faculty member because of his or her subjective views on issues (although this is a thorny issue, as occasionally a faculty member may take positions, ostensibly on the basis of facts, that are totally at variance with what factual evidence demonstrates conclusively in the minds of virtually the entire scholarly community; the denying of the existence of the Holocaust is an example). An abusive administration could use post-tenure review to punish controversial professors, using other alleged deficiencies in the professor's performance to cover up for the real reason termination is sought. I think experimentation with the concept (which is already being used in some states) should indicate whether these fears are realistic. Given the cost of tenure to universities, more such experimentation seems warranted.

There are other ways in which the tenure issue could be approached. Since tenure is a fringe benefit with real if unstated value to the faculty member, perhaps faculty members should be able to choose whether they want it included in their "compensation package," with the administration placing some value on it. This approach can also be used to deal with other costly items, such as health insurance. A faculty member would be told that she is being hired at a salary of, say, $65,000 as an assistant professor of political science. In addition, she is told she will receive $15,000 in fringe benefits and is given a menu of options to choose from. She can acquire up to $15,000 of benefits with no deduction from salary, and more, if she chooses, with salary deductibility. The menu might include the following options: university contribution to retirement (other than mandatory Social Security contributions), with varying amounts to $5,500 a year; catastrophic health insurance, $3,000 a year; medium-quality health insurance, $5,000 a year; deluxe health insurance, $7,500 a year; distant parking, $500 a year; close-in parking, $1,000 a year; tenure-track protection, $5,000 a year; life insurance, $1,000 a year.

If the faculty member took the maximum benefit on all items, it would cost $20,000 annually, and she would have to pay $5,000 from her annual salary. However, by forgoing tenure protection, she could have maximum retirement contributions, the best parking, life insurance, and blue-chip health insurance without deducting anything from her salary. If she has confidence in her professional achievement but is concerned about other forms of income security, such as having good retirement and health protection, she might choose the nontenure-track option. If concerns about academic freedom and job security are paramount, she might want to take the tenure option, but opt for catastrophic health insurance and having to walk some distance to the office. Universities would then have a tighter control on fringe benefit costs, and faculty members could elect to have tenure protection, but only at a price, in recognition of the fact that tenure confers costs on the university.

Cut and Consolidate Costly Programs. Much of the instructional capacity of universities is underutilized because students are enrolled in classes with very low head counts, or participate in programs with few majors or degree candidates. What is popular at one time loses popularity at another. Some programs started ambitiously during an era of expansion never achieve much success but are not eliminated because of inertia and lack of pressure to reduce costs. As those cost pressures mount, the move to slash programs should increase.

Particularly costly are low-enrollment PhD programs, where senior faculty members often instruct only a handful of students. Out of institutional hubris and ambition, dozens of mid-size universities began PhD programs in the 1960s and 1970s of indifferent quality and low enrollments. While some pruning of them has occurred, much more needs to be done. This is particularly true in fields where the demand for graduates is low. At one point, for example, my adopted state, Ohio, offered eight PhD programs in history, which is at least five more than desirable on any rational cost-benefit basis. History PhDs are plentiful and have trouble getting jobs, particularly ones who graduate from institutions of marginal quality.

Institutional desire to demonstrate serious research efforts by offering PhD degrees may well increasingly conflict with the necessity of funding bread-and-butter undergraduate operations. Some voluntary, albeit reluctant, dropping of some programs in the future is likely. Institutions with multiple campuses will try to have individual campuses specialize in a smaller number of disciplines rather than offer comprehensive instruction on virtually all campuses. In the midst of a huge cut in state appropriations, the University of Wisconsin (UW) raised tuition sharply (up 16 percent at the flagship Madison campus in 2003), but also reduced the number of programs. For example, it reduced engineering offerings on some regional campuses, forcing engineering students to attend UW at Platteville.

This is in keeping with a small but growing trend for universities to offer programs jointly to reduce costly duplication. UW also eliminated its Land Tenure Center and other smaller research/teaching units. The University of Colorado eliminated its program in integrated marketing communications.[3] Similar things have happened at campuses across the country. Faced with real resource reductions, universities have trimmed off operations perceived to be of marginal importance. That trend may well continue if cost pressures rise in the long term.

In some cases, universities can effect savings by sharing facilities and resources. Libraries are expanding their interlibrary loan programs, and in some states students can use materials from any of a number of universities. For example, Ohio has the OhioLINK consortium of universities, community colleges, and small private colleges that share in computerized form their catalogues of holdings, which are freely available to students at all institutions in the consortium. Volume purchases have cut costs. Some institutions forgo purchase of expensive journals or books because they are available either online or in a short time via mail from the consortium.[4]

Other Forms of Cost Reduction

The cost reductions discussed thus far have focused primarily on the instructional mission of the university. Yet a majority of typical university budgets go for expenses not directly related to the instructional mission. There are some possibilities for cost savings in these areas as well.

Reduce Bureaucracy and Noninstructional Staff. Universities are about teaching and research. An efficient university devotes as large a proportion of its resources as possible to meeting these missions. Faculty members complain incessantly about the administration of universities and the growth of administrative bureaucracies that prevent them from doing their jobs. The statistics introduced in earlier chapters suggest that the administrative apparatus of universities has grown enormously over time. Moreover, the financial statements of for-profit universities, while not definitive, strongly suggest that those institutions operate with far smaller (though better paid) bureaucracies.

It is interesting to observe that when universities have financial crunches, they tend to cut into the noninstructional staff, and in times of boom they tend to expand staff disproportionately to instructional personnel. That suggests that a significant proportion of the administrative apparatus is viewed as discretionary—not vital to the mission, but nice to have if funds are available. As budget growth slows down in real terms, the growth of this discretionary expenditure will likely come under sharper scrutiny. For years, I have said that in my relatively typical, medium-size state university, I could eliminate two hundred administrative and support positions without harming the primary academic mission by more than a negligible amount. Faced with a budget crunch, Ohio University now is doing precisely that. I suspect the same story can be told at many other institutions as well.

Cutting support staff is easier than reducing faculty personnel, in part because the former group does not have tenure, while the faculty does to a considerable extent. Without financial incentives to do so, administrators are particularly loath to reduce their own ranks, since in some cases that leads to heavier workloads for themselves. This is an argument for making state or federal subsidies to institutions of higher education inverse to the proportion of the noninstructional staff to the total. State legislatures, governors, and state higher education governing boards might experiment with providing incentives for universities to reduce the size of their noninstructional staffs. For example, they might stipulate that 90 percent of subsidies must be used to pay salaries of faculty members who actively teach and do research, forcing universities to use tuition and alumni contributions to finance administrative functions. My hunch is that this would lead to some serious cost-cutting in these areas.

Similarly, the federal government could state that it will pay overhead on research grants equal to 40 percent of research personnel costs—period. Universities that claim to have higher overhead costs would then be given incentives to reduce them. (In a perfect world, the chore of nudging the administration to move in this direction would fall to the university board of trustees, but those individuals typically are part-time volunteers heavily under the influence of the administration—a topic for further discussion below.)

Just as it makes sense to "empower" faculty members to choose from those fringe benefits that most appeal to them—including tenure—subject to a resource constraint, perhaps it is prudent also to provide administrative incentives to conserve costs, somewhat the way stock options do in the private sector. Give performance bonuses to administrators who lower their costs per student, perhaps adjusted for inflation. This might stem the pressure to perpetually demand more resources from the administration.

Incentives for reducing costs could be extended to incentives for improving outcomes or achieving mission objectives, although this is difficult to do owing to the measurement problems inherent in a nonprofit environment. Nonetheless, if an institution's average ranking in three national surveys (perhaps *U.S. News & World Report, Princeton Review*, and *Kiplinger's*) rises, a bonus would be given that would vary with the extent of the improvement. Similarly, the trustees would reduce or withhold salary increases in years in which the composite ranking fell. There are all sorts of practical problems with such incentive plans, but as budget pressures grow, the importance of sensitizing staff to cost and efficiency concerns may lead to their internal adoption.

Contracting Out and Privatization of Services. Universities know a good deal about instruction and research but are less adept at preparing food, maintaining lodging facilities, generating heat or electricity, cleaning and maintaining facilities, and running motor pools. Yet many of them do all of these things, and more. It has become more common over the last generation to contract out some of these activities, and I suspect that trend will continue. On average, private, for-profit contractors who specialize in a given function can perform it more cheaply than a university lacking expertise in that area.

Beyond auxiliary functions, it is arguably a good idea for universities to consider contracting out some instructional activities. Wal-Mart flourishes in part by leasing some of its space to outside specialty firms, such as photography studios and labs. Perhaps universities should do the same thing, contracting with, say, Berlitz (a private language instruction company) to teach elementary courses in modern languages. Certainly, the nonselective state universities and community colleges might consider contracting out their remedial instruction programs to private firms like Sylvan Learning Centers.

Beyond contracting out, universities might actually sell their noninstructional assets, redeploying the resources to activities more central to their missions. During the recent budget crunch, I urged legislators in my adopted state of Ohio to consider forcing state universities to sell their dormitories, which on average would be more efficiently run by private providers. To be sure, care would have to be taken to maintain the architectural integrity of campuses in which private facilities are intertwined with university-owned buildings, but in principle the idea is a good one, and cash-hungry schools will probably consider such options more in the future.

Reform Intercollegiate Athletics. The problem with intercollegiate sports is as much ethical and academic as it is financial. Some schools that have financially self-sustaining athletic programs have nonetheless tarnished their reputations by their unscrupulous pursuit of victory on the football field or basketball court at any cost. Nonetheless, schools facing financial crunches will look to athletics as a possible area for reform. As mentioned earlier, some schools with high athletic ambitions but small gate receipts or television revenues are spending 2 or 3 percent of their institutional budgets on subsidizing sports, especially football. On the other hand, at least one Division I school made at least $27.5 million on athletics in 2001.[5]

University presidents, knowing that reform and cost containment are highly desirable, are reluctant to act for several reasons. First, a school that unilaterally initiates cutbacks in spending will be massacred athletically. Thus, some interuniversity efforts are required. Second, the presidents fear the wrath of the alumni, key legislators, and other important "friends of the university." Third, most presidents do not like to do battle with their own staffs, particularly popular coaches and athletic directors.

Groups like the Knight Commission have made some sensible suggestions for change, but they have been largely ignored.[6] I believe that the scenario for true regime change in big-time intercollegiate athletics would have to go something like this: Several Ivy League presidents, including those at Harvard, Yale, and Princeton, often regarded as the three best universities in America for undergraduate education, would convince all the other Ivy League presidents to quietly invite the presidents of a number of key non–Ivy League universities to join them in a meeting on athletic reform. No coaches, athletic directors, or press would be invited. Indeed, the hope would be to keep the meeting secret initially.

To alter drastically the behavior of an athletic conference, at least two and preferably three schools would have to make near-nonnegotiable demands for a change in the rules of the game. Moreover, at least three highly visible athletic conferences would have to make fundamental changes to their rules to provide the political clout to change national standards, as set by the National Collegiate Athletic Association (NCAA).

Suppose that the Ivy League presidents invited the presidents of Northwestern University, the University of Michigan, and the University of Illinois from the Big Ten Conference; the presidents of Duke, Wake Forest, and the University of Virginia from the Atlantic Coast Conference; the presidents of Stanford University, the University of California at Berkeley, the University of California at Los Angeles, and the University of Southern California from the Pacific-10 (Pac-10) Conference; and the presidents of Vanderbilt University, the University of Georgia, and the University of Florida from the Southeast Conference. They also invited the president of the University of Notre Dame, a perennial independent football power and, along with Georgetown, the most prestigious of the Catholic schools.

These schools are all academically strong, and they constitute a majority of the top twenty-five universities in the *USN&WR* national research university rankings. They are also, for the most part, significant athletic powers, some of them very much so. They constitute a significant part of five athletic conferences. This group of twenty-two presidents would issue a statement saying they plan to recommend to their trustees that their institutions engage in intercollegiate athletics only under a new set of rules. What would those rules be?

First, lower significantly the scope and intensity of major sports by sharply reducing permissible team size and season length. Division I-A football teams carry well over 100 men on their rosters (far more than National Football League professional teams), yet only eleven play at any one time. Even allowing for offensive and defensive teams, a few specialists (such as kickers), and a small reserve for injuries, a team could exist with thirty members. Allowing a backup individual for every position would double that number to sixty. Therefore, permit only sixty on a team. Limit the season to ten games, *including* bowl games (teams now routinely play twelve games, and often thirteen). Prohibit games during final examination periods. Reduce practice time and preseason preparation and forbid mandatory weight and conditioning sessions except as part of regular practices. Place similar limits on seasons for other sports as well, for instance, limiting baseball to a forty-game season (some teams now play over seventy games).

Second, make athletes students first again. Prohibit "red-shirting"—the practice of having a freshman student sit out a year of eligibility. Perhaps even limit eligibility to three years, prohibiting freshmen from playing on varsity teams and permitting only some intra-university or junior varsity-freshmen sporting events—a practice common in the mid-twentieth century.

Third, limit total institutional subsidies for intercollegiate athletics to, say, 1 percent of the university budget (carefully and uniformly defined), and total spending to 2 percent. At my university, this would force a reallocation from athletics to other (presumably academic) activities of well over five million dollars annually, and I suspect that a similar story applies at dozens of other institutions. If the subsidy reduction were used to lower tuition, at my institution the level for in-state students would fall about 4 percent—not an inconsequential amount. To be sure, football coaching staffs might dwindle to three or four coaches per squad, but that number works well in high school football and can in college as well.

Fourth, insist that national television revenues be shared equally for the most part among participants in Division I-A sports, removing financial incentives to engage in unscrupulous activities. Set aside a small portion (say, 5 percent) of NCAA football and basketball television revenues to set up a completely independent Intercollegiate Athletics Rules Compliance Bureau, with which athletic directors and coaches would be forbidden to communicate except when asked to as part of a formal investigation. This group would enforce the rules, especially the financial limits.

Fifth, enact very tough and enforceable sanctions for rule violations. Serious infractions should involve suspension from intercollegiate play in the sport for at least a year (not merely prohibition of postseason play). Key officials should be banned from college sports for long periods (possibly life) for egregious violations. One might even make serious violations criminal under state law, although I am concerned about the excessive governmental regulatory apparatus that might be associated with such a provision.

Sixth, integrate the athletic department into the rest of the university—for example, making it compete in budget allocations with other units, rather than having it exist as an independent, autonomous entity. Gordon Gee, Chancellor at Vanderbilt (and former president of Brown and Ohio State), is doing just that. As Gee put it, "There is a wrong culture in athletics, and I'm declaring war on it." He also revealed that fellow presidents of Southeast Conference schools encouraged him to do it, saying, "'If you succeed we'll follow.' There is not a great deal of courage out there."[7]

This six-point program would allow active and viable intercollegiate athletic programs to continue, admittedly on a far less grandiose scale than at present. The primacy of academics over athletics would be reestablished. Costs would be reduced, along with such morale-reducing occurrences as coaches making perhaps ten times as much money as university presidents or world-renowned senior faculty members. Yet the spirit of competition, the leadership-building potential for participants, and an outlet for some alumni enthusiasm would be preserved. The plan is a decent compromise between eliminating college athletics altogether, which probably is simply not politically feasible, and maintaining the status quo, which is both expensive and debilitating to the major missions of universities.

The key to reform is united action. Individual university presidents who promote changes like those cited above will be eaten alive by alumni, trustees, and legislators who are sports fanatics. As Gordon Gee remarked regarding his reform of athletics at Vanderbilt, "If I did this at Ohio State I'd be pumping gas."[8] Yet if enough schools with lots of prestige both academically and athletically appeal for reform collectively, the momentum for it happening will be there. If the playing field is level, fierce athletic competition can ensue, even if at a less commercial and professional level than before. My guess is that total revenues received from collegiate athletics would decline somewhat, but not as dramatically as one might think. Watching college football on television would still be fun, and commercially lucrative. Moreover, costs would typically fall substantially, so on balance the move would be financially beneficial to most universities.

The proposal above does not solve all problems of intercollegiate sports. Incentives to cheat and break the rules would still exist. Athletes would still be exploited financially, although probably less than at the present (and fewer of the fruits of exploitation would likely be transferred to coaches and others running athletic programs). Still, both the financial and academic problems associated with the commercialization of college athletics would be sharply reduced.

End Formal Affirmative Action Programs. Affirmative action is not just an economic issue, but it has strong financial implications. First, the enforcement and administrative costs of diversity programs often run into seven digits at major institutions. At my rather typical state institution, with its $300 million or so basic budget, we could easily reduce expenses by $1 million without completely eliminating affirmative action simply by doing away with fifteen or so "diversity coordinators," "minority recruitment specialists," or other positions that exist to ensure a politically correct racial and ethnic mix to the student body or even the curriculum. Academic quality would not suffer. Indeed, it would probably improve, as academic decisions would more likely be based on merit; and a bureaucracy that gets in the way of faculty doing their jobs would be eliminated. The financial savings with a total elimination of affirmative action efforts would be still greater.

Would universities, however, revert to practices of two generations ago, denying admission to nonwhite students on the basis of color, or women on the basis of gender? It is extremely farfetched to think so, in my judgment, partly because of changing attitudes in American society, and also because of the voluminous rhetoric of university presidents extolling the virtues of diversity. Moving toward colorblind admissions, hiring, and contracting would also be consistent with the original vision of proponents of civil rights in the 1950s, namely that minorities wanted not special treatment, but merely a level playing field where people were judged not by "the color of their skin but by the content of their character."[9]

To the extent that the elimination of affirmative action police in university communities leads to a reduction in minority admissions, it might well also lead to improved retention rates and a decline in the highly inefficient practice of admitting marginally qualified students who then fail to make the academic grade. This is highly wasteful of resources and costly, financially and psychologically, to the student who does not make it. Thus such a move would probably promote greater productivity in the university community, broadly defined.

Improving Productivity: The Output Side Matters as Well

To this point, this chapter has focused on cost savings. Yet productivity and efficiency involve relating outcomes or performance to costs and resources. If the "output" of universities can be increased, say by improving the learning of students or the volume of meaningful research, productivity rises even if costs remain unchanged. Some productivity-enhancing reforms involve enhancing the numerator—outcomes—in the calculation of productivity (output divided by inputs) as much as the reduction in the denominator—cost of resources.

Academic Retention. The point about the dropout rate of minorities favored by affirmative action can be extended to a broader context. Dropout rates are high among students generally at NCAA Division I schools (defined as the percentage who fail to receive a bachelor's degree within six years). The NCAA with some justification can say that the athletic dropout rate is not that extraordinary.[10] The question is, can anything be done to reduce the waste in resources that arises from any students failing to graduate? And what about the particularly high dropout rates in graduate studies, where marginal instructional costs are high?

Some college dropouts will occur under almost any circumstance, and are not reducible by policy changes. Family financial circumstances change; students become seriously ill. Yet some of the high dropout rate may be the result of existing university policies. Some students are accepted despite warning signs that they will not succeed (such as low ACT or SAT scores or mediocre high school grades) because universities increasingly apply nonacademic criteria to their admissions decisions. Race and gender are not the only such criteria considered. Other things being equal, students who handle a ball well are accepted more often than those who cannot. Students who work in after-school volunteer programs are often preferred to those who read books and go to museums—even though the latter, slightly more "nerdy," students may have a greater probability of academic success.

Many students are frustrated because of the huge number of closeouts from required classes, which sometimes necessitates their taking another year or two to complete college in order to meet highly detailed requirements in their majors—perhaps too detailed for persons seeking a general undergraduate education. Since some universities receive state subsidies based on the number of students attending class, keeping them around for five or six years is actually fairly remunerative. Certainly, the incentives to graduate students in four years are fairly weak.

I am a bit surprised that state governments do not simply stop paying subsidies for students for more than four full-time-equivalent academic years. While a case can be made for public support of a basic undergraduate education, students who take lots of courses beyond those necessary to obtain their degrees are arguably somewhat frivolously using public resources. In the case of doctoral degrees, more than four years of public support is similarly indefensible. Too often universities put lots of marginal requirements on these adult learners, who often are supporting families. Dissertation advisers send students off on marginally interesting tangents that take months upon months of the students' time. No one has any incentive to force students to work in a disciplined fashion over a very well-defined, limited time span.

State governments probably should impose that discipline externally by tying funding to "productivity," which means graduating doctoral students (outputs) after a limited number of years in school. As funding pressures grow, I expect mandates of these kinds will be increasingly common.

Indeed, as some schools have successfully demonstrated, a record of getting students through a given degree program in a finite and reasonable period of time enhances the popularity of that program. Universities can improve their recruitment of students by forcing some discipline on faculty to teach the required courses for majors (rather than whatever the faculty member wants to teach), to pressure students to finish projects on time, and to move the students out of the program within a reasonable time period (four years for a BA degree, perhaps four to five years for a PhD). Administrations interested in efficiency should reward units that achieve these objectives, and punish those that do not.

An excellent way to get students to graduate in a reasonable period of time is to reduce the periods of leisure and idleness that characterize university campuses. Most campuses are nearly deserted for around four months a year, and at many schools Friday classes are a rarity. Aside from leading to a gross underutilization of capital resources such as classrooms and laboratories, this promotes the idleness and party atmosphere that are becoming increasingly serious problems at even reasonably high-quality institutions.

State governments may start to reformulate their funding formulas to provide incentives for both students and faculty to work harder in summer months, to have Friday classes, and the like. Special scholarships for summer school attendance, for example, would greatly increase the year-round utilization of human- and physical-capital facilities.

Issues of Academic Quality, Standards, and Scholarly Openness. Traditional universities and liberal arts colleges differentiate themselves from community colleges, online universities, and for-profit schools by claiming to offer a different, superior product. They project the image that their standards are higher and their learning more intense; that they are the training grounds for the "best and the brightest." Yet as the costs of these schools rise relative to the alternatives, more individuals might decide to forgo some prestige and rigor, reasoning that "a degree is a degree."

More than ever, universities must present themselves not just as places that feed information to students, but as learning communities where ideas are manufactured and disseminated in an exhilarating fashion and standards are high. Fighting grade inflation and attempts to stifle freedom of expression are highly desirable pursuits in terms of meeting the traditional goals of higher education, and I suspect they are good marketing tools as well.

Accordingly, I expect we should see some pressure on the part of university administrations (at times prodded by boards of trustees or even state legislatures) to reverse the decline in the use of the grading system as an evaluative device and to stifle heavy-handed attempts to enforce politically correct expression through speech codes and other erosions of academic freedom.

Change University Governance. Some observers of universities believe a good deal of their inefficiency arises from the very awkward and expensive ways in which decisions are made. Three groups are important in decision-making at most universities: the governing board (most often, a board of trustees), the administration, and the faculty. At state universities, the governor/legislature/state governing board often plays a major role; at private universities, prominent (wealthy) alumni are often key players.

Turning first to the traditional self-contained university with a single major campus, inefficiency, low productivity, and resistance to change among the employed university community can be overcome by leadership from boards of trustees. A good board will take its oversight function seriously, nudge administrations into cutting costs, and put brakes on expensive efforts at university self-aggrandizement. Such a board would use its business expertise to prod the institution into following more business-like, market-disciplined modes of behavior. It would insist that technology enhancements be cost-reducing and administrators be rewarded for noninstructional staff reductions, would put pressure on staff to get rid of expensive small graduate programs, and so forth.

There are two problems in attaining this ideal. First, most trustees are part-time, busy persons who are easily co-opted by the university administration. They hear one side of every debate (typically), they are wined and dined by the president and his or her close advisers, and they have little time to study the broader issues of higher education as outlined in books such as this one. Moreover, they have few independent resources to verify the information provided them. Truly independent auditors or inspector generals who report directly to the trustees provide one solution to this problem, but not an inexpensive one. Second, while the need for some oversight is desirable, there is sometimes a tendency for trustees to become too involved, interfering in day-to-day decision-making about which they have little training. Finding the right mix between being ineffectual "stooges" of the administration and being overbearing tyrants who disrupt orderly governance is easier said than done.

At the other end of the hierarchy, the faculty, especially at prestigious universities, believe they are the heart of the university and should run it. Yet they are extremely self-interested observers who tend to resist needed change, particularly when it would change their comfortable ways of doing their jobs. It is particularly undesirable for faculty to play a significant role in decision-making that is not purely academic, such as deciding whether to construct building A or B or raise tuition by 4 or 6 percent. On the other hand, it seems appropriate to give faculty members a significant say, perhaps a dominant one, on purely academic issues such as deciding on the content of required general education courses or whether to hire Professor A or Professor B. Even there, however, the administration needs to be able to veto moves that are clearly dictated purely by self-interest instead of objective evaluation of the educational merits of the issue.

State universities typically face a significant amount of "governing" from above, either from a broader university system administration and governing board (as in the case of the University of California, the state university system in California, or the State University of New York), from the legislature and governor in the form of mandates, or from a board of regents or other coordinating board with a similar name. Decision-making from the state capital or other distant location more often than not tends to be self-defeating, in my judgment robbing the local universities of the flexibility to deal with problems in the manner best befitting the unique institutional environment. At the same time, some coordinating decisions made by boards of regents or political leaders, such as forcing reductions in graduate programs, probably have had some positive impact although I prefer giving the institutions some flexibility as to how they reduce costs. Moreover, competition between, say, PhD programs, often condemned as "wasteful duplication," in some cases spurs excellence, as the programs compete for better students, offer better instruction, and so on.

In general, I am dubious that changing organizational and governance arrangements can have dramatic impacts on universities, whose behavior is largely constrained by the nonmarket, nonprofit environment in which they operate. Having said that, however, my sense is that decentralization on balance is usually preferable to decisions about university operations mandated by distant politicians or bureaucracies.

The British Experience. The United States is not unique in facing financing problems in higher education. Britain is undergoing a significant overhaul of its system of higher education in the face of cost strains and other issues. For example, the huge rise in higher education participation that came to the United States after World War II—possibly earlier—arrived in Britain after 1980. In the past two decades, total funding for higher education has risen sharply, but per-student spending in real terms has actually fallen as the enrollment explosion has strained university budgets.

Responding to these financial pressures and facing potential revenue shortfalls of billions of dollars over the next few years, the British central government, which controls higher education to a vastly greater extent than is the case in the United States, has ordered substantial changes, in large part influenced by the ideas of Nicholas Barr, a professor at the London School of Economics.[11] Among other things, student fees, now very low, will nearly triple. Faculty salaries will be based on a performance-based rewards system, enrollments will increase, and teaching loads will rise at nonresearch-oriented institutions, while expectations for research output will virtually vanish.

Perhaps the most controversial part of the plan is to introduce government loans to students to finance education. The notion of students having to finance their own educations is repellent to many in the Labour Party majority that constitutes the current (Blair) government, whose leadership ironically is proposing the changes. The Blair government's very existence was threatened in early 2004 over this issue. Unlike loans in the United States, the United Kingdom loan repayments will be scaled to income after graduation—graduates who are financially more successful will repay more.

Conclusions

Faced with the likely necessity of curbing tuition growth in coming years, universities will have to end the productivity decline that has characterized modern higher education and take other steps to prevent students from seeking alternative ways of learning and certifying themselves as vocationally competent. While market forces do not operate as vigorously in the nonprofit university sector as in private business, universities are not immune from market forces and financial pressures.

Accordingly, with the passage of time, universities can be expected to take steps to reduce costs and make themselves more efficient. The late twentieth-century reduction in teaching loads may not only end but may be reversed. Tenure will come under intensified attack. Academic programs that have low enrollments or provide training for which there is little social demand will come under greater scrutiny. Technology will finally be used more to reduce labor costs, not merely "enrich" instruction. More universities' services will be contracted out to private, for-profit specialists who can provide them more cheaply; conceivably, that approach might even be applied to some forms of instruction. The scandal in big-time college athletics possibly will be dealt with, either legislatively or, preferably, by concerted action by some of the nation's academic leaders. As cost pressures mount, manifestations of political correctness, such as the abundance of diversity coordinators and others enforcing a racially, gender-correct mixture of students and faculty, may be partially or wholly abandoned on cost grounds. Universities may experiment with different ways of making staff accountable, including increased participation by trustees in university governance. Slowly, painfully, and controversially, universities will take some steps to make themselves more affordable.

10

An Alternative Scenario: Systemic Reform

The pace and pattern of change in higher education may move faster than likely from the largely internally generated incremental reforms suggested in chapter 9. A good case can be made for largely removing public subsidies for higher education, making institutions mostly private. Absent that, an alternative approach may be to channel more aid directly to students in the form of scholarships (vouchers), reducing institutional subsidies. This likely would stimulate competition, make universities hesitate more about raising tuition, and refocus emphasis on serving undergraduates. Tying vouchers to student performance could improve learning and reduce problems of retention. An alternative approach would be to enact more regulations and tax reforms designed to alter university behavior. Examples include putting price controls on tuition, taxing tuition, tying subsidy support to efficiency gains, and mandating higher teaching loads or an end to tenure. I present arguments suggesting that the market-based approach is preferable to the regulatory one in dealing with the cost explosion in higher education.

A Tale of Two Paradigms

In the last chapter, I suggested that rising tuition would lead to greater resistance from the consumers of higher education, and that state legislators, private donors, and others might reduce the rate of increase in their largess. All of this would lead to universities gradually and reluctantly reforming themselves. Universities would become more cost-conscious and efficient, but their basic nature and missions would remain fundamentally unchanged. There would be some battles along the way—faculty might, for instance, try to fight changes by unionizing—but ultimately the economics would force some change. The availability of alternatives to current delivery systems, such as for-profit schools, online education, and private certification programs, would make students more price-sensitive, and spur some meaningful changes in the ways universities do business.

Under this first scenario, change would be directed in large part internally—the decisions would come from within the academy. A second possibility is change directed from outside, by those who provide the third-party funding presently financing a large majority of the typical, traditional, four-year university's budget.

To this point, the response of governments to the rising cost of education has been largely to throw more money at the problem. Recall the vicious circle. Tuition charges rise, so the public complains loudly. The federal government increases guaranteed student loans and other programs to help students finance the rising cost of attending college, while state governments increase subsidies to universities. More financial aid increases the demand for higher education, enabling universities to raise prices further. With no profit-based "bottom line," universities try to maximize their income or their prestige—the latter often pursued by spending more money to improve their standings in the *USN&WR* or other ratings. The universities then increase spending more, necessitating still further tuition increases.

Yet as the ratio of the cost of higher education to people's incomes and wealth continues to grow, governmental authorities may start realizing that the previous "solutions" are not working because nothing is being done to deal with the root cause of the problem. They might start trying other things, perhaps throwing less, not more, money to the universities, forcing them into quicker internal reforms than would otherwise have occurred. The fund reductions to universities following the 2001 recession may have been a harbinger of things to come.

Government might go further than merely reducing funds, directing certain changes (perhaps by mandates, perhaps by providing financial incentives) from outside the academy. The people paying most of the bills (the general taxpaying public) may become more assertive. The probability of this happening is enhanced by taxpayers' reluctance to pay higher taxes at the same time that other needs—particularly in the area of health care, but also with respect to primary and secondary education, corrections, and so forth—are crowding out the funds available to higher education.

Externally directed reform could take two fundamentally different forms. One approach would be for state governments, probably working through coordinating boards such as boards of regents, to mandate certain cost savings, or at least to make spending reductions more attractive to schools by tying subsidy payments to progress in implementing certain cost-saving practices. This would be a step toward greater centralization of higher education resource allocation. The second approach would be to go in the opposite direction, increasingly directing funds not to universities, but to students themselves. This could have interesting implications for the various activities undertaken on American college campuses, including research. Indeed, it could ultimately lead to the privatization of state universities. We will discuss this option first.

Before proceeding, however, it should be noted that there are all types of institutions of higher education, and many motives for attending or funding them. The coming changes in higher education will probably affect some types of colleges and universities more dramatically than others. For example, I would expect the most prestigious private universities to be less severely affected than, say, the medium-quality state institutions. The elite schools have six or eight applicants for every opening, and as income rises over time, the demand to buy prestige (in the form of attendance at a top university) is probably highly income-elastic. As families become more affluent, they want to direct disproportionately more of their incremental income toward buying access to financial success and good social standing for their progeny.

Therefore, the demand for higher education will rise faster for the schools in, say, the top twenty-five in the USN&WR rankings than for others. Thus, the Harvards and Stanfords of the world will be able to raise their tuition more than other schools and maintain their positions of leadership. For such schools, the online institution or local for-profit university center is not a serious competing substitute. High ($50,000 or even $100,000) tuition will not deter applicants—or at least not enough to keep these schools from fielding classes of relatively well-qualified students. Just as people spend far more lavishly than they did even a couple of decades ago on large houses, luxury cars, club memberships, and other conspicuous forms of luxury, so they will spend more on colleges. Harvard, Yale, Princeton, and other elite institutions offer what economists call a "superior good."

That is less true of, say, Slippery Rock University, a medium-quality institution that accepts most applicants and faces perhaps serious erosion in their numbers if costs rise too much. In an increasingly affluent society, the demand for Slippery Rock (and other secondary state institutions) may be income-inelastic, or even have a negative income elasticity—as people grow wealthier, they want to avoid the Slippery Rocks and send their kids to schools perceived to be of better quality. Already, there are some signs that that has happened with community colleges—they are perceived as "inferior goods," much as bus transportation is an "inferior good" while private jet travel is a "superior good." Harvard is the private-jet equivalent in higher education; the local community college may be the bus transportation, and the mainline state universities are somewhere in between, as are most private liberal arts colleges below the top ranks.

The Optimal Solution: Defund Higher Education. Recall from the discussion in the early chapters that there is actually very little evidence that governmental subsidization of higher education is beneficial. Even the most favorable evidence suggests that many previously observed positive externalities of higher education have become internalized as the earnings differential between high school and college graduates has risen. The big beneficiaries of universities are the students themselves. The correlation between university funding and economic growth is negative; governmental funding does very little to increase student access; people tend to migrate out of states with a tradition of strong governmental support of schools. College students are woefully ignorant of basic cultural facts that might justify some subsidies on the grounds that they promote production of the intellectual glue that binds us together as a culture, a nation, and a civilization. Universities today may well have greater negative than positive externalities. This provides a strong case simply to defund universities by gradually withdrawing state subsidies, and, in the reauthorization of the federal Higher Education Act, to end most federal grants as well.

The Second-Best Solution: Reduce Public Support. Although defunding is a worthy goal of reformers, and despite growing concern about some excesses of higher education, a complete withdrawal of governments from university life is unlikely to occur in the near future. The benefits of subsidies are concentrated among the university community and their costs disbursed among the taxpaying public. Public-choice theory tells us that under such conditions, the special interests—in this case public universities with strong lobbies—are likely to emerge triumphant. Therefore, reform of higher education is likely to take some "second-best" approach. That second-best approach likely will involve a transitional period (which may be quite long), where public financial support of higher education declines. What is the second-best approach that will enhance the general welfare most—or inhibit it least?

The First Paradigm:
Scholarships (Voucherization) and Privatization

As any university president will tell you, institutions of higher education spend every dollar they receive. The "marginal propensity to consume" out of income is one. In years of rapidly rising revenues, schools usually squirrel a little money away in reserve accounts, and they spend it in years of fiscal austerity; but little in incremental funds goes to contain costs to customers or enhance endowments (unless explicitly earmarked by donors). Under one set of assumptions, by directly reducing the inflow of funds to college campuses, governments can reduce their spending growth. An alternative approach would be to mandate certain outcomes directly, constraining the freedom of universities to manage as they see fit.

By strictly controlling third-party funding, governments can almost certainly force a reduction in the rate of growth in tuition and per-capita real spending, and in the process nudge universities into taking some of the cost-containment measures discussed in chapter 9. At the same time, they might wish to try to deal with universities' seeming neglect of undergraduate instruction. One promising approach, first suggested by Milton Friedman over forty years ago, would be to move funding away from the producers (the universities themselves) and toward the consumers, giving students vouchers redeemable toward tuition at state universities and, perhaps, all other institutions, public or private.[1] In the fullest extension of this approach, "state universities" as such would be abolished, and all of higher education (with a few minor exceptions perhaps, such as the service academies) would be privatized.

To illustrate how this might work, let us use a simple example—one too simple to be completely realistic, but realistic enough to drive a point home. Looking for the moment at funding just of state colleges and universities, let us assume that a mid-size state has three types of public institutions of higher education: one moderately prestigious flagship public research university, somewhat selective in its admissions; several somewhat smaller but fairly comprehensive state universities less oriented toward research; and a series of community colleges. This nicely describes states like Washington, Colorado, and Tennessee. Let us assume that, currently, the flagship state university spends $20,000 for each of its thirty-five thousand full-time-equivalent students, or a total of $700 million. This figure excludes break-even commercial operations, such as dormitories and dining halls, and research grants, mostly federally funded (which might easily represent an additional $200 million or more). Let us assume that $6,000 of that $20,000 per-student expenditure (30 percent) comes from tuition and related charges, $9,000 (45 percent) comes from state subsidies, and $5,000 (25 percent) comes from other sources, such as endowment incomes, donations, and royalty payments.

Let us assume the other universities collectively spend $16,000 per student (excluding commercial operations and funded research) on seventy thousand students, or $1.12 billion, with $6,000 per student funded by tuition, $6,000 by state subsidies, and $4,000 from other income, such as grants or gifts. Finally, let us assume that community colleges spend $9,000 for each of forty-five thousand students ($405 million total), of which $3,500 comes from tuition, $4,500 from state subsidies, and $1,000 from other income. All told, one hundred and fifty thousand students are attending universities that receive $937.5 million in state funding, or an average of $6,250 per full-time-equivalent student.

Let us also assume that federal student loan and scholarship programs remain at current levels of funding on a per-student basis, correcting for general inflation. Let us now take all subsidy monies currently given to

universities directly and give them to students in the form of vouchers—
$9,000 vouchers at the flagship university, $6,000 for the other universities,
and $4,500 for the community colleges—and allow the universities to raise
their tuition by any amount, with the presumption that most will raise them
by the amount of revenue lost from the end of subsidies (that is, the amount
of the voucher).

Initially, the impact on students and universities of this change would
be almost close to zero, as total university funding would remain unchanged,
along with the out-of-pocket costs to consumers of university services.
Over time, however, the value of student vouchers would rise only with
the rate of inflation, and student loan aid likewise would be frozen in
real enrollment-adjusted terms. Thus, *universities could not increase their real
per-student spending except by raising costs to the consumers themselves or getting larger gifts from donors or grants for research.* Paying tuition at five-digit
levels and providing a majority of university funding, students would
become more price-sensitive—and their money would be far more critical
than before. The notion of "consumer sovereignty" would come to higher
education. Universities would be far less cavalier than at present about closing students out of classes, offering classes taught by graduate students
barely literate in English, and continuing other dubious practices common
at the present.

Would tuition rates continue to rise faster than inflation? It is impossible to say with certainty, but with the incremental burden falling directly on
students and their taxpaying parents and their sensitivity to price increasing, my hunch is that institutions would become constrained in their ability
to raise tuition by much more than the inflation rate. While it is possible
that universities might act in an implicit or explicit cartel fashion to try to
increase fees faster, I suspect the probability of this tactic being successful is
not high.

Moreover, the voucher plan could be modified to incorporate other
dimensions of public policy regarding higher education, such as issues of
access. Even with a $9,000 voucher, attendance at the $15,000-tuition flagship state university is very expensive for low-income families. Currently,
discounting in the form of scholarships is practiced to ease that problem. If
desired, as a condition of winning political support from some constituencies skeptical of vouchers at the K–12 level, the size of vouchers could be

means-tested. For example, the value of the voucher for attending the flag-ship university, while averaging $9,000, could be varied from $3,000 to $15,000, depending on family economic circumstance.[2]

Political considerations aside, it might be argued that giving large subsidy payments to provide income-enhancing educations to the children of affluent professional or managerial workers is a dubious use of public funds in any case. Given how questionable positive externalities in higher education have earlier been shown to be, the case for providing subsidies at all is already somewhat suspect. However, the income differential associated with college training may justify subsidies of those disadvantaged by economic circumstance on the grounds of income redistribution and equity. The "progressive voucher" approach, pursued aggressively, would improve access of low-income individuals to college, yet be revenue-neutral to the colleges themselves. It would essentially end the need for state universities to give need-based scholarships and presumably reduce tuition-discounting, making the financing of higher education more transparent and uniform.

The voucher approach also would sharply reduce the perception that state governing bodies (such as boards of regents) need to regulate the university system. Since the universities would not be receiving state money of any kind directly, the oversight previously provided by governments could be more efficiently provided by the marketplace: If a university were to behave abysmally, it would pay the price, as budgets suffered from declining enrollments. This "site-based management" approach encouraged by vouchers has been found in other levels of education to work better on average than centrally directed decision-making.[3]

The idea of vouchers for higher education is, of course, not a new one. The GI Bill, first approved in 1944, gave money to students, not institutions, and allowed them to go wherever they wanted—public or private school, religiously oriented or nonsectarian. Similarly, federal loans and grants, such as Pell Grants, are directed toward students, not institutions. Some states have scholarship programs of modest size already in place.

Moving state funding from institutions to students (with $2400 vouchers) is actually happening, beginning in 2005, in Colorado. In that state, strict constitutional spending limits under the Taxpayer Bill of Rights (TABOR) have constrained total state university spending, including the part funded by tuition. Since vouchers will be directed to students, that spending possibly will not count against the constitutional limits on spending by state agencies. These conditions led presidents of major Colorado universities to support the voucher approach successfully.[4]

Vouchers are no panacea, however, and detractors cite problems that might develop. An increased sensitivity of universities to the concerns of their primary instructional customers—students and their parents—could lead to a neglect of the research function. America's primacy in university research, which has led to U.S. domination of the Nobel Prize awards and acknowledged world leadership in basic research, could decline.

There is no reason, however, that research should suffer, at least not initially. If voucher size is related to existing state subsidy levels, the vouchers will incorporate the higher per-student funding levels associated with high levels of research intensity. For example, instructional costs per student are higher in large universities not because of smaller class size, but because professors have lighter teaching loads, usually reflecting the fact that they are doing more research. Subsidy levels currently reflect this, so implicitly taxpayers are financing in part the research activities of the leading research universities. Moreover, a large portion of research is independently funded by government agencies like the National Institutes of Health, and by private businesses. That funding would not be affected by the change in the state subsidy-tuition system.

In a conversation with me, former Secretary of Education William Bennett, a strong proponent of vouchers at the K–12 level, raised a second objection, which he succinctly summed up with a question: "What would happen to the Classics Department?"[5] By that, Bennett meant that areas of low enrollment but considerable importance to our heritage as a civilization would be neglected and suffer a loss of funds, as universities, in their quest for efficiency and to provide students with what they want, reallocated funds away from the humanities. This is a valid issue.

From a strictly empirical point of view, a decline in the humanities has already occurred to a considerable extent *without* vouchers. Under the status quo, that erosion is likely to continue. Already, universities internally allocate resources in large part according to student interest. Also, the implicit assumption that classics education (and education in other disciplines in the humanities and social sciences, like philosophy and history) will disappear because of its unpopularity is dubious at best. First of all, many universities have moderately flourishing departments in these areas. For example, at the moment of this writing, my university's classics department (which recently also took in world religions, presumably for administrative efficiency reasons given the small number of faculty in each discipline), has over 180 students in Latin and Greek classes, plus more than 200 others in world religion courses. Excellent instructors are teaching a respectable number of students in classics at a cost per student not radically out of line with other disciplines (particularly given the modest salary levels for instructors in this area). I suspect my university is far from unique. My guess is that voucherization would do little to classics education (or that of allied humanities) that is not happening already.

When I posed Bennett's question to the father of the voucher approach, Milton Friedman, he replied:

> I think we can say that if the market won't support a classics department, I have very little doubt that private beneficence would do so. Private philanthropy supports art institutes, ballet, opera. Why should it not be capable of supporting a classics department if there are many people who feel the way Bill Bennett does?[6]

As usual, Professor Friedman's logic is impeccable.

Transitional Issues with Voucherization. Although a quick conversion to full voucherization could be done without immediate radical changes in the overall budgets of affected universities, concern about such a significant shift would probably lead individuals to resist it unless it were phased in less abruptly. A five- or ten-year phase-in, for example, would give universities and people some time to adjust, acknowledging the fact that many university costs are fixed in the short run (in part because of tenure).

Suppose we were to phase in vouchers over ten years, holding state support per student constant in real terms over that entire period. Suppose we were to take a typical mid-size university receiving $6,000 in subsidies per student and begin the program immediately, assuming 2 percent inflation. If we removed the subsidy and converted it to vouchers in a linear fashion over ten years, each year $600 less per student in direct subsidy payments would be provided to the university. This year, the direct subsidy would be $5,400, and the students would receive a voucher worth $600. Next year, the direct subsidy would be $4,800, and the students would receive $1,320 (giving the inflation adjustment entirely to the student). In the third year, the direct subsidy payments to the university would be $4,200, while the student voucher would be $2,042.

By this stage, the university would already be far more tuition- (and voucher-) driven in terms of revenues than it was before the program began. Some would persist in complaining that the funding formula threatened the existence of the institution (largely because of forced efficiencies arising from a stagnation in total real per-student funding levels). But the complaints would be somewhat reduced by the certainty implicit in such a phased-in approach that still-critical state subsidy funding, though diminishing, would continue.

Ultimate Privatization. In a world where no subsidies are paid by state governments to universities for instructional costs, to what extent are universities "public" or "state" in nature? Only in a very limited way. The "state" universities benefit in that only they are eligible to receive students' vouchers, giving them an advantage over other institutions.

The question then arises, why not let students go anywhere they want to college? Why should public policy favor students attending university X, which is "public," over those going to university Y, which is "private"? Would not fairness and equity allow all students, not merely those attending historically state-funded schools, to receive funding from the state? Would not the government better serve the welfare of the citizenry by creating a level playing field, allowing students to exercise unlimited free choice in institutions attended, including, perhaps, institutions located out of state?

State universities would fiercely fight a system of vouchers usable at any institution, arguing that private schools have large endowments that substitute for state institutional subsidies. Yet that argument, while generally true, is trumped, in my judgment, by the fact that universities exist to serve the welfare of the citizenry, and that welfare would be ill-served if the choice of where to attend college were distorted by the state's subsidizing attendance at some institutions and not others.

Again, a transitional scheme could be devised that gradually opens up vouchers for universal use, allowing universities that are presently state institutions to adjust to the impact of subsidy-broadening. For example, if $6,000 vouchers were provided to attendees at four-year state universities, over a period of five years vouchers could be extended to all institutions, with those for private schools equaling 20 percent of those of public universities in the first year, 40 percent in the second year, and so forth. Also, during a transitional period, the state would continue to provide capital improvement funds for traditional state institutions, but not private schools.

Under such a scheme, within a few years the "public" and "private" distinction would become meaningless. To ease their angst over the inclusion of private schools, the public universities should be freed of close oversight; indeed, coordinating or governing boards over multiple institutions, such as boards of regents, should be dissolved. The reduction in regulation in some states would be of great value to these institutions, particularly where the state-level governing board exercises close control, such as in the California state university system. Within a decade or so of implementing a voucher approach, we truly could privatize state universities and allow students an unlimited choice of institutions.

The cost of extending vouchers to private school participants would vary sharply by state, as the level of private school participation would vary greatly—it would be high in eastern states with a strong private university tradition, perhaps, and lower in areas with few private schools. If the funding of private schools were gradually introduced, the incremental annual cost of funding would not be onerous, and inflation-adjusted subsidies would probably rise no more than at present (since the assumption is that vouchers per student would be kept constant in real terms).

Making vouchers progressive would address another objection to their use, namely that the idea itself is highly regressive, taking funds from the general taxpaying public and giving them to generally affluent kids attending private schools. Under progressive vouchers, the highly affluent students would receive relatively little (perhaps even zero), and those most economically disadvantaged would receive much more. By providing those from lower socioeconomic backgrounds with currently unavailable public assistance to attend first-rate private schools, the goal of greater educational access and economic opportunity would be served.

One further objection, raised by some engaged in the voucher debate at the primary and secondary education level, is that private school participation in voucher programs potentially will compromise the advantages that the "private" status provides. State governments will increase their regulatory grasp over private universities, which might also raise costs. For example, a university might be required to agree to pay "prevailing wages" on construction projects as a condition for participation in the voucher program. Certainly, that would be a disadvantageous outcome.

The experience with the GI Bill and other scholarship programs administered previously by the federal government suggests that fears here are overblown. In any case, a good argument can be made that the obvious advantages to students of greater university access and choice outweigh this rather theoretical disadvantage.[7]

The Second Paradigm:
Other Regulatory and Financial Options

The switch of public financial support from the producer to the consumer of education services might appear too radical for some, even if it is implemented over a significant transitional period. An alternative approach is for state governments to impose new rules or regulations on universities designed to reduce spending, or provide financial incentives for them to engage in cost-cutting. Such an approach has a danger of leading to excessive bureaucratic interference in university affairs, reducing the entrepreneurial initiative of individual institutions and creating distortions in the allocation of resources. However, it is likely to prove popular with politicians wishing to show they are "doing something" about the rising costs of attending college.

Price Controls. An approach used in some states, including my own, is for either the legislature or a statewide governing board to set tuition levels for all institutions (strong version), or place caps on the size of tuition increases decided upon by each institution (weaker version). To be meaningful, the permitted tuition levels are lower than what universities themselves would have established on their own.

As with any kind of price control, this approach has its problems. Rigid control of tuition levels might lead universities to deny access to some students, as the mandated fee will be below the market-clearing one. Price controls universally create shortages, and higher education is no exception. Alternatively, universities will try to circumvent the fee limits either by reducing the quality of the offerings or by charging fees for activities currently provided "free," such as use of recreational facilities. The assessing of "technology fees" has grown exponentially in recent years, in part to circumvent limits on tuition growth.

Another way to evade tuition caps is to charge instructional fees at the individual college level on top of the basic university fee. Where uniform fees are established for all campuses of a large university (such as the University of California), or for various independent universities in a multi-institutional system, market forces are not allowed to work efficiently. The high-demand school will be forced to turn many students away (more than it perhaps wants to), while the low-demand schools may well have below-optimal (from their perspective) enrollments. Individual institutions should be encouraged to engage in price competition, not be prohibited from it.

Tax Tuition. In an e-mail to this author discussed in an earlier chapter, Milton Friedman mused that instead of subsidizing instruction at universities, the government perhaps, on net, should tax them.[8] An approach I find preferable to tuition price controls is for state governments to reduce subsidies to universities that raise their tuition levels a lot, lowering the revenue gain from such increases but not prohibiting them. Suppose university X charges $6,000 in in-state tuition. Suppose the state imposes a tax, payable by the university, of 50 percent of any tuition increase in excess of, say the annual increase over the past 12 months in the Consumer Price Index for All Urban Consumers (Consumer Price Index-U, or CPI-U, the Bureau of Labor Statistics index most often used to gauge inflation in the United States). Suppose the CPI-U rises 2 percent. University X could raise its tuition by $120 (2 percent) without paying a tax. If it chose to raise it by $300, however, it would have to pay the state a payment equal to $90 per student (one-half of $300 minus $120). Since universities typically increase student financial aid by 10 or 20 percent or more of incremental tuition, the tuition tax would sharply limit revenue gains from raising tuition.

A variant on the model above would be to increase subsidies to universities that raise tuition *less* than the rise in the CPI-U (or whatever the base chosen). If university X in the above example froze tuition at the previous year's level, for example, it would receive 50 percent of the permissible ($120) tuition increase per student in added state assistance. For most state universities, to freeze tuition (or come close to that) would require some cost reduction from normal practice. The subsidy/tax could have some positive impact on cost containment, albeit in a somewhat bureaucratic, one-size-fits-all approach imposed from above.

End State-Subsidized Prepaid Tuition Plans. A significant number of states have created plans that allow individuals to buy tuition credits in advance. Each credit pays for, say, one semester of tuition at any university in the state. These plans issue an open invitation to universities to raise tuition, and to engage in all sorts of chicanery in doing so. Students with ample prepurchased credits have a perfectly inelastic demand for university education with respect to price. The tuition is irrelevant to the student, since the state has guaranteed it will cover the cost for a given time period. When the proportion of students with such plans is large, universities have enormous incentives to raise tuition substantially. In 2003, Miami University, a highly selective Ohio school, announced that it was eliminating the tuition differential between in- and out-of-state students, raising the fee for in-state students from the current $7,600 to the out-of-state rate (currently $16,324), and giving generous scholarships to in-state students. It is my suspicion that the reason for this is that Miami plans to bill students on the state's prepaid tuition credit plan the full fee, thus enhancing its revenues without hurting students.[9]

Change Tax Benefits. A whole host of tax benefits has contributed to the sharp increase in tuition costs at both public and private institutions. Tuition tax credits administered federally and in some states have lowered the tax liability of families sending children to college, increasing demand for university education and raising tuition. One way to put the brakes on surging tuition would be to reverse the process, reducing or eliminating such tax benefits and making families far more sensitive to price in college selection.

States or the federal government could use the threat of tax credit elimination as a way of moderating tuition increases, forcing universities into some of the cost-containment measures discussed in the previous chapter. One approach would be to restrict eligibility for tax credit relief to students attending those universities that have raised tuition less than X percent over the previous year, or perhaps over the previous three years (or both). Universities would have powerful incentives to make the list of eligible institutions.

An alternative (or additional) tax-related approach involves tax deductions for charitable contributions. Why should individuals giving money to universities that are sharply increasing their prices pay lower taxes than otherwise financially identical individuals who make no such contributions, or who make contributions to schools whose commitment to affordability is demonstrated by modest tuition increases over time? To be sure, some university contributions go to finance non-instructional missions, such as worthy research efforts like finding cures for cancer, or college sports, so tying tax deductibility solely to policies relating to instruction is a questionable strategy (although an out-and-out prohibition on tax deductions for contributions to support college athletics might be justifiable by itself, given the often scandalous commercialization of intercollegiate athletics).

As universities build ever-more luxurious facilities to lure students and provide tax-free enjoyments for university staff, the case for subsidizing those activities through favorable tax treatments becomes highly suspect. Why should a person giving funds for a fancy recreational center, stadium loges, or a student union building at an expensive university get a tax deduction? Why is this use of funds favored over giving money to build a new clubhouse at an upscale country club?

Subsidy Reduction or Realignment. As the federal and state governments face growing financial pressures arising from the inefficient health care delivery system and demographic changes (such as an aging population, or, in some states, rapidly growing young immigrant communities), the temptation on the part of states is to reduce the rate of growth in university subsidy support. Previously I argued that the case for support is intellectually and empirically rather weak. Therefore, I would not be surprised if state support for higher education grows fairly tepidly over the next decade or so, and possibly even falls on a real per-student basis.

This development would, in turn, increase the desire on the part of university administrations to raise fees even more. In the long run, however, as tuition rises relative to income levels, the price-elasticity of demand for traditional higher education will almost certainly also rise, particularly in the face of proliferating substitutes, such as private certification, for-profit schools, and online learning. As customers become more price-conscious, universities will, reluctantly to be sure, be forced into cost-saving reforms such as those suggested in the previous chapter.

Consumers already are showing a rising sensitivity to price as tuition goes higher. For example, in fall 2003, Ohio's institutions of higher education, like those around the country, raised tuition far more than typically.[10] The increases were greatest at the four-year residential universities. As a consequence, enrollment at the main campuses of those institutions was barely changed from the previous year (up 0.5 percent), while enrollment at the low-cost community colleges and university branch campuses increased proportionally seven times as much (over 3.6 percent).[11] As the absolute and relative price differential between the high-cost and low-cost alternatives grew, more students picked the low-cost option.

In some states, the government gives largely lump-sum grants to the universities, while in many others the subsidy is determined by a formula, often somewhat elaborate. By tinkering with the formula, state governments can force some changes in the way universities do business. For example, if there is a general perception that the push for research has gone too far and is yielding low marginal returns on the investment, a state could sharply lower subsidies per doctoral student while raising them for undergraduates, putting some pressure on schools to get rid of expensive, low-demand graduate education and give more attention to undergraduates.

Mandated Cost Reductions. Rather than try to effect change by altering revenue streams in a way that they hope will lead to more cost-conscious behavior, states might directly mandate certain forms of cost reductions. They might, for example,

- Forbid the granting of tenure, or require rigorous post-tenure review.

- Mandate minimum teaching loads for all faculty members, or a stated average teaching load, allowing some flexibility for individual faculty members.

- Limit administrative staff, insisting, for example, that the number of support staff not exceed the number of full-time-equivalent faculty members.

- Forbid the continuance of doctoral programs with fewer than five full-time resident students, or ones that graduate fewer than five students over a five-year period.

- Limit university subsidies to intercollegiate athletics, including private donations, to 2 percent of the instructional budget, with severe financial penalties for violating the rule.

- Limit overseas travel of university administrators, or the purchase of luxury cars, university aircraft, or posh SUVs, even with privately provided funds.

To ease the pain of complying with such rules, special compensation increases for those institutions that successfully implement them might be provided as a carrot to go along with the stick of state regulations.

I would not be surprised to see moves along these lines implemented as angry legislators seek to "do something" about rising tuition costs. And, no doubt, some of the mandates suggested would be cost-reducing and maybe even desirable on other grounds. At the same time, however, I view this as a distinctly less-desirable, second-best approach to reinventing college education.

Why? Top-down mandates fail to take into account particular conditions and traditions of institutions, and thus often prove counterproductive. If the legislature mandates that all professors shall teach two courses per term, Professor X, an eminent scholar hired as a research scholar with an expectation that he will teach one course every other year, might leave on the grounds that the mandate violates the conditions of his employment contract. State-imposed mandates are often inconsistent with the imperatives of the academic marketplace. If the legislature states that "average teaching loads shall equal nine credit-hours per week," universities will do interesting things in defining what an "hour" is, for example, giving four credit-hours for a class that meets three hours per week. (Actually, the three hours is more likely three fifty-minute lectures, or two and a half hours, according to the nonacademic definition of "hours.") The small school with twelve-hour teaching loads might actually lower its loads, using the law as an excuse. When all is said and done, probably little teaching time would be gained, but there would be lots of energy and resources expended in interpreting, fulfilling, and/or evading the mandate.

It would be far better to foster cost-consciousness in less rigid ways. Providing vouchers, for example, would give consumers greater clout in resource allocation, thereby stimulating greater competition for students. If mandates are to be imposed, it should at least be done in a manner that allows some institutional flexibility in meeting their intent.

Conclusions

An excellent case can be made simply to defund public support of higher education. The evidence of net positive externalities—or spillover effects—is very limited. Political reality, however, makes this an unlikely option in the near future.

There are two politically realistic approaches to public policy designed to reform higher education. The first emphasizes decentralized decision-making and allowing market forces to nudge university participants into voluntarily taking those actions consistent with institutional objectives that would reduce costs. The second emphasizes centralized mandates, enforced presumably by an arm of the state government, such as a board of regents or equivalent group. University autonomy and freedom of action would be more severely circumscribed than at present in an attempt to stem the decline of productivity.

A very strong case can be made for granting more higher education subsidies directly to students, gradually reducing and perhaps eliminating altogether general institutional subsidies. If done comprehensively, "state" universities as we know them today would disappear. Support to individuals via vouchers could be altered to take into account differential socioeconomic status, if desired. Inasmuch as the evidence that universities on balance have positive externalities deserving public support is increasingly suspect, part of the reform effort should be to reduce the continued growth in aggregate governmental support.

As they do in nearly every other human endeavor, entrepreneurship and individual initiative can promote progress in higher education. University entrepreneurship is best served by allowing administrators considerable freedom of action. While state governments can set the parameters for decision-making by their financial decisions, they will stifle creativity and endanger the ability of institutions to carry out their distinct missions if they impose one-size-fits-all mandates from on high. By contrast, accountability and discipline are better fostered using a market approach, increasing competition, and giving the customers—students and their parents—more clout. Accordingly, it is hoped that greater attention will be given to moving toward a voucher approach to funding higher education, ultimately opening vouchers for use at both private and public schools—a move that ultimately might render the distinction between the two types of institutions largely meaningless.

11

The Future of the American University

The functions of universities are eternal—the passage of knowledge from one generation to another and the creation of new knowledge are at the heart of what universities do, and those functions will always continue. Yet this book began with the observation that universities are not the only institutions available to perform those functions, and it demonstrated that several new substitutes for traditional forms of higher education already provide competition for conventional universities, which have become costly, inefficient, and complacent.

The heart of economic theory is the theory of relative prices, which says that if the price of something rises relative to the price of other (substitute) goods, people will want to buy less of it—and more of the substitutes. The price of a conventional college education has risen sharply, however measured, and already there is a sharp increase in the use of substitutes, such as for-profit schools.

In some mathematical sense, the high rate of tuition growth at the traditional universities is unsustainable in the long run; at some point, tuition will absorb a huge proportion of lifetime family income. Consequently, without major reform of traditional universities, students will flee them for the new substitutes—for-profit institutions, computerized instruction beamed into the home, certification programs offered by private companies or organizations, and the like. This book devoted two chapters to discussing ways that universities, bowing to this imperative, will fight back by cutting costs, either voluntarily or under coercion from the governments that provide a large proportion of their funding.

Many problems of modern American universities relate to their being highly subsidized, sheltered institutions that have been too immune to pressures from the market to be efficient in a financial sense. Some would argue they have not even been very accountable in terms of faithfully serving their main educational missions. Supporters assert, with some justification, that "we have the best universities in the world," and that there is far more to universities than providing schooling for undergraduate students. We lead the world in cutting-edge research, and universities sometimes play other positive roles in the communities they serve.

Still, at the margin, the evidence is far less positive. Costs are rising sharply with little evidence that educational quality is increasing. Much "research" is highly marginal, serving little utilitarian purpose and not even spreading humanistic ideals. The corruption of college athletics, the occasional scandals over college admissions, the growing politicalization of the academy, lax standards, the construction of extremely luxurious facilities, and excessive student party-going threaten public trust in our institutions of higher education, along with the immense subsidies that allow universities to operate as they do.

The existence of universities as ivory towers somewhat insulated from the pressures of modern societies is both one of their strengths and their greatest weakness. One dilemma relates to universities' legitimate role as refuges for unpopular ideas and heretical thoughts. Conventional wisdom should not be allowed to intimidate dissenters or completely monopolize the public discourse, since out of unconventional ideas often comes progress. As President Lee Bollinger of Columbia University recently put it, "With all the pressures toward the closing of our minds that come with conflict in the public arena, it's not a bad idea to have special communities like universities distinctly dedicated to the open intellect."[1]

Yet the assumption that universities promote "the open intellect" is increasingly questionable in American academic life. One commentator responding to Bollinger declared that "American academia is a forum for destructive political and social propaganda, for conventional wisdom, for mindless adherence to dogma in the name of, ironically, open-mindedness."[2] Another commented, "There is a distinct lack of academic freedom and a pervasive effort to squelch unpopular theory, research and opinion on the American campus."[3]

Yet "open-mindedness" is the key to progress and the evolution of a prosperous, civilized society. The rise of Christianity two millennia ago and of the modern scientific method half a millennium ago are examples of how unconventional thoughts became important, positive factors in the evolving lives of the population. Universities can and often do play constructive roles in effecting social and technological change. How can this dissent, these unconventional ideas, be protected while still allowing market forces, with their tendency to provide needed financial discipline, to play a constructive role in making universities affordable and accessible to the citizenry? In several chapters of this book, we wrestled with some specifics related to this broader question, asking, for example, how universities can obtain the advantages of faculty tenure without all of the current costs.

As I see it, the "root causes" of the tuition price explosion in universities are fourfold. They are:

- *The impact of third-party payments.* Third-party payments have reduced the sensitivity of the consumers of higher education to its costs. This is precisely the same thing that happened in medical care, with similar results. The third parties here, of course, are governments providing subsidies, loans, and the like, but also private philanthropists giving money. It is a simple fact of human nature that when someone else is paying a large portion of the bills, consumers pay less attention to price.

- *Price discrimination.* Universities have taken increasing advantage of the fact that upper-income individuals are less price-sensitive than those with more modest means, boosting the price differential charged to students from more affluent families through the device of scholarships.

- *Cross-subsidization.* By diverting resources from instruction to other purposes, universities have increased their need for higher tuition to cover the costs of instruction.

- *Lack of financial discipline.* The absence of any important incentives for universities to reduce costs and achieve efficiency has arisen from the lack of a bottom line of profits. In private enterprise, the quest for profits leads firms to offer rewards to managers and employees who follow a strategy of minimizing costs for goods or services of any given quality. In the public sector, without a clearly defined measure of success, there is a lot of "rent-seeking,"—using public funds to enrich individuals. This lack of financial discipline is implicit in a nonprofit environment where markets are only allowed to work to a limited extent.

As tuition increases begin to lead even the affluent to revolt, universities are going to have to change their ways to some extent. The pressures on governments to fund other activities have grown in recent years. Most notable are the health care obligations that will continue to grow over time with an aging population, and an inefficient health care delivery system. As push comes to shove, politicians will be faced with the choice of raising taxes, cutting health care benefits, slashing aid to public schools, or reducing higher education support. The health of the elderly and the education of younger children have, to this point at least, proved to be the politically more pressing needs, so the higher education share of state budgets has actually declined modestly in recent decades. For example, in fiscal year 1980, higher education accounted for 9.23 percent of the direct general expenditures of state and local governments, declining to 9.01 percent by fiscal year 2001.[4]

This decline accelerated in the aftermath of the 2001 recession. For example, in 2003–4, Colorado reduced state appropriations by double-digit percentages, allowing large tuition increases; the University of Colorado estimated only about one-tenth of its expenditures would be covered by state appropriations. These conditions helped in the May 2004 adoption of Governor Bill Owen's proposed voucher system, which will also include three private colleges. Moreover, the upsurge in private support for universities that began in the late 1990s is not permanently sustainable, given that the stock market boom that led to a spectacular increase in personal wealth is not likely to be replicated on a sustained, substantial basis at any time in the near future. Thus, the past rate of growth in third-party payments, both public and private, is slowing.

Universities bemoan this reduction in relative support from third parties, especially the government. Yet the theoretical justification for the support is weak and declining over time. As Milton Friedman indicated, there are negative as well as positive externalities to higher education. Externalities are hard to measure, but the statistically significant negative correlation between university funding and economic growth in the United States suggests that, at the very minimum, state funding should be reduced, if not eliminated.

Rationalizing Public Policy: Piecemeal Approaches

Even in the absence of any governmental action, inevitably some changes will come to higher education that will slow down the productivity decline and introduce some needed reforms. Government subsidization has made people less sensitive to cost considerations than they otherwise would be, but not totally insensitive. At some stage, more and more Americans are going to "just say no" to higher university costs.

Yet this process is likely to be accelerated by governmental interventions of various kinds at both the federal and state levels. Political entrepreneurs are going to want to score points with the public by "doing something" about the cost explosion in higher education. Already there are signs that this is occurring, with moves at both the federal and state levels designed to discourage universities from raising tuition charges as much as they have in the past. Alternatively, other politicians, including President George W. Bush, are proposing to deal with the tuition explosion with increases in such things as student loans and tuition tax credits.

These moves are no more than a second-best approach to solving the problem, and they may actually worsen the existing situation. Take, for example, the expansion of federal student loan programs and increased tax credits for college tuition expenses. These moves increase third-party payments, a root cause of the problem. They increase the demand for higher education at existing price levels, providing incentives for universities to raise their tuition further and increasing economic rents (payments made with nothing provided in return). As Congress debates reauthorization of the Higher Education Act, I hope that it does not simply adopt a large election-year increase in appropriations that would worsen the problem. While there is great merit in giving assistance directly to students (the federal approach) as opposed to institutions (the main state governmental approach), doing both simultaneously is a recipe for inefficiency and inflation, both of which have been produced in abundance in recent decades.

While other steps that might be taken still do not deal with root causes, they are less egregiously wrongheaded than expanding student assistance. Some might even be modestly beneficial. For example, the notion of "taxing" universities for tuition increases above a certain level actually serves to reduce the net subsidies provided universities by government—on the whole a good thing. If I were a state legislator, I might well support such legislation. Legislation removing subsidies for extremely expensive doctoral programs might fall into the same category, although on balance I think it is highly preferable to allow individual institutions flexibility in how they distribute reduced subsidies. For example, a doctoral program at some middling-quality state university may be small and rather costly—but it may also be the best program of its kind in the country, and the jewel in the university's crown. In such a case, the university might well want to reduce other less costly, but qualitatively less-distinguished, programs if faced with reduced state subsidies. It is reasonable to allow it to do so.

Generalized edicts on spending or subsidy reductions issued from state capitals or Washington fail to take into account the individual circumstances of institutions, and implicitly assume, wrongly in my judgment, that the people in the state or national capital know better how to reduce costs than those intimately familiar with university operations. To be sure, the individual university presidents do not *want* to make cuts, but they will do so if forced by financial circumstance. The reduction in state support after the 2001 recession brought about numerous instances in which state universities "bit the bullet" and cut whole programs—but ones that *they* felt were marginal to their missions.

I would predict that there will be increased efforts by legislators to mandate certain practices at state-supported universities. The two leading possibilities are legislation abolishing tenure and efforts to increase the teaching loads of faculty. As indicated earlier, I am highly ambivalent about tenure. It can be an extremely costly device that robs universities of the ability to reallocate resources in a timely fashion. Tenured professors use their power to block new initiatives and to maintain costly, outmoded programs. Its role in higher education certainly needs to change. Yet tenure is a relatively effective means of protecting free speech and expression—which is critical to a vibrant academic community.

My own preference is to make tenure optional for *individual* faculty members, something that can be "purchased" from a fixed sum provided faculty as part of the fringe benefit compensation package. Faculty members wanting tenure would be charged an amount equal to the estimated cost that this contractual arrangement imposes on the institution, and would have either to take less of other fringe benefits, such as costly health insurance, or accept an implicitly lower salary. Out-and-out legislative abolition of tenure is a crude, one-size-fits-all approach to the problem. The costs of tenure need to be realized and made explicit. But *prohibiting* one type of contractual arrangement between universities and their employees is not the answer.[5] It would be particularly ironic in this age of five- and sometimes ten-year contracts for college athletic coaches and even presidents to prohibit faculty members from having contracts of, say, more than one year in duration.

Mandating minimum teaching loads is a similarly crude way of trying to increase allocation of resources toward instruction. Blanket-minimum teaching loads for all faculty members is a truly bad idea, as some faculty are much stronger in research than in teaching. Legislative mandates of this sort would lead to well-known scholars deserting state universities where such restrictions exist, as those mandates are inconsistent with market conditions for superstar faculty.

Not nearly as bad are restrictions placed at the institutional level mandating some minimum average teaching load for all faculty members. Again, however, my preference would be to give institutions flexibility on resource usage. For example, a university wishing to expand faculty participation in online instruction should be able to give its faculty fewer classroom contact hours in return for some online instructional participation. New technologies are leading to more nonclassroom types of instruction, and laws mandating teaching loads very possibly could retard the development of promising new cost-reducing approaches that are instructionally effective, substituting relatively cheap capital for expensive labor resources.

Rationalizing Public Policy: More Systemic Reform

In short, I do not see a great deal of promise in piecemeal efforts on the part of legislators at either the state or federal level to reform higher education.

However, a much more compelling case can be made for more fundamental reforms, moving in the direction of privatization and reducing the negative effects of third-party payments.

Returning to first principles, there is no particular justification for massive government subsidies of higher education unless it can be shown that there are net positive externalities. At the most, it could be argued that in order to promote goals of equal economic opportunity, some subsidies for lower-income children might be appropriate. Claims of vast positive externalities of higher education are just that—claims, usually articulated by scholars who benefit from governmental support of their institutions.

While it is hard to measure externalities, the little empirical evidence I was able to analyze is more consistent with the position that universities, on net, have negative externalities—economic growth is less in states with large state subsidies of higher education, for example, and, with other things being equal, people tend to "vote with their feet," moving out of high-subsidy states. To the extent this evidence is reliable, there is actually, as Milton Friedman suggests, a better argument for taxing rather than subsidizing higher education.

A more cautious position would be to say that, on balance, the hypothesis that there are net positive externalities to higher education is not supported by the evidence. That conclusion would suggest that governments should be neutral toward higher education—neither promoting nor discouraging it through tax and regulatory policies. That, however, is current governmental policy toward, say, used car dealers. It would suggest that optimal policy would be for governments to disentangle themselves from assisting in the financing of instruction. With respect to private donations, the case for charitable tax deductions would largely vanish as well.

There are two caveats: First, universities perform some research activities that conceivably could be worth subsidizing independent of the instructional functions of those institutions. Second, it is empirically a fact that there are large earnings differentials associated with higher education attainment, and thus a case can be made for providing some subsidization of students for whom access to higher education would otherwise be difficult. This, however, would have to be done in a way where the spending truly improved access significantly, and that is not the case at the present.

Even these caveats, however, may not be particularly valid. For example, in the absence of government, there is a high likelihood that charitable contributions would fund more research that might have long-term positive externalities. Private research efforts have risen sharply in recent years. Research institutes, both privately owned, like the Battelle Memorial Institute and the American Enterprise Institute, and government-funded, like the National Institutes of Health and the Rand Corporation, can and do support efforts to expand the frontiers of knowledge. There is some evidence that when public assistance payments are reduced, a significant minority of the slack is picked up by private contributions.[6] It is very likely the same thing would happen with respect to financial assistance to lower-income students wishing to attend college.

Thus a strong case can be made for government gradually (or perhaps even less gradually) withdrawing from financing higher education altogether. Since people plan financially on having government support for college funding, it probably would be prudent to withdraw funding over an extended time period, say ten or even fifteen years. To make such a move palatable politically, a governor could call for a phase-out of state subsidies over a ten-year period, with the funds saved used to finance reductions in taxes, such as the personal income tax. State budgetary data indicate that elimination of higher education funding would allow reductions of income taxes on the order of 30 percent or more in many states—hardly an inconsequential amount. Since there is an abundant scholarly literature suggesting that a negative relationship exists between state and local taxes and economic growth, such a proposal would stimulate economic growth as well.[7]

Already, there are some early moves in the direction of privatization. The University of Virginia's graduate business and law schools no longer receive state subsidies and will formally end their funding association with the Commonwealth of Virginia within the year. Thus, in a sense, the University of Virginia is being partly privatized, a little at a time. The idea of full privatization has been mentioned. In South Carolina, Governor Mark Sanford recently proposed that state colleges be given the option of freedom from oversight by a strengthened higher education commission, in return for an end to government funding.[8]

Notwithstanding the above, the out-and-out elimination of support for higher education will probably not be politically feasible in the near term, despite the manifestly strong arguments for it and the possibility of dangling tax relief before voters as a reason to support it. Universities and their friends have strong lobbies, while the lobby to end government support for higher education, even with lower taxes, is likely to be small indeed.

Move to Student-Centered Funding. Following Colorado's move to shifting public funding from providers to consumers, however, may well have far more appeal, and is a start in the direction of privatization. Vouchers are proving relatively popular at the primary and secondary level, although even here the political forces supporting the status quo have thwarted most attempts to introduce them. However, the tradition of vouchers is fairly well established at the university level. The GI Bill implemented after World War II led to a massive increase in university enrollments—and it was, in effect, similar to a voucher program, since individual students controlled the disbursement of federal payments to institutions based upon their choice of university. Many states have scholarship programs that give scholarships to citizens usable at any institution in the state. Moreover, unlike government primary and secondary schools, public universities already charge tuition, and vouchers are merely another form of scholarships. Indeed, given the antipathy of some toward the word "vouchers," politically it probably is more desirable to speak of expanding state scholarship programs.

The elimination of university subsidies and replacement of them with expanded student scholarships would have many advantages over the existing system. First, it would make universities more responsive to their primary customers, the students. Funding, at least for state universities, would be tuition-driven, and schools would have to be popular, in high demand, to increase their revenues. Universities that treated their undergraduates with contempt and gave them third-rate instruction would suffer relative to institutions that genuinely put a good deal of emphasis on meeting students' needs. Institutions that engaged in unreasonable practices, such as attempting to censor some sorts of speech, or forcing students to take politically correct but unpopular courses, or massively subsidizing intercollegiate athletics at the expense of instruction, or allowing students to engage in rioting, could face some significant negative financial ramifications as enrollments declined in the wake of adverse publicity.

Second, the transition to scholarship funding can be an opportunity to end, and even reverse, the growth in real third-party payments per student that is a major cause of the tuition cost explosion. Indeed, the legislation creating scholarships might very well state that they will stay the same in nominal dollars over time, or be increased only at the rate of inflation, as measured by the CPI-U.

Third, over time, the inequity created by providing state assistance to some students (those attending public schools) but not others (those attending private schools) could be eliminated.

My suspicion, based on some casual empiricism, is that vouchers would lead to significant increases in the productivity of universities. I taught for a couple of years at a remarkable institution that incorporated many of the attributes of a voucher approach, namely the Economics Institute (EI) at the University of Colorado, sponsored by the American Economics Association. The EI provided intensive training in English and some introduction to graduate work in economics to foreign students planning to enter graduate programs at American universities. Run for decades by an energetic academic entrepreneur, Professor Wyn Owen, the EI was tuition-driven financially, with virtually no direct government support. Whenever enrollments fell because of a crisis in some region of the world, the Institute instantly adjusted its staff size and teaching loads accordingly. (There was no tenure.) Administration was lean and mean. Faculty members who did a mediocre job were not rehired, but those who excelled were well compensated. The Institute bought its own facilities out of cash flow and offered first-rate instruction, with some lectures provided by faculty from top schools, such as Yale and Stanford. I believe the pressure of having to please students (and their scholarship sponsors) was a key to the EI's being high quality, cost effective, and successful.[9]

As successful as the EI was, however, it ultimately went into decline, partly, no doubt, as a consequence of managerial mistakes, but also as a result of something it could not control or compensate for: the impact of the September 11, 2001, terrorist attacks. Sharp restrictions on the issuance of visas, a problem for many institutions, had a devastating impact on the EI. Like other market-driven institutions, the EI prospered and suffered with changing conditions, and it is being closed down.

As indicated earlier, the move toward a scholarship-based funding system almost certainly would have to be accomplished over a period of years, hopefully not exceeding ten and preferably closer to five. To me, the best approach would be to lower the absolute dollar-per-student subsidy in a straight-line fashion over a number of years, reducing uncertainty to university administrators about the transition process. Other variants, however, are feasible.

The voucher-scholarship approach can and probably should be modified in a way that ought to appeal to groups at opposite ends of the political spectrum. A "progressive" voucher approach would vary the amount of student grants inversely with income. For example, a student from a very low-income household might receive a voucher for $12,000, while a student from a very wealthy family would be excluded from eligibility, or receive a voucher of, say, $3,000. This approach would be very appealing to liberals worried about equal educational and economic opportunity, since students from low-income homes would receive greater guaranteed support than is currently the case while having access to high-quality private institutions. Libertarians and some conservatives might like the approach because it would reduce or even eliminate subsidy support for a significant subset of the population (say the 25 to 50 percent most affluent college students), reducing the role of government in higher education and potentially reducing total expenditures, and allowing for lower taxes than otherwise would be the case. This is a way of moving closer to the ideal public policy, which is essentially defunding public education.

A five- to ten-year transition to scholarship funding could gradually increase the costs to children of higher-income families of attending state universities. Universities would raise their tuition significantly during the period in which subsidies were being withdrawn, but there would be no dramatic immediate increase in fees.

The Ultimate Reform—Privatization of Higher Education. A move to scholarships is a large step toward privatizing higher education. This could involve converting schools to private, not-for-profit institutions. Private schools have some advantages over public. Their boards of trustees are usually selected on the basis of dedication to the university, not political considerations. A host of state regulations that govern public agencies would be ended. Universities would be rid of the costs of lobbying legislatures for funds.[10]

An even more radical reform would combine a move toward vouchers with the conversion of universities to for-profit institutions. Universities could be sold to for-profit companies (like Apollo Group, owner of the University of Phoenix), with the proceeds—net of university debt obligations—going toward taxpayer relief or endowing part of the future voucher obligations of government. An alternative would be to give a significant proportion of the shares to university employees, providing them with incentive to engage in cost-reducing strategies designed to make the institution more profitable in the new market setting. Faculty would be more willing to teach more students, for example, if they thought it could lead to an increase in their wealth. The gift to faculty and administrators of a significant portion of the educational enterprise would be an inducement to accept the loss of job security that might come with privatization. The experience of existing for-profit institutions suggests that the market capitalization of universities converted to a for-profit basis might be several hundred thousand dollars per employee, meaning a gift of part of the universities to the employees would significantly increase their net worth, a powerful inducement to favor the change. The conversion would also almost certainly lead to dramatic increases in efficiency, but because it is so radical, it is unlikely to be adopted anytime soon. Elsewhere, I have outlined in detail such a proposal for primary and secondary schools.[11]

Performance-Based Vouchers (Scholarships). The case for subsidization declines sharply as students perform abysmally. Why should hard-working, middle-class taxpayers subsidize the college costs of students from high-income backgrounds who "goof off" in college and perform poorly academically? Private donors and universities that give scholarships usually attempt to remedy this state of affairs by setting conditions that must be met for a scholarship to be maintained. Typically, for example, a student has to have a cumulative grade-point average of at least 3.0 (a B average) for the individual to renew the grant. State governments could impose similar performance standards as a condition for receipt of aid.

One minor problem is that students need the scholarship assistance *before* they take courses, but their performance is not known until *after* the courses have been completed. This dilemma could be resolved by legally defining the scholarships as "loans," with the written understanding that the loan would be completely forgiven if the student performed satisfact-orily. Students failing to do so would be required to repay the loan, ideally with interest. Indeed, to provide incentive to do well in college, the amount of loan forgiveness could be positively related to student performance. For example, students graduating with a GPA of 2.5 or under might have to repay their loan completely, with 2 percent of the loan forgiven for each hundredth of a point that the GPA exceeds 2.5. Under that formula, only students graduating with a GPA of 3.0 or more would receive the full scholarship.

Many students study too little in college because the subsidy received from the state is independent of their level of performance. Tying students' cost of education to academic achievement more directly would place them under much great financial pressure to perform adequately, if not spectac-ularly, and presumably would lower somewhat the scandalously high attri-tion rate that contributes to the high cost of college education.

This idea, of course, is not new, although it gets relatively little attention these days. A performance-based subsidy scheme for Canadian universities was recently proposed by Rod Clifton, a professor of the sociology of edu-cation at the University of Manitoba.[12] Clifton would give universities more money the further a student progressed toward a degree, aiming to lower attrition rates on the order of 40 percent. My proposal by contrast transfers the responsibility and rewards for good performance directly to the student.

A problem with my plan is that tying scholarship support to students receiving a certain absolute grade-point average, say, a 3.0 GPA, would put pressure on professors to give even higher grades than they already do. Ways of counteracting that tendency and perhaps even rolling back some of the more egregious instances of grade inflation include tying scholarships to rank in class, giving them, for example, only to students ranked in the top 80 percent. Or a rule could state that for universities to be eligible to receive scholarship students, at least 25 percent of grades given in under-graduate courses must be lower than B.[13]

An alternative or additional requirement would be to have a standard exit examination from college, perhaps half on general topics and half on the subject of the student's major field. Ideally, the examination would be a national test fairly similar to the Graduate Record Examination. Perhaps in addition to meeting grade-point criteria as outlined above, students would be required to pass the national exit examination to have their "loans" forgiven upon graduation. Such an exam would give us new ways of evaluating universities, perhaps reducing the cost-enhancing dimensions of some private rankings, such as those of *U.S. News & World Report*. In addition, a strong general education component could help counteract the contemporary tendency of students to be ignorant of basic facts relating to our heritage. Universities would be under pressure to teach the types of basic factual information useful to appreciating our cultural heritage and maintaining our cultural capital.

The concept of performance-based scholarships could be used to address another, very large problem: prolonged stays. Currently, students change majors, take light loads, and continue to take courses after meeting graduation requirements, in part because it is relatively cheap to do so, and in part because of class closeouts, arcane requirements that make changing majors costly, and so on. Since subsidies are typically enrollment-driven, universities have incentives to encourage students to hang around for a fifth or even sixth year. Scholarships could be limited to four years, period. The pressure on students to get through would be enhanced. The pressure on universities to offer courses to meet student needs would also increase. The taxpayer interest, ignored now in curricular decision-making, would be represented.

New Approaches to Funding Research: More Competition

The emphasis of this chapter to this point has been on the teaching function of universities. Universities also play an important role in expanding our intellectual capital through the creation of knowledge, ideas, and artistic works. A large part of that research is funded separately by research grants from governmental agencies and private foundations, but institutions also fund such activities themselves from tuition revenues, endowment income, and government subsidies.

Government-funded research typically involves a grant to a principal investigator to cover direct costs of the research project, along with an indirect—or overhead—cost component that goes to the university. Many resources go into trying to measure the overhead cost component and to make it as large as possible. It seems to me that some of the bloated administrative structure of universities is either involved in arcane details of grant administration or funded from the generous overhead funds provided.

Perhaps the time has come to set a uniform national overhead rate for research to reduce considerably the accounting costs associated with grants. That rate ideally would be set to the levels of the more efficient institutions, defined as those that expend the least resources to provide overhead services. Let's say institution X will do the research with a 60 percent overhead charge, but if the same researchers were at institution Y, the overhead rate would be 40 percent. The total cost to taxpayers would be reduced substantially by having the researchers do their work at institution Y. While that may not be feasible, a uniform overhead policy imposing a relatively low rate would force institutions claiming high overhead costs to economize and reduce costs to taxpayers.

A more fundamental question relates to the wisdom of having the federal government fund research in the first place. There is no question that some academic research is highly beneficial to society. I would submit, however, that in the absence of federal grants to universities, a significant portion of that research would be done anyhow, and some that would be discontinued is of dubious value in any case. Moreover, as was pointed out earlier in this book, a majority of funded research in the United States is already done outside universities, and the university share of research resources has already declined significantly.

On the first point, I am influenced by personal experience. For example, I remember once when my colleague Lowell Gallaway and I decided to do some research related to human migration. We decided to do the research using summer periods when we were free of teaching duties, plus some time in the academic year when our teaching absorbed, at best, twenty hours per week. We successfully sought funding from two prestigious private foundations—the Ford and Rockefeller foundations—but because we were genuinely intellectually curious about the topic, and since the publications from the research would increase our marketability and prestige in academia, we would have been wholly prepared to do much of the work without the grant. The grant merely provided us with economic rent—that is, income in exchange for which no incremental service is provided.

Talking with colleagues from many universities over the years, I have heard of numerous cases in which this has occurred. Indeed, some researchers successfully write proposals to fund research that is already well underway (although that is not revealed in the grant application). They then use the grant money to move on to their next project, creating the appearance of successful use of grant funds to the grantor.

To be sure, grants often cover travel, expensive pieces of research equipment, needed graduate assistance, and other things that facilitate more elaborate research. But sometimes I even question these expenditures on cost-benefit grounds. For example, very often in social science research, grants finance massive studies using microdata—data based on observations of individuals—that yield similar results to findings derived using published aggregated data—say, observations grouped by state, or by year—that are far cheaper to perform. The microdata results confirm, at considerable cost, what less-expensive research investigations financed without grants reveal. I suspect occasional expensive microstudies are needed to confirm findings of studies using the less-expensive research methodologies and to discover nuances of human behavior not observable otherwise, but that the marginal rate of social return on these studies on average is not terribly high.

With respect to big-ticket scientific research, I wonder whether gains from it are largely internalized—that is to say, that the fruits of the research ultimately are financially rewarded. Certainly, that is the case with pharmaceutical research. If universities are doing promising research that could lead to new forms of pharmaceutical therapies, it is almost certain that in the absence of universities the research would be conducted by private companies, assuming, of course, that intellectual property rights can be captured by patents and other means.

But what about basic research? Do not the gains from it provide positive externalities, justifying public support through devices such as the National Science Foundation? Perhaps, but so-called basic research often opens doors for practical applications, and the empirical evidence is already clear that private firms are increasingly willing to fund it. Big companies fund hundreds of projects. Some are obviously practical ideas for which a short-term payoff is anticipated. Others have low probabilities of payoffs that will be substantial if they do occur. Research involves many blind alleys, false starts, and perplexing findings. The large technology-based entrepreneur accepts that, and makes a multiplicity of research investments in the hope that enough of them will have payoffs—a few of them very considerable—to make the investments collectively worthwhile. Given the sharp rise in private R & D funding, increasingly for basic research, it appears that more businesses are proceeding this way. The question then is, who needs universities to do research?

Having said this, I would add that the instructional and research missions of the university are not rigidly separate, and at advanced levels of learning, student involvement in research helps them learn, and helps the researcher as well. There are sometimes synergies facilitating both the teaching and research functions, especially in graduate education, where the advanced student is expected to demonstrate an ability to conduct research as a prerequisite of receiving either a master's or doctoral degree.

The issue, however, is not whether research should be conducted at major universities, but rather the extent to which public funds should be used to subsidize it. Given the high level of economic rent in much research funding, a decent case can be made for significant reductions in government funding, starting with standardizing overhead reimbursement at a relatively lower rate than the current average.

One particularly disturbing recent trend is for Congress to give research awards to politically favored institutions without a competitive process. This new form of pork-barrel funding surely leads often to monies going to support unneeded research done by individuals of marginal competence. In the revision of the Higher Education Act, one would hope that an out-and-out prohibition on such grants will be included, even though such provisions tend to be ineffective, as they can be easily overridden by later legislation.

Competitive Funding. A considerable problem with attaining cost efficiency relates to the way we fund grant research in our country. Typically, the funding body solicits proposals for research in a general area of interest, and then a body of scholars reviews them almost entirely on the basis of scholarly merit. Since each proposal typically covers a somewhat different topic than others, there is effectively a single proposal for each very specific body of research—the researcher is a monopolist, and there is no competition for that particular project. There are exceptions, of course, such as when funding agencies invite proposals for a very specific research project from multiple teams of investigators.

An alternative paradigm would be to have a larger proportion of research projects be funded on the latter basis, thus injecting more competition into the research projects. A committee would decide upon a project and review applicants to determine if they were capable of doing it, with the award going to the lowest bidder among the applicants. Since committees often stifle creativity, some research probably needs to be funded on the basis of ideas suggested by the broader scholarly community; but getting more competition into the process seems possible.

Alternative Delivery Systems for Research. It would be interesting to compare the rate of discovery of new ideas for each dollar expended on university research with that of private, for-profit companies, and non-profit research institutes. While research "output" is notoriously hard to quantify, some crude measures, such as patent awards, are available. The federal government, which spends billions annually funding research, should be measuring the relative efficiency of alternative approaches to delivering research results.

A Final Word

Universities are luminous places. They light up the world intellectually, and have contributed importantly to the advancement of modern civilization. America is a better place because a large proportion of its adult citizens have spent some time in the university environment—learning, maturing, asking questions, seeking answers. Yet all of this is becoming very costly—so costly that the old ways will have to change. Adding to the problem in terms of public support, some believe that universities seem to have lost sight of their missions, watering down standards, promoting conformity and political agendas, and huckstering entertainments only remotely connected with the dissemination and production of knowledge.

Market forces have been partly suppressed, but only partly. Competition will force change, and public policy may speed the process, introducing new concepts like the transfer of funding from the universities to their customers. I think this is a good idea that will work to improve the efficiency of universities without sacrificing the quality of their product. Performance-based scholarships can increase competition, enhance efficiency, promote renewed emphasis on instruction, reduce problems of attrition and lackluster student performance, and even deal with grade inflation, if properly devised.

Am I predicting that traditional universities will eventually die and wither away, to be replaced by for-profit institutions, certification programs, and distance learning? No. There is another trend that works in favor of preserving the high-cost, labor-intensive prestige university, if not more ordinary institutions. With economic growth, incomes rise, and so do aspirations of adults for their children. Just as many more Americans today drive luxury cars than did a generation ago, so more Americans want "the very best" for their kids. Thus, the ratio of applicants to admissions has actually risen at the elite universities, despite soaring tuition costs. There always will be a demand for some extremely expensive, highly personalized instruction—even at inflation- and income-adjusted prices that are two, three, or even four times current levels. Harvard's future is not in doubt, nor is the future of most of the other institutions in the top twenty-five universities or liberal arts schools on the *USN&WR* list.

Even these institutions face customers who are not immune to the law of demand—as prices rise, less is demanded. But these schools can likely retain much of their current ambience, and perhaps even much of their inefficiency. The recent trend toward building luxury housing facilities and fancy recreational facilities at universities reflects the affluence of today's students and a desire to live better than previous, less wealthy generations. While attending college is partly an act of investment in human capital, it is also an act of consumption.

Schools of more average quality, however, face a more daunting future than Harvard and Princeton. Their prestige is not so great that applicants will automatically reject nontraditional alternatives. Their past arrogance and insensitivity to public concerns over costs make them politically more vulnerable and may even lead to a partial defunding of higher education by the public sector, which actually would be good for society, given the ambiguity over the universities' external contributions. As schools become more tuition-driven, many of the inefficiencies of current university life—the massive labor inputs used, high student attrition rates, large numbers of high-cost, noneducational activities of dubious worth—will be squeezed out of the system as they struggle to survive.

In 2050, America will still have universities, and they will still play a vital role in American life. But they mostly will be quite different places than they are today in the way they operate, and that, by and large, is to the good of society.

Notes

Chapter 1: The Cost Explosion

1. William G. Bowen, *The Economics of the Major Private Research Universities* (Berkeley, Calif.: Carnegie Commission on Higher Education, 1967).

2. Calculations are from tuition amounts listed in the undergraduate catalogue for Ohio University, various years.

3. See Michael J. Boskin et al., "Toward a More Accurate Measure of the Cost of Living," Final Report to the Committee on Finance, United States Senate, 1996. For a review of the vast literature on the subject, see David E. Lebow and Jeremy B. Rudd, "Measurement Error in the Consumer Price Index: Where Do We Stand?" *Journal of Economic Literature* 41, no. 1 (March 2003): 159–201. See also the papers from a symposium on the CPI included in the *Journal of Economic Perspectives* 17, no. 1 (Winter 2003): 3–58.

4. Greg Winter, "Jacuzzi University? A Battle of Perks to Lure Students," *New York Times*, October 5, 2003.

5. Data are taken from the National Center for Education Statistics, *Digest of Education Statistics: 2002* (Washington, D.C.: Government Printing Office, 2003), 354. This reference source is referred to throughout this book. It provides indispensable statistics on enrollment, financing, student performance, staffing, and other important variables impacting higher education. The 2002 edition became available only after this manuscript was largely completed, and some references are from the 2001 edition.

6. U.S. Census Bureau, *Statistical Abstract of the United States: 1989* (Washington, D.C.: Government Printing Office, 1989), 22; *Statistical Abstract: 1984*, 34.

7. National Center for Education Statistics, *Digest of Education Statistics: 2002*, 364.

8. Ibid., 365.

Chapter 2: Why Are Universities Inefficient and Costly?

1. Ludwig von Mises, *Socialism: an Economic and Sociological Analysis*, trans. J. Kahane (New Haven: Yale University Press, 1951).

2. Nicholas Thompson, "The Best, The Top, The Most," *Education Life* supplement to the *New York Times*, August 3, 2003, 24–26.

3. Ibid., 26.

4. There have been a few instances when institutions have done something similar, especially at liberal arts colleges, but none of the truly top universities has done so. Rice University, a very good institution, has historically charged tuition at least one-third below that of its private school peers. Of course, there is no charge for attending one of the nation's military academies, all of which are very selective and have fine academic reputations.

5. These data come from the Current Population Survey as reported by the Census Bureau. See their *Income in the United States: 2002, Current Population Reports Series P-60*, no. 221, available at http://www.census.gov/hhes/wwww/income02/html.

6. Of course, population projections tend to be notoriously inaccurate over long periods. The numbers to the year 2020 are probably fairly reliable, however, since the cohort involved has already been born. The one big imponderable is net immigration, whose contribution to the size of the pool can be moderately important.

Chapter 3: Productivity Decline and Rent-Seeking

1. Published annually by Resource Associates of Washington and included in the annual U.S. Census Bureau, *Statistical Abstract of the United States*.

2. National Center for Education Statistics, *Digest of Educational Statistics: 2002*, 393. Calculations are based on the Higher Education Price Index, which I find less satisfactory than either the CPI or GDP price deflator, but use of these other indices would not change the conclusion materially.

3. Two representative pioneering studies are William A. Niskanen, Jr., *Bureaucracy and Representative Government* (Chicago: Aldine, Atherton, 1971), and Thomas E. Borcherding, Jr., ed., *Budgets and Bureaucrats: The Sources of Government Growth* (Durham, N.C.: Duke University Press, 1977).

4. I am somewhat skeptical about the relatively significant rise in the faculty/ student ratio reported for the 1990s, almost as great in percentage terms as the growth in the "other professional" category. Some change in the classification of workers is possible.

5. Caroline Hoxby, "The Productivity of Schools and Other Local Public Goods Producers," *Journal of Public Economics* 24, no. 1 (November 1999): 1–30.

6. Ronald G. Ehrenberg, *Tuition Rising: Why College Costs So Much* (Cambridge, Mass.: Harvard University Press, 2002), 6.

7. For whatever it is worth, this assessment is remarkably similar to my own, teaching in a moderately high-quality state university (Ohio University). Typically my

students in 1965 were clearly superior to my students of 1980, but my students of today are superior to those of 1980—but probably not quite as good as the ones I had in 1965.

8. Frank H. T. Rhodes, *The Creation of the Future: The Role of the American University* (Ithaca, N.Y.: Cornell University Press, 2001).

9. The author expressing that view best perhaps is the late Allan Bloom. See his *The Closing of the American Mind* (New York: Simon and Schuster, 1987).

10. I do not know what the standard deviation is on the GRE average composite score, but based on the standard deviations for the verbal and quantitative tests, it is unlikely that the rise in the composite score was more than one-tenth of a standard deviation—a very modest improvement.

11. The education test changed somewhat in the 1990s, so this conclusion makes some assumptions about the convertibility of the new scoring method to the old norms.

12. National Center for Education Statistics, *Digest of Education Statistics: 1981*, 133; *Digest of Education Statistics: 2002*, 344.

13. Total factor productivity in private business from 1980 to 2000 rose about 18 percent, according to the U.S. Bureau of Labor Statistics. See their website at http://www.bls.gov for a wealth of productivity data.

14. That statistic is a bit misleading compared with the one for the pre-1945 period because of the addition of the Nobel Memorial Prize in Economic Science in the late 1960s.

15. See U.S. Census Bureau, *Statistical Abstract of the United States: 2002*, 514. Available online at http://www.census.gov/statab/www/.

16. "American Dominance of Nobels Continues as Research Pays Off," *USA Today* online, October 9, 2003. The quote is from Jonas Foerare.

17. Ehrenberg, *Tuition Rising*, 279.

18. The report of the Boskin Commission on this point has been echoed in several scholarly commentaries. See, for example, Boskin et al., "Toward a More Accurate Measure of the Cost of Living," 1996, or David E. Lebow and Jeremy B. Rudd, "Measurement Error in the Consumer Price Index: Where Do We Stand?" *Journal of Economic Literature* 41, no. 1 (March 2003): 159–201.

Chapter 4: The New Peculiar Institution

1. See, for example, Kenneth M. Stampp, *The Peculiar Institution: Slavery in the Ante-Bellum South* (New York: Alfred A. Knopf, 1956).

2. Christopher Avery and Caroline M. Hoxby, "Do and Should Financial Aid Packages Affect Students' College Choices?" in *College Decisions: The New Economics of Choosing, Attending and Completing College*, ed. Caroline Hoxby (Chicago: University of Chicago Press, forthcoming, 2004).

3. Daniel Golden, "A Look at Who Got in Where Shows Preferences Go Beyond Racial Bias," *Wall Street Journal*, April 25, 2003, A1.

4. Daniel Golden, "Bill Would Make Colleges Report Legacies, Early Admissions," *Wall Street Journal*, October 29, 2003, B1.

5. Ibid.

6. Ibid.

7. Although I suspect it is relatively rare, overt corruption occasionally enters the admissions process. I know of two instances in my college career when students were admitted on what would universally be agreed to have been an inappropriate basis. In the first case, the college dean was, in effect, bribed, accepting an interest-free loan from the parent of an admitted student. (The dean left the university upon the news breaking in the press.) In the second instance, an admissions officer promised admission in the process of trying to develop a sexual relationship with a prospective student (who chose to go elsewhere).

8. Universities can get creative in their attempts to ease out tenured faculty. I once was involved in an attempt to get a faculty member who likely would have taught for another ten years to retire. The faculty member was offered a three-year contract with large salary increases—if he agreed to retire at the end of the three years. The salary increases, however, raised the salary base on which his pension was calculated, thereby shifting a large portion of the cost of obtaining earlier retirement onto his retirement system. Still, the move cost the university and society far more than if the individual had not had tenure.

9. An excellent statement of this perspective is found in Rhodes, *The Creation of the Future*, 30–44.

10. There are some positive signs on the horizon. For example, in my field of economics, the profession's most prestigious award for young scholars was recently given to Steven Levitt, of the University of Chicago. His theoretical work is not terribly abstract, and he is multidisciplinary in his interest. A news article about Levitt noted that "young economists of every stripe are more inclined to work on real-world ssubjects and dip into bordering disciplines—psychology, criminology, sociology, even neurology—with the intent of rescuing their science from its slavish dependence upon mathematical models." See Stephen J. Dubner, "The Probability That a Real-Estate Agent Is Cheating You (and Other Riddles of Modern Life)," *New York Times Magazine*, August 3, 2003, 22–27.

11. See, for example, Thomas Sowell, *Inside Education Today: The Decline, the Deception, the Dogmas* (New York: Free Press, 1993).

12. National Center for Education Statistics, *Digest of Education Statistics: 2002*, 294.

13. Rhodes, *The Creation of the Future*, 130.

14. William G. Bowen and Neil L. Rudenstine, *In Pursuit of the Ph.D.* (Princeton, N.J.: Princeton University Press, 1992), chapter 8.

15. "What Americans Think About Higher Education," *Chronicle of Higher Education*, May 2, 2003, A10–A17.

Chapter 5:   American Higher Education: Past and Present

1. Data are for academic years ending in the year in question (for example, 1970 is for the 1969–70 school year). Data are reported by the National Center for Education Statistics (NCES), except population data, which are from the decennial population censuses conducted by the U.S. Census Bureau. See the *Digest of Education Statistics* for details.

2. Ibid., 220.

3. U.S. Census Bureau, *Statistical Abstract: 2002*, 374.

4. Ibid., 372.

5. Ibid., 168.

6. Ibid., 138.

7. U.S. Census Bureau, *Historical Statistics of the United States, Colonial Times to 1970* (Washington, D.C.: U.S. Government Printing Office, 1975), 386.

8. National Center for Education Statistics, *Digest of Education Statistics: 2002*, Table 217.

9. Statistics in this paragraph came from U.S. Census Bureau, *Statistical Abstract: 2002*, 168–69.

10. In 2003, 70.1 percent of white males over the age of sixteen worked, compared with 59.5 percent for African American males. *Economic Report of the President*, 2004, 333. Available at http//www.gpoaccess.gov/eap/index.html.

11. See Sandra E. Black and Amir Sufi, "Who Goes to College? Differential Enrollment by Race and Family Background," National Bureau of Economic Research, Working Paper W9310, November 2002, available for purchase online at http://papers.nber.org/papers/w9310.

12. U.S. Census Bureau, *Historical Statistics*, 383.

13. Based on Current Population Survey estimates. See U.S. Census Bureau, *Statistical Abstract: 2002*, 155. Because of relatively small sample sizes, there is a possibility of moderately severe error, but vast differences between the most and least university-intensive states would almost certainly persist even after correction for statistical error.

14. The SAT scoring system has also changed; the numbers reported here are adjusted to the scoring basis in effect in 1970.

15. The characteristics of college freshmen are based on the annual surveys of the Higher Education Research Institute at the University of California at Los Angeles, published in *The American Freshman: National Norms*; see U.S. Census Bureau, *Statistical Abstract: 2002*, 170. The GPA statistics reported here are based on certain

assumptions about the distributions of grades within the categories A, B, and so forth, as reported in the UCLA survey.

Chapter 6: Why Do We Need Universities?
First Principles of Higher Education

1. Charles Dickens, *A Tale of Two Cities* (New York: Sheldon, 1863). Dickens opens this epic novel with this observation.

2. "What Americans Think About Higher Education," A11.

3. See Adam Smith, *An Inquiry into the Nature and Causes of the Wealth of Nations* (Oxford: Oxford University Press, 1976), 758–88, for an interesting discussion of the financing and other practices of universities in the eighteenth century.

4. John Donne, *Devotions Upon Emergent Occasions* (New York: Oxford University Press, 1986). The famous quote is from Devotion No. 17.

5. Rhodes, *The Creation of the Future*, 45.

6. See U.S. Census Bureau, *Statistical Abstract: 2002*, 502.

7. Derek Bok, *Universities in the Marketplace: The Commercialization of Higher Education* (Princeton, N.J.: Princeton University Press, 2003), 111.

8. Ibid.; and also U.S. Census Bureau, *Statistical Abstract of the United States: 1996*, 602. Available online at http://www.census.gov/statab/www/

Chapter 7: Universities and Society

1. James J. Heckman, "Policies to Foster Human Capital," *Research in Economics* 54, no.1 (2000): 3–56, 71–74.

2. Milton Friedman, *Capitalism and Freedom* (Chicago: University of Chicago Press, 1962), 85–6.

3. John Henry Newman, *The Idea of a University* (Notre Dame, Ind.: University of Notre Dame Press, 1982), 134–35.

4. Data were obtained at the website for the Bureau of Labor Statistics, U.S. Department of Labor, http://www.bls.gov.

5. Milton Friedman, e-mail to Richard Vedder, September 12, 2003.

6. "What Americans Think," A11.

7. Theodore W. Schultz, "Investment in Human Capital," *American Economic Review* 51, no. 1 (March 1961): 1–17.

8. A recent study arguing that wages of nonuniversity-educated workers are enhanced by the presence of college-educated persons in the community is

Enrico Moretti's "Estimating the Social Return to Higher Education: Evidence from Longitudinal and Repeated Cross-Sectional Data," National Bureau of Economic Research, Working Paper W9108, August 2002, available for purchase online at http://papers.nber.org/papers/w9108. Obviously, this is consistent with the argument that the social rate of return to higher education is higher than the private rate of return, thus justifying some public support.

9. The data sources for all the statistical analysis in this chapter are the U.S. Census Bureau website for university spending data, specifically www.gov/govs/www.estimate.html, and *Statistical Abstract of the United States*, various years, from which came the data for the various control variables. Economic growth data are derived from the U.S. Bureau of Economic Analysis; their website is at www.bea.doc.gov. Some of the older data on state and local governmental spending on higher education are found in U.S. Census Bureau, *Government Finance in (Year)* (Washington, D.C.: U.S. Government Printing Office, various years).

10. The college–high school earnings differential has widened over time, but the precise magnitudes vary with gender, whether one looks at year-round, full-time workers or all workers, and so forth. The earnings differential is discussed in greater detail in later chapters.

11. Again, the precise differential depends on the groups examined (males vs. females, full-time, year-round workers vs. all workers, and so forth.) Moderate changes in the differentials will not change the basic conclusion: At the margin, the benefits of college have increasingly been internalized by the recipients of the education.

12. For 2000, the income accruing to the college graduates themselves rose to 0.70–0.75 percent per capita (multiplying 1.00—resulting from the 100 percent earnings differential existing by 2000—by 0.70 or 0.75, labor's share of the national income). Dividing 0.70 or 0.75 by 1.02, the coefficient for the change in participation variable from the regression equation, gives a number approximating 0.70.

13. I am indebted to Professor James Bennett of George Mason University for suggesting this point.

14. See Mancur Olson, *The Rise and Decline of Nations* (New Haven: Yale University Press, 1982).

15. Ronald G. Ehrenberg, *Tuition Rising*, 275.

Chapter 8: New Alternatives to Traditional Higher Education

1. The source of this and other information is Yahoo Finance on the Internet. Go to http://finance.yahoo.com. From this entry point, I acquired annual reports, SEC

financial statements, research reports, and other information that forms the factual basis for the information in this part.

2. The data on "revenue per student" are not precisely the same thing as "tuition per credit hour," as they are not corrected for changing average student course loads; also, there is a small amount of nontuition revenue as well, such as from earnings on investments. Thus, the factual data support the suspicion that Apollo is raising tuition charges at a rate modestly below the not-for-profit institutions, but they by no means prove it.

3. Because there are a number of privately held for-profit institutions, it is impossible to say with precision what the overall market valuation of all for-profit companies is.

4. E-mail from Kelly Tabah, University of Phoenix Admissions Counselor, to Karen Vedder, October 8, 2003.

5. National Center for Education Statistics, *Digest of Education Statistics* (Washington, D.C.: Government Printing Office, 2003), table 428.

6. U.S. Census Bureau, *Statistical Abstract: 2002*, 171.

7. George Archibald, "College-by-Computer Growing," *Washington Times*, July 21, 2003, A10.

Chapter 9: Evolutionary Change on the Campus: One Scenario

1. The best authority here is Eric Hanushek of the Hoover Institution at Stanford and the National Bureau of Economic Research. See, for example, his "The Evidence on Class Size," in *Earning and Learning: How Schools Matter*, ed. Susan E. Mayer and Paul Peterson (Washington, D.C.: Brookings Institution, 1999), 131–68.

2. This accounting is a consequence of conversations between the author and President Hammond on September 2–3, 2003, in Wichita, Kansas.

3. Mary Beth Marklein, "Colleges brace for bigger classes and less bang for more bucks," *USA Today* online edition, August 27, 2003.

4. See Ron Feemster, "Volume Discounts," *National Cross Talk*, National Center for Public Policy and *Higher Education 11*, no. 3 (Summer 2003): 6.

5. The largest reported revenue in 2001 was $79.6 million, while the largest reported expense was $52.1 million, suggesting that one school must have made a $27.5 million profit, although because of implicit or explicit institutional subsidies that number may be overstated. See Daniel L. Fulks, *Revenues and Expenses of Division I and II Intercollegiate Athletics Programs: Financial Trends and Relationships: 2001*, p. 20, available on the Internet via http://www.ncca.org.

6. To be sure, there have been some modest nonfinancial improvements. The NCAA has reported that six-year graduation rates of scholarship athletes had risen to 62 percent by 2002. This, however, masks important differences—the black athlete

graduation rate was significantly lower (52 percent); for Division I basketball, it was much lower yet, 42 percent. The national champion in football at this writing, Ohio State, had a graduation rate of 41 percent in football, well below the 54 percent rate for the male student body as a whole (itself a somewhat scandalously low rate). These statistics were derived from Steve Wieberg, "Grad Rates for Athletes on Rise," *USA Today*, September 3, 2003, 1C, 9C.

7. "Vanderbilt Cuts Athletic Department," AP story reported on www.msnbc.com, September 12, 2003.

8. Ibid.

9. Borrowing, of course, from the "I Have a Dream" speech of Martin Luther King delivered in 1963 at the Lincoln Memorial in Washington, D.C.

10. According to an NCAA press release, 62 percent of athletes entering Division I schools in 1996 had graduated by 2002, "three percentage points better than the overall student-body." NCAA News Release, September 2, 2003, available at http://www.ncaa.org/releases/research/20039020re.htm.

11. Jon Marcus, "A Massive Overhaul," *National Cross Talk* 11, no. 3 (Summer 2003): 1. Available online at the for the website National Center for Public Policy and Higher Education, http://www.highereducation.org/crosstalk/ct0303/front.shtml

Chapter 10: An Alternative Scenario: Systemic Reform

1. Friedman, *Capitalism and Freedom*, 98–100. See also his very good "The Higher Schooling In America," *The Public Interest* 3, no. 11 (Spring 1968): 108–12. In that piece, Friedman seems to question strongly the validity of most governmental subsidies for higher education. I am indebted to Professor Friedman for providing me with a copy of this paper.

2. The idea of the "progressive voucher" was first advocated publicly, I believe, by Robert Reich, former secretary of labor in the Clinton administration. See his "The Case for Progressive Vouchers," *Wall Street Journal*, September 6, 2000; also available at American Prospect Online at http://www.prospect.org/page.ww?section=root&name=ViewWeb&articleId=249.

3. See, for example, John Chubb and Terry Moe, *Politics, Markets and America's Schools* (Washington, D.C.: Brookings Institution, 1990), or James S. Coleman, Thomas Hoffer, and Sally Kilgore, *High School Achievement: Public and Private Schools Compared* (New York: Basic Books, 1982), for two classic studies that make this point.

4. Pamela Burdman, "Colorado's 'Grand Experiment': Voucher Program Could Give the State's Colleges a New Lease on Life," *National Cross Talk* 11, no. 2 (Spring 2003). Available online at the website of the National Center for Public

Policy and Higher Education, http://www.highereducation.org/crosstalk/ct0203/front.shtml.

5. William Bennett, in a private conversation with the author, Austin, Texas, February 2003.

6. E-mail from Milton Friedman to Richard Vedder, September 12, 2003.

7. Another potential objection to a comprehensive voucher scheme is that it violates the establishment clause of the U.S. Constitution. That argument, however, has been drastically weakened by the Supreme Court's decision in *Zelman v. Simmons-Harris*, the Cleveland voucher case.

8. E-mail from Milton Friedman to Richard Vedder, September 12, 2003.

9. I am indebted to my colleague Lowell Gallaway for this insightful idea.

10. According to the College Board, the average four-year public institution raised tuition and fees by 9.6 percent, an inflation-adjusted increase of well over 7 percent, which is on the high end of modern historical experience.

11. Ohio Board of Regents, "Fall Enrollment Increases 1.8 Per Cent Over Last Year for Ohio's Public Colleges and Universities," press release, October 16, 2003.

Chapter 11: The Future of the American University

1. Lee C. Bollinger, "The Idea of a University," *Wall Street Journal*, October 15, 2003, A20.

2. Thomas Merry, "The 'Devastating' Climate at Our Universities," *Wall Street Journal*, October 23, 2003, A21.

3. Richard M. Stanaro, letter to the editor, *Wall Street Journal*, October 23, 2003, A23.

4. U.S. Census Bureau, *Governmental Finances in 1979–80* (Washington, D.C.: Government Printing Office, 1981), 84, and http://census.gov/govs/www.estimate00.html.

5. At the time of this writing, a new book dealing with tenure and its role in higher education was about to be released by the Independent Institute. See Ryan C. Amacher and Roger E. Meiners, *Faulty Towers: Tenure and the Structure of Higher Education* (Oakland, Calif.: The Independent Institute, 2003).

6. For evidence, see Burton A. Abrams and Mark D. Schmitz, "The Crowding Out Effect on Governmental Transfers of Private Charitable Contributions: Cross-Section Evidence," *National Tax Journal* 37, no. 4 (December 1984): 563–68.

7. For two representative studies from the vast literature, see Eric Engen and Jonathan Skinner, "Taxation and Economic Growth," in *Tax Policy in the Real World*, ed. Joel Slemrod (Cambridge: Cambridge University Press, 1999), and L. Jay Helms, "The Effect of State and Local Taxes on Economic Growth: A Time Series-Cross-Section Approach," *Review of Economics and Statistics* 67, no. 4 (November 1985): 574–82.

8. John Boyanoski, "Universities Look Hard at Going Private," *Greenville News*, December 11, 2003.

9. I am indebted to my colleague David Klingaman, who also taught at the Economics Institute, for reminding me about this remarkable institution and the close parallels to the proposed student-centered educational funding.

10. That is a point emphasized by Ryan Amacher and Roger Meiners. See their "Free the State Universities to Better Serve Students," *San Francisco Business Times*, September 29, 2003.

11. I have outlined in detail such a proposal for primary and secondary schools in Richard K. Vedder, *Can Teachers Own Their Own Schools?* (Oakland, Calif.: Independent Institute, 2000).

12. Rod Clifton, "What Can be Done About the 'Under-funding' of Canadian Universities," *Background Brief Analysis* (Winnipeg, Manitoba: Frontier Centre for Public Policy, September 2003).

13. There are early signs that universities are themselves considering moving to "quotas" designed to reduce grade inflation. At this writing, the faculty of Princeton University are considering a proposal to restrict the number of "A" grades. See Karen W. Arenson, "Princeton Proposes Curbing the Growing Number of A's Awarded to A-List Students," *New York Times*, April 8, 2004, available online at http:www.ny times.com/2004/04/08/education/08princeton.html.

Index

About the Author

Richard Vedder is distinguished professor of economics at Ohio University and an adjunct scholar at the American Enterprise Institute. Trained as an economic historian, much of his work has dealt with the history of American labor markets and issues such as immigration, internal migration, slavery, and unemployment. After serving as an economist with the Joint Economic Committee of Congress, Mr. Vedder focused on public policy issues dealing with labor markets and governmental budgetary policy. In the past decade he has worked on issues relating to education at both the primary/secondary and university levels.

Mr. Vedder's previous books include *The American Economy in Historical Perspective*, *Unemployment and Government in Twentieth-Century America* (with Lowell Gallaway), and *Can Teachers Own Their Own Schools?* He has authored over two hundred scholarly papers, which have appeared in *The Journal of Economic History*, *Agricultural History*, *Explorations in Economic History*, and numerous other academic journals. His writing has appeared in the *Wall Street Journal*, *USA Today*, *Investor's Business Daily*, the *Christian Science Monitor*, and the *Washington Post*. The winner of numerous teaching awards, Mr. Vedder is a popular public speaker, having lectured on public policy issues across the country and in Europe and Asia. He has advised numerous political leaders on tax and fiscal policy or education issues. Mr. Vedder is a graduate of Northwestern University and the University of Illinois.

Nelson W. Polsby
Heller Professor of Political Science
Institute of Government Studies
University of California, Berkeley

George L. Priest
John M. Olin Professor of Law and
Economics
Yale Law School

Jeremy Rabkin
Professor of Government
Cornell University

Murray L. Weidenbaum
Mallinckrodt Distinguished
University Professor
Washington University

Richard J. Zeckhauser
Frank Plumpton Ramsey Professor
of Political Economy
Kennedy School of Government
Harvard University

Research Staff

Gautam Adhikari
Visiting Fellow

Joseph Antos
Wilson H. Taylor Scholar in Health
Care and Retirement Policy

Leon Aron
Resident Scholar

Claude E. Barfield
Resident Scholar; Director, Science
and Technology Policy Studies

Roger Bate
Visiting Fellow

Walter Berns
Resident Scholar

Douglas J. Besharov
Joseph J. and Violet Jacobs
Scholar in Social Welfare Studies

Karlyn H. Bowman
Resident Fellow

John E. Calfee
Resident Scholar

Charles W. Calomiris
Arthur F. Burns Scholar in
Economics

Liz Cheney
Visiting Fellow

Lynne V. Cheney
Senior Fellow

Thomas Donnelly
Resident Fellow

Nicholas Eberstadt
Henry Wendt Scholar in Political
Economy

Eric M. Engen
Resident Scholar

Mark Falcoff
Resident Scholar

J. Michael Finger
Resident Scholar

Gerald R. Ford
Distinguished Fellow

David Frum
Resident Fellow

Reuel Marc Gerecht
Resident Fellow

Newt Gingrich
Senior Fellow

James K. Glassman
Resident Fellow

Robert A. Goldwin
Resident Scholar

Michael S. Greve
John G. Searle Scholar

Robert W. Hahn
Resident Scholar; Director,
AEI-Brookings Joint Center
for Regulatory Studies

Kevin A. Hassett
Resident Scholar; Director,
Economic Policy Studies

Steven F. Hayward
F. K. Weyerhaeuser Fellow

Robert B. Helms
Resident Scholar; Director,
Health Policy Studies

Frederick M. Hess
Resident Scholar; Director,
Education Policy Studies

R. Glenn Hubbard
Visiting Scholar

Leon R. Kass
Hertog Fellow

Herbert G. Klein
National Fellow

Jeane J. Kirkpatrick
Senior Fellow

Marvin H. Kosters
Resident Scholar

Irving Kristol
Senior Fellow

Randall S. Kroszner
Visiting Scholar

Desmond Lachman
Resident Fellow

Michael A. Ledeen
Freedom Scholar

James R. Lilley
Senior Fellow

Lawrence B. Lindsey
Visiting Scholar

John R. Lott Jr.
Resident Scholar

John H. Makin
Resident Scholar; Director,
Fiscal Policy Studies

Allan H. Meltzer
Visiting Scholar

Joshua Muravchik
Resident Scholar

Charles Murray
W. H. Brady Scholar

Michael Novak
George Frederick Jewett Scholar
in Religion, Philosophy, and Public
Policy; Director, Social and Political
Studies

Norman J. Ornstein
Resident Scholar

Richard Perle
Resident Fellow

Sarath Rajapatirana
Visiting Scholar

Michael Rubin
Resident Scholar

Sally Satel
Resident Scholar

William Schneider
Resident Fellow

Daniel Shaviro
Visiting Scholar

Joel Schwartz
Visiting Scholar

J. Gregory Sidak
Resident Scholar

Radek Sikorski
Resident Fellow; Executive
Director, New Atlantic Initiative

Christina Hoff Sommers
Resident Scholar

Fred Thompson
Visiting Fellow

Peter J. Wallison
Resident Fellow

Scott Wallsten
Resident Scholar

Ben J. Wattenberg
Senior Fellow

John Yoo
Visiting Fellow

Karl Zinsmeister
J. B. Fuqua Fellow; Editor,
The American Enterprise